THE EU
*Understanding
the Brussels Process*

THE EU
*Understanding
the Brussels Process*

Christopher Bright
Partner, Linklaters & Paines

John Wiley & Sons

Chichester, New York, Brisbane, Toronto, Singapore

First published in the United Kingdom in 1995 by
Chancery Law Publishing Ltd
Baffins Lane
Chichester
West Sussex PO19 1UD

National (01243) 779777
International (+44) 1243 779777

Reprinted July 1995

Published in North America by
Wiley Law Publications
7222 Commerce Center Drive
Colorado Springs
CO 80919 USA

International (1) 719 548 1900

Typeset in 11/13pt Times by Acorn Bookwork, Salisbury, Wiltshire
Printed and bound in Great Britain by Biddles Ltd, Guildford and King's Lynn

This book is printed on acid-free paper responsibly manufactured from
sustainable forestation, for which at least two trees are planted for each one
used for paper production.

ISBN 0471 95608 2

British Library Cataloguing Data

A Copy of the CIP entry for this book is available from the British Library.

©
Christopher Bright
1995

CONTENTS

PREFACE

Jacques Delors, former President of the European Commission, forecast that 80% of economic and social legislation of Member States will flow from the European Community by the end of the century. Despite this, many remain unaware of the growing importance of the Community as a source of law. EC Regulations, Directives and Decisions already affect, and will increasingly influence, the rights of individuals and the way in which companies carry on their businesses. Consequently, it is no longer sufficient simply to focus on national law and national legislative and administrative processes.

Many people focus on EC initiatives only after they have been finalised. By then it is too late. An example of this is the Unfair Contract Terms Directive. The UK implementation of this has been much criticised. In many respects, however, its faults are inherent in the Directive. It simply mirrors those faults. Had the effort expended by so many in trying to shape the UK's implementation been expended on the process leading to the Directive these faults may have been avoided.

It is not only the process of Community law making to which attention needs to be paid but also recognition of the existence of EC law, both legislative and judge made. Whether or not the EC system is regarded as a federal one, it is clear that countries within the EC have at least two tiers of law – EC and national – for their citizens to contend with. Understanding the inter-relationship of these tiers is essential. By and large EC law takes precedence, sometimes with unexpected consequences for the rights and remedies of those subject to the law. An understanding of the EC, its institutions and its powers is fundamental to ensuring effective participation in future developments and opportunities.

The Treaty on European Union ("Maastricht Treaty"), which entered into force on 1 November 1993, introduced many new elements to this process. The Maastricht Treaty establishes a European Union ("EU") adding two so-called "pillars", dealing with foreign and security policy and with justice and home affairs, to the existing economic and monetary "pillar" embodied in the EC. The economic and monetary pillar was significantly strengthened by the Maastricht Treaty.

This book explains the workings of the economic dimension of the EU (the EC and its institutions), sets out the processes which those interested can use to make their interests known at EC level, and points to how EC law and the Brussels process can be used to advantage. The other dimensions of the EU, foreign and security policy and justice and home affairs, are touched on briefly. The relationship between the EC and other European nations, currently in a state of flux, is examined. The text of the EC Treaty, as amended at Maastricht, is included so that reference can be made to the principal constitutional document of the Community. Protocols relating to monetary union and social policy have been included to aid an understanding of the UK's own position. The book does not attempt to describe substantive areas of EC law: there are numerous texts that can be turned to for this.

For the purpose of this publication the terms European Community ("EC" or "Community") are used to refer to matters governed by the Treaty of Rome, as amended. Reference to the European Union ("EU") is only made where it is intended to cover all three Communities and the second and third pillars of common foreign and security policy and justice and home affairs. It is, however, likely that in practice and over time the distinction between EU and EC will become more and more blurred and the term EU will prevail.

Short as this work is it is the product of considerable effort during which many have helped. A number of people in the EC and Competition Law Group at Linklaters & Paines, both in London and Brussels, have contributed. In particular, mention should go to Christiane Williams, Gavin Robert and Emma Turnbull together with my secretary Joyce Fairweather whose efforts made this work possible.

Christopher Bright
February 1995

GLOSSARY

AmCham	American Chamber of Commerce
BEUC	The European Consumers Organisation
CEN	European Standards Committee
CENELEC	European Electrotechnical Standardisation Organisation
CFI	Court of First Instance
CFSP	Common Foreign and Security Policy
CIS	Commonwealth of Independent States
Commission	European Commission
COREPER	Committee of Permanent Representatives
Council	Council of the European Union
DG	Directorate General
DTI	UK Department of Trade and Industry
EAGGF	European Agricultural Guidance and Guarantee Fund (FEOGA)
EC	European Community
ECB	European Central Bank
ECHR	European Convention on Human Rights
ECJ	European Court of Justice
EcoSoC	Economic and Social Committee (ESC)
ECSC	European Coal and Steel Community
ECU	European Currency Unit
EEA	European Economic Area
EEC	European Economic Community
EFTA	European Free Trade Association
EIB	European Investment Bank
EIF	European Investment Fund
EMI	European Monetary Institute
EMU	Economic and Monetary Union
EP	European Parliament
EPC	European Political Co-operation
ERDF	European Regional Development Fund (FEDER)
ERT	European Round Table of Industrialists
ESCB	European System of Central Banks
ESF	European Social Fund (FSE)

ETSI	European Telecommunications Standards Institute
ETUC	European Trade Union Confederation
EU	European Union
EURATOM	European Atomic Energy Community
GATT	General Agreement on Tariffs and Trade
IGC	Inter-Governmental Conference
Maastricht Treaty	Treaty on European Union
MEP	Member of the European Parliament
Merger Treaty	Treaty establishing a Single Council and a Single Commission of the European Communities (1967)
NATO	North Atlantic Treaty Organisation
OJ	Official Journal
PHARE	Poland and Hungary Assistance to the Restructuring of Economies
SEA	Single European Act (1986)
TACIS	Technical Assistance to the CIS and Georgia
Treaty	In this publication, refers to the Treaty establishing the EC (Treaty of Rome) unless specified otherwise
Treaty of Paris	Treaty establishing the ECSC (1951)
Treaty of Rome	Treaty establishing the EC (1957)
UNICE	Union of Industrial and Employers' Confederations of Europe
WEU	The Western European Union

Member States
of the
European Union

IRELAND

UNITED
KINGDOM

DENMARK

SWEDEN

FINLAND

NETHERLANDS

GERMANY

BELGIUM

LUXEMBOURG

FRANCE

AUSTRIA

ITALY

PORTUGAL

SPAIN

GREECE

1. INTRODUCTION

The creation of a European identity has been slow in the making. The European Community was founded four decades ago, although efforts to forge a closer European identity date back much further. In that time huge strides have been taken, expanding the Community from 6 to 15, developing the institutions of the Community and creating a new legal order to which Member States and their nationals are subject. In the last decade the pace of change has speeded up. The creation of a real single market among the 15 Member States has progressed significantly since the Commission White Paper on the Internal Market in 1985 and the Single European Act in 1986. Constitutional reforms have allowed institutions in Brussels to set, and push forward, the agenda within the EC, while the Maastricht Treaty has opened the door to the creation of a European Union. The Maastricht Treaty builds on the EC (essentially an economic community) to move forwards to a European Union involving powers over foreign and security policy and justice and home affairs. These developments may gather pace in 1996 when an Inter-Governmental Conference is due to review the current arrangements.

Alongside the so-called "deepening" of relationships among existing EC Member States the structure of relationships within neighbouring European states is changing rapidly. The creation of the European Economic Area on 1 January 1994 expanded the EC single market programme to five EFTA countries, creating a free trade area across the territory of 17 European states. Three of these EFTA countries have now become members of the European Union giving them full rights of participation. The EU has entered into agreements with several countries of central and eastern Europe giving them in effect associate membership of the EU, while looser free trade agreements are currently being negotiated with the CIS countries. Closer relations with other countries along the Mediterranean axis are also sought and Poland, Hungary, Cyprus, Malta and Turkey have already applied for EU membership. The EU has become the focal point for the development of a New Europe.

(i) The European Community and European Union

The first step towards the creation of the EU was taken with the establishment in 1952 of the European Coal and Steel Community (ECSC) by the Treaty of Paris, bringing together Belgium, France, Germany, Italy, Luxembourg and the Netherlands with the aim of creating a common market in coal and steel. Six years later, on 25 March 1957, in two separate treaties, the same countries agreed the creation of a European Atomic Energy Community (EURATOM) and the European Economic Community (EEC). Each Community had its own Council and Commission (or, in the case of the ECSC, a High Authority). The institutions were merged by the Merger Treaty of 1967 to form a single "Commission of the European Communities" and "Council of the European Communities". Since the Maastricht Treaty, their respective titles have been changed yet again to the European Commission and Council of the European Union respectively. The six founder members of these three Communities were joined in 1973 by the United Kingdom, Denmark and Ireland, in 1981 by Greece, in 1986 by Spain and Portugal and in 1995 by Austria, Finland and Sweden.

The EEC focused on the economic objectives of establishing a common market, progressively approximating the economic policies of Member States and promoting throughout the Community a "harmonious development of economic activities, an accelerated raising of the standard of living and closer relations between the states belonging to it".

The ECSC and EURATOM are concerned with relatively limited areas of competence and the ECSC Treaty expires in 2002. It is the EEC which has been the cornerstone for the development of European integration. The EEC developed a supra-national character that is overreaching and pervasive; its law is both above and part of the national law of each Member State.

In 1986, the Single European Act breathed new vigour into the EEC by making the completion of the internal market by the end of 1992 a Treaty goal and introducing the necessary institutional changes to the Treaty of Rome. All measures connected with the internal market could now be adopted without the need for unanimity. The "single market" programme saw significant developments in many EEC policies, such as environmental, social and fiscal policies. Although the 1992 deadline has long passed and a number of its objectives have not yet been achieved, the single market legislative programme is largely now complete. A true single market depends also, of course, on the removal of non-legal barriers. Linguistic and cultural factors play a significant role. The removal of the legal barriers may, however, in time lead to greater economic integration. That process continues. The Treaty on European Union (the "Maastricht Treaty") is intended to develop integration in a different way, in a political rather than simply an economic direction.

The Maastricht Treaty entered into force on 1 November 1993. One of the immediate consequences of this is that the European Economic Community has now been renamed the European Community (the "EC"). Under the Treaty, the Member States have agreed to establish a European Union based on three pillars – the three European Communities, a common foreign and security policy (CFSP) and also co-operation between Member States in the spheres of justice and home affairs. These latter two pillars are not currently within the normal institutional structure but are focused on the Council and are inter-governmental in nature and, as a form of political co-operation, go beyond that which previously existed, which was known as European Political Co-operation (EPC). It is intended that ultimately they will be absorbed into the institutional structure of the Community.

The European Community will continue to evolve. The Maastricht Treaty set out detailed provisions for the achievement of economic and monetary union and new areas of non-exclusive competence for the Community including, for example, health protection, consumer protection, education and training and culture. A

Key dates in the development of European Union
1952 ECSC Treaty
1957 EEC Treaty
Euratom Treaty
1967 Merger Treaty
1973 Accession of UK, Denmark and Ireland
1981 Accession of Greece
1986 Accession of Spain and Portugal
Single European Act
1992 Maastricht Treaty
1995 Accession of Austria, Finland and Sweden
1996 Inter-Governmental Conference
1999 Target for European Monetary Union
2001 ECSC Treaty expires

description of and a timetable for achievement of economic and monetary union are set out at Section (iii) *infra*.

(ii) Institutional Framework

The Treaty of Rome, as amended by the Single European Act and the Maastricht Treaty, sets out the EC's constitution and framework. It sets up a complex institutional structure: the **Council of the European Union** which has the law-making role (see Chapter 2); the **European Commission** which fulfils an executive and civil service function and is the source of all legislative proposals (see Chapter 3); the **European Parliament** which has an advisory and supervisory role (see Chapter 4); the **Court of Justice** which is the supreme judicial authority on EC law issues (see Chapter 5); and the **Court of Auditors**, which is the Community's financial watchdog (see Chapter 6 Section (i)). The roles and powers of the Community institutions reflect a complex and elaborate framework designed to give representation to the interests of the Community as a whole and those of the individual Member States and its citizens.

The text of the EC Treaty, as amended by the Single European Act and by the Maastricht Treaty, is included in Appendix D. The text indicates, for ease of reference, those parts of the Treaty that were amended (by deletion, modification or insertion) at Maastricht. Reference to the text of the Treaty is important. It is the constitution of the EC and as such familiarity with relevant provisions is essential. Anecdote has it that UK Cabinet Ministers freely confess they have not looked at the text. The following excerpt from Lord Cockfield's book, describing a discussion he had with Margaret Thatcher (Prime Minister at the time), shows the dangers of this:

"Sensing that all was not well I said that I had not invented harmonisation of indirect taxation, it was accepted Community policy long before we joined the Community and indeed was specifically provided for in the Treaty of Rome. The following conversation then took place:

Myself:	It was in the Treaty of Rome.
The PM:	It was not.
Myself:	It was.
The PM:	It was not.
Myself:	It was.

This unproductive conversation was brought to an end by the Private Secretary being sent to find a copy of the Treaty of Rome. I asked him to read out Article 99, which reads as follows:

'The Commission shall present proposals for the harmonisation of indirect taxes . . .'.

This was greeted in complete silence."

(Cockfield, *The European Union: Creating the Single Market* (Wiley Chancery, 1994)

As the EC has developed, the role of the Community institutions in European government has increased apace, to the detriment of the influence of individual Member States. The Single European Act 1986 and the Maastricht Treaty both increased the powers of the European Parliament in the legislative process, giving it greater influence through the powers of delay and veto (see Chapters 4 and 7). The Commission's role as initiator of legislation has become highly prominent as a result of the push for completion of the Internal Market and, more importantly, as a result of a ruling by the European Court of Justice which has established the Commission's ability to act independently of the Member States in order to achieve open markets. The competences of the Council and the European Council (see Chapter 2) now embrace aspects of foreign and security matters as well as home affairs and judicial co-operation, in their inter-governmental capacity. These matters were formerly the exclusive and separate competences of the individual Member States.

There is no doubt that the full potential of the EC Treaty is yet to be realised. Just as the US Constitution is a reference document for the constant reassessment of rights and remedies, so the EC Treaty is a document from which new issues will emerge and which will enable the re-assessment and revision of long-held assumptions. The Treaty affects not only the relationship between individuals and companies on the one hand and EC and Member State institutions and governments on the other, it also affects rights among individuals and companies. Article 101 of the Treaty is an illustration of the development, interpretation and application of the Treaty. A virtually overlooked Article in the Treaty until recently, it is now beginning to be mulled over by the Commission as a way of bringing reluctant Member States into line. It provides:

"Where the Commission finds that a difference between the provisions laid down by law, regulation or administrative action in
Member States is distorting the conditions of competition in the
common market and that the resultant distortion needs to be
eliminated, it shall consult the Member States concerned.

If such consultation does not result in an agreement eliminating the distortion in question, the Council shall, on a proposal
from the Commission, acting unanimously during the first stage
and by a qualified majority thereafter, issue the necessary directives. The Commission and the Council may take any other
appropriate measures provided for in this Treaty."

This Article clearly has as yet unrealised potential as the Community moves towards harmonisation, the more so as it can now
be operated by a qualified majority.

(iii) Economic and Monetary Union

The Maastricht Treaty set out in detail for the first time the stages
for achievement of Economic and Monetary Union (EMU) by the
end of the century. The co-ordination of the Member States'
economic policy is largely to be carried out by the existing EC institutions. However, monetary policy has to a great extent been
entrusted to an array of new independent institutions with their
own consultative and decision-making functions.

The provisions on EMU are necessarily complex. The activities
of the Community are extended to cover "the adoption of an
economic policy based on the close co-ordination of the Member
States' economic policies, on the internal market and on the definition of common objectives". In accordance with a timetable, this is
to include the irrevocable fixing of exchange rates leading to the
introduction of a single currency and a single monetary and
exchange rate policy. A European Central Bank (ECB) and a
European System of Central Banks (ESCB), made up of the ECB
and the national central banks, are to be set up.

There are three stages of EMU:

- the **first stage** began on 1 July 1990, at the same time as the
  liberalisation of capital movements, with work towards progressive convergence of economic performance by Member

States, adherence to the Exchange Rate Mechanism, and a system for the co-operation of the Central Banks of the Member States;

• the **second stage** began on 1 January 1994. This is a largely transitional phase in which central Community financial institutions are to be put in place and Member States are to align their economic performances in a way that will allow movement to a true economic union in the third stage.

During the second stage, the Commission and the European Monetary Institute (a transitional body replacing the pre-existing committee of central bank governors) will examine Member States' economic performance to see if there is a high degree of economic convergence, measured by:

– price stability (inflation rate must be within 1.5 percentage points of the three best performing Member States);

– avoidance of excessive budget deficits;

– observance of ERM fluctuation margins without devaluation; and

– durability of convergence (assessed by long-term interest rates);

• if a majority of Member States fulfil the set criteria, the heads of government are to decide whether it is appropriate to set a date for the beginning of the **third stage**. If no date has been set by the end of 1997, the third stage will begin on 1 January 1999. This means that whichever Member States fulfil the criteria at this date will go on to the third stage. On the setting of the date the Governing Board of the ECB is to be appointed, constituting the establishment of the ECB and ECSB. However, both the United Kingdom and Denmark, by virtue of respective Protocols to the Maastricht Treaty, have secured the ability to opt out of the third stage of EMU.

At the beginning of the third stage, the ECB and ESCB become fully operational. Their tasks will include the definition and implementation of the Community's monetary policy and the management of the Member States' foreign reserves. The ECB will be consulted on all proposed Community and national legislation in this area and will also have exclusive power to authorise the issuing of bank notes. The ESCB will be responsible for defining and implementing monetary policy including the carrying out of all foreign exchange transactions, the management of Member States' official reserves, and the supervision of credit institutions. The ECU will be the single currency in the states which are ready to move to the third stage. There are special provisions for countries which have not met the conversion criteria. Their position will be reviewed at least every two years.

Although the ECB and ESCB have yet to be established, 1 January 1994 saw the beginning of the second stage toward EMU and the establishment of the European Monetary Institute (EMI) in Frankfurt. The EMI replaced the Committee of Governors and the European Monetary Co-operation Fund and its tasks are to strengthen co-operation between national banks and Member States' monetary policies, monitor the functioning of the European monetary system and to prepare for the third stage of economic and monetary union including, for example, facilitating the use of the ECU and setting up the ESCB. Progress towards economic and monetary union and the forging of a single currency was, however, thrown into considerable doubt by the crisis in the Exchange Rate Mechanism in 1992 which saw Italy and the United Kingdom withdraw and the bands within which other currencies are allowed to fluctuate against each other significantly widened. The ensuing period of recession throughout the EC has meant that the criteria of economic convergence for monetary union to take place are unlikely to be met in the near future. It seems that the basis for monetary union may need to be adjusted and that the most likely result is that a core of countries may proceed when they judge the time is right. Belgium and Luxembourg already have a monetary union and maintain close economic and monetary co-operation with the Netherlands. Germany and France are, together with these three, the most likely participants.

(iv) 1996 Inter-Governmental Conference

The next major milestone in the development of the structure of the European Community is the Inter-Governmental Conference planned for 1996. This will provide an opportunity for the role of, and balance between, institutions of the Community to be revised. The European Parliament has, as a price for its supporting the accession of Austria, Finland and Sweden, obtained a commitment from the Member States that it will be given a role in the Conference. It is likely that this, and the perception of the existence of a democratic deficit in the EC, will lead to some strengthening of the role of the European Parliament, continuing the trend of transforming that body from an advisory to a real legislative chamber.

Other issues are on the agenda. The streamlining of the Commission and the voting balance between Member States in the Council are two major issues. The part that Community institutions should play in the two new pillars of the European Union, the common foreign and security policy and justice and home affairs, is another. A further issue which may be up for consideration is the possibility of creating independent agencies particularly in the utility regulation field and with a view to hiving off the supervision and enforcement functions of the Commission in the field of competition to a new independent cartel authority.

(v) EU Enlargement

The sign of the EU's success is the number of applicant countries waiting to join what is seen increasingly as a worthwhile economic, and political, community. Austria, Finland, Norway and Sweden moved speedily in 1994 to agree terms of membership. These were agreed by the Council and Commission in March and by the European Parliament in May 1994. The terms were negotiated vigorously by the applicants and the EU – with special arrangements emerging on alpine transit, arctic farming and budget contributions. At the last stage of negotiations the United Kingdom sought an accommodation on the voting arrangements in the Council. Despite being unsuccessful this is a clear marker for the 1996 Inter-Governmental Conference. All but Norway are now EU members.

Other applicants include Poland, Hungary, Turkey, Malta and Cyprus. The first two of these have moved ahead of other former Soviet-bloc states to formally request membership. The Czech Republic and Slovakia are expected to follow as indeed are other Central and Eastern European States. Malta and Cyprus are moving towards membership with the European Commission having published its opinion on the terms of accession. Cyprus has the problem of being a divided territory and the Maltese financial, economic and budget structures (it has a heavily protected and regulated economy) need restructuring. However, the Commission

have already stated they expect accession negotiations with Malta
to begin six months after the end of the 1996 Inter-Governmental
Conference and as no serious economic problems are foreseen,
these two countries are likely to be included in the next phase of
enlargement. The Commission's opinion on Turkey concluded that
economic dislocation would be too great: emphasis is now being
directed towards realisation of the customs union foreseen in the
EC/Turkey Association Agreement of 1964. Early in February 1995
a proposal was agreed in principle whereby Greece would lift its
veto on an EU/Turkey customs union in exchange for setting a
date of around 2000 for Cyprus to join the EU. Greece has yet to
accept this proposal.

Accession requires a number of formal moves. Once an application is formally made, the Commission must produce an opinion
on the application, after which the Council takes its decision acting
by unanimity. The terms of accession must be agreed and ratified
by the applicant and the Member States. This will involve a referendum in the applicant country. Recent referenda have produced
mixed results. Those in Sweden, Finland and Austria, as with the
referenda held in some Member States on the Maastricht Treaty,
produced a narrow margin of voters in favour. These narrow
margins of support and significant numbers of Euro-sceptics in at
least three Member States – France, Denmark and the United
Kingdom – are likely to be a significant brake on the speed at
which European integration progresses. The no vote in Norway
and the rejection in Switzerland of the EEA, and by implication the
EU, will also give pause for thought.

Whether the EC institutions in their present form will be equal to
the challenge posed by enlargement is very much a live issue. This
will be but one of the elements considered in the institutional
review set for the Inter-Governmental Conference in 1996. One
very significant practical – and often emotive – problem is that of
official Community languages. The EU's current operations and
legislative process are already burdened by the need to translate
documents into [eleven] official languages (English, Danish, Dutch,
Finnish, French, German, Greek, Italian, Portuguese, Spanish and
Swedish). As the EU expands further, whatever compromise is
essentially adopted – and that some compromise solution will have
to be found is almost inevitable – the EU cannot expect its new
"citizens" to be subject to laws and regulations issued in a
language they do not understand.

(vi) The European Economic Area

In May 1992, the European Economic Community, the European Coal and Steel Community, the then 12 Member States of the EEC and the seven members of the European Free Trade Area signed an agreement creating the European Economic Area (EEA). The Agreement seeks to create a common market, based on the four freedoms of people, goods, capital and services, within the EC/EFTA territory, supported by policies on competition, where the EC rules are more or less entirely transposed to the EEA, and by closer co-operation in other fields such as environmental and social policy.

The EEA Agreement required ratification by all participating countries and in December 1992 it was rejected by a Swiss referendum. Although many expected Liechtenstein, which has close ties with Switzerland including a customs union, to follow Switzerland, it did not. The EEA survived Swiss rejection. An amending protocol simply provided for the deletion of Switzerland from the Agreement in all relevant places and participation by Liechtenstein when this was possible. An agreement has now been reached to allow Liechtenstein to participate in the EEA from 1 May 1995. Future membership of Switzerland in the EEA is possible, but in the meantime, it has observer status in EFTA on matters relating to the EEA. The Agreement finally entered into force on 1 January 1994, one year behind schedule and without Switzerland and, initially, Liechtenstein.

During the course of 1994 four EFTA members – Norway, Sweden, Finland and Austria – negotiated terms of entry into the EU. All but Norway held successful referenda on EU membership and became EU Member States from 1 January 1995. Norway voted against EU membership in its referendum and it remains outside the EU but within the EEA.

While the EEA's institutional structure may survive to admit further members, for at least three out of the six participating EFTA states the EEA has been little more than a waiting post before full EU membership.

(vii) A Wider Europe

Looking further east, several central and eastern European countries have set EU membership as their goal. The EU has concluded association agreements (known as the "Europe Agreements") with Hungary, Poland, Romania, Bulgaria and the Czech and Slovak Republics. Negotiations are now also under way with Slovenia. These Agreements, which are the EC's most sophisticated form of trade association agreement, contain provisions to promote closer political dialogue and economic ties with the Community. Their aim is to gradually create a free trade area through the progressive dismantling of trade barriers. They also include provisions on competition law and establish Association Councils to monitor the operation of the Agreements. Only the Agreements with Poland and Hungary have so far entered into force (on 1 February 1994) but in the meantime interim trade agreements, which implement provisions relating to the free movement of goods and competition, are in operation in the other countries.

Lesser order economic and co-operation agreements were concluded with the Baltic states, Latvia, Lithuania and Estonia, and Albania in May 1992 and, later, with Slovenia. While they do provide for the removal of import quotas and most-favoured nation treatment for customs duties and internal taxes, they do not provide for free trade in the same way as the Europe Agreements, and nor do they contain any competition rules. In July 1994, the agreements with Latvia, Lithuania and Estonia were replaced with free trade agreements coming into force on 1 January 1995.

Partnership and co-operation agreements have been signed with the Ukraine, Kazakhstan, the Russian Federation, Belarus, Kyrgyzstan and Moldova. Negotiations are under way with Morocco. These agreements are similar to those entered into with countries further afield - India and South Africa. These are intended to develop political dialogue and economic co-operation between them and the EU.

(viii) A Multi-Speed Europe?

Both the prospect of further enlargement of the EU and the strengthening of trade and economic links with other central and eastern European countries has fuelled speculation that Europe is developing into a multi-speed or perhaps, more accurately, a multi-tiered entity. To some extent, there already is a multi-speed Europe, both within and outside the European Union itself.

Within the EU, a core of nine Member States have signed (but Italy and Greece have not yet ratified) the Schengen Convention which provides for the removal of all controls for travellers at internal land and sea frontiers of the EU, and establishes common procedures for customs and other controls at external borders at airports. The date for the entry into force of the Schengen Convention was 26 March 1995. When the Schengen Convention entered into force, the three Member States which are not party to it – the UK, Denmark and Ireland – were already in the "slow lane" of European integration, although Denmark is currently negotiating to accede to the Convention, initially as an observer country. Moreover both the UK and Denmark have secured an "opt-out" enabling them to retain a national currency when the other 13 Member States move to the third stage of economic and monetary union and a single currency. The United Kingdom, by virtue of a Protocol, has also opted out of the Social Charter annexed to the Maastricht Treaty. The legal effect of this opt-out is, however, diluted by the ability of the Council to adopt much social legislation under the "health and safety of workers" provisions in the Treaty of Rome and by the practical efforts of companies deciding to extend new practices to the whole of their European operations. Nonetheless, the effect in the UK will be the opportunity for reduced labour market regulation and, in many cases, lower labour costs.

Perhaps even more striking is the way in which the "wider Europe" is developing in tiers with different countries developing free trade links and integration with the EU at different speeds. The arrangement closest to full integration and indeed EU membership was the EEA Agreement, three out of the six original members of which have already acceded to and joined the EU. Snapping at their heels are the Europe Agreement signatories, all of which regard EU membership as a long-term goal (the year 2000 has been cited by Poland and Hungary) and all of which can be expected to progress to more developed free trade arrangements some time before then. Similarly, the Baltic states, who have more diluted free trade agreements in the form of "trade and economic co-operation agreements", are already aspiring to transform these agreements into Europe Agreements. It is intrinsic to the Partnership Agreements with the CIS countries that, as progress is made, they will also proceed to more developed free trade agreements.

With all the controversy and discussion that has accompanied the "deepening versus widening" debate in recent years, a multi-speed Europe may not only prove to be a possibility but may emerge as a necessity.

Table of European relationships

	EU	Schengen Convention	EEA	EFTA	Free trade agreement	Europe Agreement	Trade and Economic Co-operation Agreement	Partnership Agreement	WEU	NATO	CIS	Visegrad	WTO	ECHR
Belgium	✔	✔	✔						✔	✔			✔	✔
Denmark	✔		✔						×	✔			✔	✔
Germany	✔	✔	✔						✔	✔			✔	✔
Greece	✔	✍	✔						✍	✔			✔	✔
Spain	✔	✔	✔						✔	✔			✔	✔
France	✔	✔	✔						✔	□			✔	✔
Ireland	✔		✔						×				✔	✔
Italy	✔	✍	✔						✔	✔			✔	✔
Luxembourg	✔	✔	✔						✔	✔			✔	✔
Netherlands	✔	✔	✔						✔	✔			✔	✔
Portugal	✔	✔	✔						✔	✔			✔	✔
UK	✔		✔						✔	✔			✔	✔
Austria	✔	×							×				✔	✔
Finland	✔								×				✔	✔
Sweden	✔								×				✔	✔
Norway	!		✔	✔					○	✔			✔	✔
Iceland	✱		✔	✔					○	✔			✔	✔
Liechtenstein	✱		C	✔										✔
Switzerland	!		!	✔	✔									✔
Cyprus	✱													✔
Malta	✱												✔	✔
Turkey	✱								○	✔				✔
Poland	✱					✔			●			✔		✔
Hungary	✱					✔			●			✔	✔	✔
Romania						✔			●				✔	✔
Bulgaria						✔			●				×	✔
Czech Rep						✔			●			✔	✔	✔
Slovakia						✔			●			✔	✔	✔
Estonia					✔		✔		●				†	✍
Latvia					✔		✔		●				†	✍
Lithuania					✔		✔		●					✍
Slovenia							✔							✔
Albania							✔							
Belarus								✔			✔		×	
Kazakhstan								✔			✔			
Kyrgyzstan								✔			✔			
Russia								†			✔		×	
Ukraine								✔			✔		×	
Moldova								✔			✔			
San Marino														✔
Morocco								†					✔	
Andorra														✍

Legend

✱	application for EU membership submitted	×	observer
□	member of NATO but not military alliance	C	conditional membership agreement
○	associate membership	†	subject of negotiations
●	associate partnership	!	rejected
✍	signed but not ratified		

2. THE COUNCIL OF THE EUROPEAN UNION

(i) Role

The Council of the European Union (the "Council") is the political and legislative organ of the EU. The national interests of each Member State are represented on it. It is the principal and ultimate decision-making body of the EU. Prior to the entry into force of the Maastricht Treaty in November 1993, the Council's full title was the Council of the European Communities (colloquially known as the Council of Ministers). It has now renamed itself to take into account its additional role under the Maastricht Treaty in the context of the foreign and security policy and justice and home affairs (see Chapter 2 Section (iv) *infra*).

(ii) Composition

The Council has no fixed composition and its membership will vary according to the subject area under discussion. Representatives on the Council are politicians or civil servants from each Member State selected by each national administration to represent its interests at the appropriate rank for the issue under discussion. Each of the 15 Member State governments is represented at meetings of the Council. These meetings range from meetings of Heads of Government to meetings of Ministers holding responsibility in each Member State for a particular policy area. The General Affairs Council, for instance, considers external affairs and matters of general Community concern, and is attended by foreign ministers of each Member State. More specialised Councils include Ecofin, at which finance ministers meet, and the Internal Market Council (IMC), at which those ministers responsible for particular single market issues meet. There are also specialised Council meetings in respect of the following subject areas: agriculture, budget, consumer affairs and protection, cultural affairs, development co-operation, education, energy, environment, fisheries, health, immigration, industry, judicial affairs, labour and social affairs, research, telecommunications, tourism and transport. The composition of each Council may vary depending on the difficulty or seriousness of the issue under discussion, in which case a more senior Minister may attend, and on the exact subject under discussion. Member States may have different Ministers responsible, for example, for air transport and inland transport. The relevant Minister will attend.

The Council is assisted by a committee of permanent representatives, colloquially known as COREPER, and a number of "expert" working groups. Each Member State has a permanent delegation in Brussels, roughly equivalent to an embassy (its "representation to the EC"). The delegation is made up of national civil servants covering all major policy areas who work in conjunction with officials from the relevant national ministries. The UK delegation is known as "UKRep". The purpose of COREPER (and the working groups) is to negotiate and reach agreement on proposals and policy and to avoid their discussion at ministerial level. COREPER I is made up of deputy ambassadors, whose responsibilities are divided by subject. It considers proposals on technical subjects such as financial services, transport or environment. COREPER II is made up of the ambassadors themselves and considers the more general and political issues such as third country relations and institutional problems. Working groups formed of the national civil servants of the relevant government departments, officials from the Member States' permanent representatives at the EC and Commission officials discuss and negotiate the details of particular proposals and report to COREPER. As national Ministers are only able to come to Brussels for short periods, the working groups and COREPER do a substantial amount of preliminary negotiation of proposals and, wherever possible, reach agreement on Community policy. In practice, the working groups will settle the detail of proposals and identify issues on which agreement cannot be reached or areas where guidance is needed. Those issues will go to COREPER for resolution. The remaining contentious issues are referred to the Council for debate. Where agreement cannot be reached or cannot be finally given by a delegation, for instance because national Parliamentary approval is needed first, "reservations" are made by the delegation and recorded in the working documents. These documents are very often not made widely available.

The Council is based in Brussels, where the majority of its meetings take place. However, during April, June and October its meetings are held in Luxembourg. Council meetings are chaired by the Member State holding the Council Presidency, which rotates every six months between the Member States according to an order laid down by the Council. The Council has laid down the holders of the Presidency for eight and a half years from accession of the three new members. We are currently in the course of the second cycle. Each presidency issues an action list of priorities for its presidency during its first month of office. The Secretariat of the Council is responsible for co-ordinating and assisting the work of the Council, COREPER and various working groups.

Holders of the Presidency of the Council from 1994 until the end of 1999

From:

January 1994: Greece	January 1997: Netherlands
July 1994: Germany	July 1997: Luxembourg
January 1995: France	January 1998: United Kingdom
July 1995: Spain	July 1998: Portugal
January 1996: Italy	January 1999: Germany
July 1996: Ireland	July 1999: Finland

The country holding the Presidency will be represented in two capacities at Council meetings – in its national capacity and as President. The President's role is to move matters forward and to search for consensus. In practice, and by convention, this means that the national interest of the country holding the Presidency will be tempered during the course of its custodianship of that position.

The Presidency is responsible for setting the priorities for the Council for each six months of office and will usually set particular objectives which it hopes to achieve. There is a degree of competition among Member States to run the Presidency in an efficient and effective way. Each country holding the Presidency likes to feel it has made a contribution to the progress of EC affairs.

(iii) Decision-Making Procedure

Council meetings are convened by the Council President either on his own initiative or at the request of a Member State or the

The Structure of the Council

COUNCIL OF MINISTERS

Attended by the relevant Minister
from each Member State, depending
on the policy area under discussion.
Meets monthly (at least).

↓

COMMITTEE OF
PERMANENT REPRESENTATIVES

("COREPER")
Composed of national civil servants
based permanently in Brussels*.
Responsible for preliminary negotiation
of proposals and reaches agreement on
non-contentious issues.

↓

COUNCIL WORKING GROUPS

Composition as for COREPER.
Responsible for negotiating details of
proposals.
Reports to COREPER.

---

* Each Member State has a permanent delegation in Brussels roughly equivalent to an embassy (its "Representation to the EC"). The delegation is made up of national civil servants covering all the major policy areas, who work in conjunction with officials from the relevant national ministries. The UK's delegation is referred to colloquially as "UKRep".

Commission. A timetable of Council meetings is planned in advance and papers setting up the matters to be considered are circulated. A Council agenda will be divided into so-called "A" and "B" items. "A" items are those upon which agreement has been reached during the preparatory meetings of COREPER and the Council working groups and these may be approved by any Council with little debate. "B" items are those upon which agreement has not been reached and which the Council with responsibility for that subject area will have to debate more fully.

Council decisions are usually taken either by unanimous vote or by a qualified majority vote (essentially 62 votes out of 87 using a weighted voting system, see table below for details), depending upon the Article of the Treaty of Rome upon which the decision is based. A limited number of Council decisions, mainly those relating to questions of internal procedure and to calling an Inter-Governmental Conference, can be taken by simple majority. Even where decisions are taken by simple or qualified majority, as a last resort it may, in theory, be possible for a Member State to invoke the so-called Luxembourg Compromise. While this allows a Member State to assert its national interests to block a proposal, it has no legal status and has very rarely been deployed. Indeed, some commentators believe it no longer exists. Since it is a matter of convention rather than law, its existence inevitably depends on a consensus between Member States at any given time.

The legal basis of a proposed measure is therefore of fundamental importance for it may determine whether unanimity is required and thus whether a particular Member State can block its adoption. The Commission and the Council have on a number of occasions disagreed over the correct legal basis of a measure, with the Commission endeavouring to base the majority of its proposals on Articles of the Treaty providing for qualified majority voting.

Qualified majority voting ensures a system of limitation or redressing of powers between the Member States by preventing the large Member States from imposing their will on the other Member States. The number of votes required to block a proposal is currently 26 (i.e. 30%).

The number of votes required to block a proposal was the subject of considerable debate during the negotiations for the accession of Austria, Finland and Sweden. While the majority of Member States favoured a proportional increase in the number of

The Treaty of Rome weighted voting structure in the Council

Austria	4	Ireland	3
Belgium	5	Italy	10
Denmark	3	Luxembourg	2
Finland	3	Netherlands	5
Germany	10	Portugal	5
Greece	5	Sweden	4
Spain	8	United Kingdom	10
France	10		

TOTAL   87

Votes required for a qualified majority 62

votes required to block, from 23 to 26, so as to keep the blocking minority at 30%, the UK wanted to retain the blocking minority at 23, fearing that any increase would give smaller states an unfair advantage. The compromise eventually reached raises the blocking minority to 26 votes, although a dissenting minority of at least 23 will be entitled to a "reasonable delay" before a final vote is taken. During that period, the Commission will be obliged to try to reach agreement. Once a Member State considers a reasonable delay to have elapsed, it can request a final vote to be taken. If a simple majority agrees, the proposal may then only be blocked by a dissenting minority of 26 votes. As a last resort, it may still be possible to invoke the Luxembourg Compromise.

The qualified majority voting rules work differently in the area of social affairs. Since the UK does not participate in the Social Protocol, the majority required for proposals being dealt with under that Protocol is 52 votes out of a total of 87. They also work differently in the second and third pillars of the EU. If the Council is dealing with a proposal which does not have to originate from the Commission the 62 votes must come from at least 10 Member States to count as a qualified majority. This will apply, for example, to the adoption of common positions on Common, Foreign and Security Policy and Justice and Home Affairs, if unanimity is not required.

The relative distribution of votes in an enlarged EU is one of the subjects to be discussed at the 1996 Inter-Governmental Conference. The large number of small countries likely to accede would significantly alter the internal balance as it currently stands.

Although it is the final legislative body, Council meetings are not open to the public, nor reported, although members of the Commission will usually attend by invitation to discuss proposals with the Council. This adds to the feeling of intrigue and conspiracy surrounding Community legislation and certainly makes the process more opaque. In December 1993, the Council amended its rules of procedure to allow for televising policy debates on the six-monthly work programmes of the Council. Televising other debates may be permitted on a case-by-case basis. As part of a general policy of increased openness and transparency, the voting record at Council meetings, which up until now has been confidential, will be made public. The Council also adopted, together with the Commission, a Code of Conduct on public access to Council documents.

(iv) The Inter-Governmental Pillars of European Union

Although the second and third pillars of the European Union established by the Maastricht Treaty, namely a common foreign and security policy (CFSP) and co-operation in the fields of home affairs and justice, are technically separate from the European Community and are essentially to be carried out at inter-governmental level it is intended these will eventually merge within the Community. The EC institutions do have roles to play, even if they are limited (except the European Court of Justice whose jurisdiction is excluded).

(a) Common Foreign and Security Policy

The CFSP replaces European Political Co-operation (EPC), which was established in 1984 and formally institutionalised by the Single European Act 1986 as a means by which Member States could informally co-ordinate their foreign and security policies. The Maastricht Treaty talks of the eventual framing of a Common Defence Policy. Unlike EPC, Member States are under an obligation, arising not under Community law but international law, to carry out and comply with agreed policies and joint actions (except in cases of urgency). In addition, the President of the Council is given the power to represent the Member States at, for example, international organisations and international conferences.

A complicated procedure has been set up according to which the Council, having agreed unanimously on a common policy, will also decide, again unanimously, whether certain measures needed to implement the policy should be taken by qualified majority vote. Nevertheless, once Member States have agreed on a common policy, countries will be allowed to act on their own "in cases of imperative need".

The nine-member Western European Union (WEU) is recognised by the Maastricht Treaty to be an integral part of the development of the European Union. The WEU is an inter-governmental organisation for European co-operation in the field of security and exists as an organisational structure in parallel to the European Union. It aims to establish an ongoing dialogue amongst its members (Belgium, France, Germany, Italy, Luxembourg, the Netherlands, Portugal, Spain and the United Kingdom) in order to arrive at common positions on politico-military issues. The WEU was established by the participating countries so that co-operation on such matters could take place on an inter-governmental level and outside the EC's supranational structure. This also enabled them to do so, notwithstanding Ireland's neutrality and the objections of Denmark and Greece. The European Union may request the WEU to elaborate and implement decisions under actions of the European Union which have defence implications. On 9 May 1994, Poland, Hungary, the Czech Republic, Slovakia, Bulgaria, Romania, Estonia, Latvia and Lithuania become "associate partners" of the WEU. The defence arrangements will be reviewed in 1996 as part of the 1996 IGC, although these will still have to be compatible with NATO. Norway remains outside full membership of the WEU.

(b) Co-Operation in Judicial and Home Affairs

In co-operation in the fields of justice and home affairs, a division of competences is made between those areas which are "primarily" Community matters and those which are "primarily" inter-governmental. There is provision for a subject to be transferred from the inter-governmental to the EC framework, with asylum being the priority candidate for this.

The maintenance of law and order and the safeguarding of internal security remain within the exclusive competence of the individual Member States. The EC is given some new, if limited, competences, namely the determination of third country nationals that must be in possession of a visa and the adoption of measures relating to a uniform format for visas. Nine inter-governmental competences are listed, namely asylum, crossing external borders, immigration, drugs, international crime, judicial co-operation in civil and criminal matters, co-operation between customs services, policing co-operation and a system of exchange of police information.

The Council may adopt joint action and draw up conventions for adoption by the Member States. It is clearly intended (but not expressly stated) that the Council should act unanimously; but, as in the case of CFSP, the Council can decide that implementing measures can be adopted by qualified majority. A co-ordinating committee has been established to assist the Council in co-ordinating action in these areas.

(v) The European Council

The habit of holding a regular "summit", grandiosely styled the European Council, began in 1974 and was formally recognised by the Single European Act in 1986. It meets at least twice a year, usually coinciding with the end of a Council presidency, although it may meet at any other time if required. For example, an extraordinary European Council meeting took place at the end of October 1993 to smooth the entry into force of the Maastricht Treaty on 1 November 1993. European Councils are attended by the heads of state or government of each Member State and the President of the Commission together with foreign ministers and a member of the Commission. It should not be confused with the Council, since it does not adopt Community legislation as such, but rather provides a forum for policy formulation at a political level and for resolving any matters on which the Council has been unable to reach agreement. Since the coming into force of the Maastricht Treaty, the European Council has additional responsibility for "ensuring the development of the European Union" and, in particular, advising and providing guidelines to the Council on economic policy and joint action in the fields of common foreign and security policy and justice and home affairs.

(vi) Foreign Missions to the EU

The accession countries and several other third countries interested in European affairs maintain foreign missions in Brussels. They have no formal role in the decision-making process, but keep themselves informed about EU developments and may make informal representations in matters where their country's interests may be affected. Recently, as part of the integration process, certain of the representatives of the missions from the accession countries have been invited to take part in meetings of COREPER as observers.

Monitoring and influencing decision-making

- Given its political character, decision-making at the level of the Council is the result of extensive dialogue between the Commission, the various Council organs and the European Parliament.

- Contact should be made with the relevant national ministries in as many Member States as possible, such as the DTI in the United Kingdom, and with the permanent representations to the EC which are based in Brussels. The permanent representations are also a valuable source of information. In particular, it is important to have good contacts with COREPER officials since COREPER will liaise between the national administrations closely involved in negotiating agreement on proposals and the EC institutions. Although useful, one does have to be aware that even if the Member State accepts your concerns, it will only have one voice among 15 Member States. Particularly if the proposal is to be adopted by majority voting, its wishes may be overridden, or it may become the victim of "horse-trading" and conceded in exchange for winning an unrelated argument. National delegations in Brussels are, however, an excellent source of information on the status of proposals and the tensions that surround them. Whilst they are interested in third party views they only have a limited role in formulating policy. In the United Kingdom at least, it is probably more effective to lobby the relevant department.

- Each Member State will have its own arrangements for ensuring that its national parliament is kept informed of EC developments. Contact with individuals who take an active part in a national parliament's surveillance of Community legislation can be useful. For example, in the United Kingdom, the House of Lords Select Committee on the European Communities has special responsibility for scrutinising in great detail all EC proposals and its conclusions may form the basis of the UK government's position on a proposal as well as being forwarded to the Commission and Council. In the House of Commons, there is a Select Committee on European Legislation and European Standing Committees A and B, all of which keep track of and scrutinise European legislative developments.

- Proposed legislation is often highly technical. Both COREPER and national governments consult pan-European trade associations, standards bodies such as CEN, CENELEC and ETSI and other interest groups who will be well placed to put forward the interests of a particular industry. Such associations often allow non-Europeans to be members and can provide useful contacts for non-EC businesses.

3. THE EUROPEAN COMMISSION

(i) Introduction

The European Commission is the initiator and co-ordinator of EC legislation. It supervises both the application or implementation of Community legislation and the application and day-to-day running of Community policies, including the various Community funding programmes. In addition, the Commission also has extensive decision-making powers of its own in certain specific areas, particularly in competition policy.

(ii) Composition

The Commission is comprised of 20 members ("Commissioners") appointed by national governments – two each from France, Germany, Italy, Spain and the UK and one each from Austria, Belgium, Denmark, Finland, Greece, Ireland, Luxembourg, the Netherlands, Portugal and Sweden. Traditionally, the United Kingdom has appointed one Commissioner from each of the two main political parties. Clearly, the number of Commissioners will change to take account of the accession of new countries. Each Commissioner undertakes not to take instructions from his respective national government and to act independently in the best interests of the Community. Nonetheless, Commissioners will naturally be sensitive to issues which concern their own countries. Under the new procedure laid down in the Maastricht Treaty, the current Commission was appointed for a renewable five-year period beginning on 23 January 1995 following approval by the European Parliament. The Commission has a President, currently Jacques Santer, and two Vice-Presidents, currently Sir Leon Brittan and Manuel Marin.

The Commission is at present composed of 23 Directorates-General and each is allocated a policy area or administrative function. In addition to the 23 Directorates-General, the Commission also has several "services" or departments including the Secretariat-General, the Legal Service, the Statistical Office, the Joint Interpreting and Conference Service, the Spokesman's Office and the Consumer Policy Service. Each Commissioner is allocated one or more policy areas, and the Directorate-General dealing with those areas, for which he will be responsible during his term of office. However, despite this allocation of responsibility, the Commission acts as a "college" and is therefore collectively responsible for all its acts. Each Commissioner is served by a private office or "*Cabinet*", formed of personal political advisers. The *Cabinet* acts as a link between the Commissioner and his or her Directorate(s)-General. A Commissioner's *Chef de Cabinet* will normally be of the same nationality as the Commissioner and may deputise on his or her behalf. A list of the current Commissioners and their respective portfolios is contained in Appendix A.

Each Directorate-General is headed by a Director-General. A Directorate-General will itself be divided into several Directorates. The Commission publishes an organigram identifying the officials responsible for policy areas within each Directorate. Appendix B contains simplified tables showing, by way of example, the structure of three different Directorates-General: DGIII (Industry), DGIV (Competition) and DGXV (Internal Market and Financial Affairs).

The Commission is based in Brussels although a number of its services and Directorates-General are located in Luxembourg. The Commission also has representative offices in all Member States providing general information for example to the media and trade organisations. Delegations and Representative Offices have also been established in third countries.

The Directorates-General

DG I: External Economic Relations
DG IA: External Political Relations
DG II: Economic and Financial Affairs
DG III: Industry
DG IV: Competition
DG V: Employment, Industrial Relations and Social Affairs
DG VI: Agriculture
DG VII: Transport
DG VIII: Development
DG IX: Personnel and Administration

DG X:	Audiovisual, Information, Communication and Culture
DG XI:	Environment, Nuclear Safety and Civil Protection
DG XII:	Science, Research and Development
DG XIII:	Telecommunications, Information Industries and Innovation
DG XIV:	Fisheries
DG XV:	Internal Market and Financial Services
DG XVI:	Regional Policies
DG XVII:	Energy
DG XVIII:	Credit and Investments
DG XIX:	Budgets
DG XX:	Financial Control
DG XXI:	Customs and Indirect Taxation
DG XXIII:	Enterprise Policy, Distributive Trades, Tourism and Co-operatives

(iii) Legislative Role

Much of the Commission's importance rests on the fact that, in the first pillar of the Union – the EC, it is the only institution with the ability to initiate legislation, although both the Council and the European Parliament can (and frequently do) request the Commission to formulate proposals. A Directorate-General will develop proposals for legislation internally in consultation with various interested parties including governmental authorities, trade associations, experts and the Commission's Legal Service. It is quite common for proposals to remain at this preparatory stage for a number of years and to undergo many internal drafts. Once the responsible Directorate-General has formulated a firm proposal it is then circulated to all the Directorates-General for comment and amendment. Finally it will be submitted to the College of Commissioners for approval by simple majority, ie 11 out of 20. Only then will it be presented to the Council as a formal Commission proposal, translated into the 11 official Community languages and published in the Official Journal.

The Commission has often been criticised for not making its working documents available for public comment. The Commission recently announced that it would make more use of so-called white and green discussion papers to allow for wider consultation prior

How a proposal is adopted by the Commission

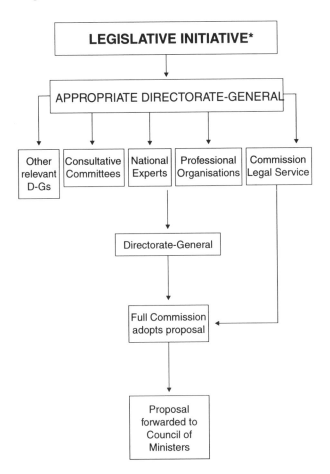

* Although it is the Commission which has the power to initiate legislation, the European Parliament (in the form of Parliamentary resolutions) and the Council of Ministers will often request the Commission to formulate a proposal in a particular area. In addition, the European Council, as part of its role of providing a political forum for discussion of future EC policies, will often invite the Commission to present proposals on specific issues to the Council.

to formulating its proposals and would ensure that all Commission documents are made public in all the Community languages. Furthermore, the Commission is to publish its annual work programme in October of each year to encourage debate on it in national parliaments and will publish in the Official Journal a brief summary of any measure planned by the Commission together with a deadline by which interested parties may submit their comments. The Commission, with Council, has adopted a Code of Conduct on public access to Commission documents which, while falling short of a Freedom of Information Act, will bolster rights to obtain information.

Contrary to popular belief, the Commission is not a large bureaucracy, at least in comparison to national Ministries. It suffers from a lack of resources and consequently is open to views and information being provided from outside the Commission. National administrations play a constant part in informing the Commission of the facts relevant to proposals through the expert working groups of the Council and *ad hoc* working groups or representatives where the proposal is in its early stages or can be adopted by the Commission on its own initiative. Private bodies are able to contribute in an *ad hoc* way. In some cases the Commission will actively seek views on proposals before they are formally adopted. Once formally adopted, proposals are published in the Official Journal, which provides an opportunity for comment.

(iv) Enforcement Role

The Commission's other major role is that of ensuring that Member States, companies, private organisations and individuals comply with the Treaty and legislation made under it. The Commission has the power to investigate, either on its own initiative or following a complaint, any alleged breaches of Community law. If not resolved at the administrative stage, such investigations may result in the Commission bringing proceedings before the European Court of Justice. This may be against Member States for failure to comply with Treaty obligations, for example non-implementation of Community legislation; against the Council for failure to adopt measures required under the Treaty (although this has never in fact happened); or against individuals, including companies and private organisations, for breach of certain EC provisions, such as the competition rules.

As well as the right to bring actions before the European Court of Justice, the Commission also has wide decision-making powers of its own. In a number of areas the Commission not only investigates a complaint but will also be the final arbiter of whether the complaint is justified (subject to an appeal to the European Court of Justice). For example, under the competition rules it is the Commission, without reference to the Council, which applies Articles 85 and 86 of the EC Treaty and the Merger Control Regulation and which can, if necessary, prohibit transactions and/or impose significant fines. Furthermore, in respect of most state subsidies, the Commission alone has responsibility for deciding their compatibility. In other areas, such as dumping, the Commission will carry out the investigation and determine whether there has been a breach of Community law and impose, if necessary, provisional duties. However, it will be the Council of Ministers who definitively collect the provisional duty and impose the definitive duty.

The Commission's enforcement role is not limited to supervising the application of existing legislation. In certain areas, the Council may delegate to the Commission the power to adopt implementing rules either in the form of Regulations or Directives, without recourse to the usual legislative procedures (see Chapter 7). The Council has done this in particular in respect of agriculture and competition. In addition, the Treaty of Rome itself, in certain limited areas, allows the Commission to lay down rules without recourse to the other institutions. Article 90, in particular, gives the Commission power to legislate to control publicly owned enterprises and businesses given special or exclusive rights by Member States. Article 90 has been the cornerstone of the Commission's policy of opening up state monopolies in sectors such as postal services, telecommunications, air transport services, and energy. The Member States, not surprisingly, have questioned the extent of this right. The European Court of Justice has held, in a recent judgment, that the Commission had not exceeded its competence in adopting a Directive on competition in the telecommunications sector. The European Court of Justice upheld the Commission's interpretation of Article 90 of the Treaty that it was empowered, in relation to certain undertakings specified under Article 90(1) and 90(2), to adopt Directives specifying Member States' obligations under the Treaty, in particular where the Council has failed to do so.

How to ensure your views are represented

- The Commission is often the most important EC institution to lobby both during the formulation of a legislative proposal and once a proposal has been referred to the Council. Indeed the Commission encourages companies, governments and associations, both European and non-European, to submit their views when it is formulating policy.

- It is important to put forward views at a very early stage in the legislative process to ensure a greater chance of them being reflected in eventual legislation.

- Views should, in the first instance, be expressed to the officials responsible for the initiative in question rather than at the political level of the Commissioners, although contact with a Commissioner's Cabinet is productive as the Cabinet is closely involved in the formulation of policies.

- Several Directorates-General may be interested in any proposal and it may be possible to identify a Directorate-General not directly responsible for the proposal which may be sympathetic to your views.

- The Commission will usually consult interest groups who often provide the Commission with research data as well as presenting a particular industry's viewpoint. UNICE, ETUC, BEUC, ERT and AmCham are the most influential and can represent not only the views of European but also non-European businesses.

4. THE EUROPEAN PARLIAMENT

(i) Membership

The European Parliament is the only directly-elected EC institution, each Member State being allocated a number of MEPs. Following the accession of the three new Members, the number of MEPs was increased from 567 to 626. This increase takes account of the additional East German *Länder* after German reunification. The number of members allocated to most other Member States was also increased to ensure that Germany was not thereby given disproportionate voting power in the European Parliament. Elections are held throughout the Community every five years.

Member State allocation of MEPs

Austria	21	Finland	16
France	87	Greece	25
Germany	99	Portugal	25
Italy	87	Belgium	25
UK	87	Denmark	16
Spain	64	Ireland	15
Netherlands	31	Luxembourg	6
		Sweden	22

MEPs sit in multinational political groupings and not according to their nationality.

Multinational political groupings

European People's Party (including UK Conservatives)	Rainbow Group
Socialists (including UK Labour Party)	European Right
Liberal and Democratic Reformist Group	Green Group
European Democratic Alliance	Left Unity
Technical Group of the European Right	Non-attached

The Parliament's Bureau is responsible for its organisation and administration. It is elected for two and a half years and together with the chairman of the political group sets the details and agenda of the Parliamentary sessions. The European Parliament is also assisted by a Secretary-General and Secretariat.

After several decades of debate, the Edinburgh European Council in December 1992 resolved the issue of the European Parliament's location. The 12-monthly plenary sessions including the budget session are to be held in Strasbourg whilst additional sessions and Committee meetings are to be held in Brussels. The Parliament's Secretariat, however, is to remain in Luxembourg.

(ii) Legislative Role

Unlike the Commission and the Council, which between them are the effective legislators, the European Parliament has not been a legislative body, and its role has essentially been an advisory and supervisory one. The extent of the European Parliament's influence depends on the legislative procedure required to be followed in each particular case (see Chapter 7). Generally, the European Parliament has the right to be consulted on proposed legislation and to put forward amendments. However, it has no right to have its amendments incorporated into a proposal, although a significant proportion of its amendments are in fact included in legislation ultimately adopted. Following the Single European Act, which introduced the co-operation procedure for adopting legislation, its influence increased as it was given the capacity to delay the adoption of proposed legislation for a period if its amendments are not incorporated into a proposal.

Given the strict time limits enforced in the co-operation procedure, the European Parliament's power to influence the legislative process in fact was not very strong. Its power has now been strengthened through the co-decision procedure introduced under the Maastricht Treaty (see Chapter 7). The aim of this new procedure is to give the European Parliament greater involvement in the legislative process and its significance lies in the fact that the European Parliament can now prevent the adoption of legislation if the Council will not incorporate the Parliament's amendments. The cynics' view is that obtaining the absolute majority required will be difficult because there is rarely the sufficient number of MEPs sitting in Parliament. The European Parliament's planned veto – its first ever – on a Council decision to ban motorcycle engines above 100-brake horsepower failed to occur, because too few MEPs attended. However, the Parliament has succeeded with amendments to some pieces of EC secondary legislation, notably the proposed Directives on waste packaging and VOC emissions.

The clearest example of its exercise of its new powers occurred in relation to the dispute over minority blocking rights during the enlargement negotiations. The European Parliament threatened to veto enlargement if the Commission made the concessions demanded by the UK. That threat constrained Member States to make only the most cosmetic of concessions. Nevertheless, in comparison with the Council and the Commission, the European Parliament remains relatively weak. Despite failing to obtain its much hoped-for power to initiate proposals, the European Parliament was given by the Maastricht Treaty the power to request the Commission to submit to the Council any appropriate proposal on matters on which it considers that a Community act is required for the purpose of implementing the EC Treaty.

In relation to CFSP and co-operation in justice and home affairs, the European Parliament's role remains purely advisory and supervisory. The Council is required to consult the European Parliament and to keep it informed but the European Parliament is not involved in the detailed decisions in these areas. The European Parliament will no doubt attempt to increase its role through its committees by exercising its right to ask questions.

(iii) Other Powers

The European Parliament also has the right to approve the nomination of the President of the Commission, to dismiss the entire Commission after a vote of censure (yet to be invoked) and to approve the Community budget and spending programmes. In addition, the Single European Act significantly increased the European Parliament's power in relation to the enlargement of the Community and the conclusion of association agreements with third countries. The European Parliament's assent is required in such cases, albeit within potentially strict time limits, thus effectively granting it the power of veto.

(iv) Decision-Making Process

The general rule is that the European Parliament takes its decisions by an absolute majority of the votes cast. Any exceptions to this rule are specified in the EC Treaty itself. In particular, in certain circumstances, the European Parliament may only take decisions by an absolute majority of its **members**. This, in practice, imposes a quorum requirement on the European Parliament for such decisions and it is this which, due to the frequent inadequacy of attendance at the European Parliament, has hampered its ability to act effectively.

If the co-decision or co-operation procedure is required, the European Parliament may only amend or reject the common position of the Council by an absolute majority of its members. In contrast, a common position may be approved by an absolute majority of votes cast. In the exercise of its budgetary powers over non-compulsory expenditure, the European Parliament may amend the Council's text by a majority of its members. Following a second reading under the procedure, the European Parliament may only amend or reject the Council's modifications to its own amendments by a majority of its members and by three-fifths of the votes cast. It may only reject the budget entirely by a majority of its members and two-thirds of the votes cast and if it has "important reasons" for doing so.

Other important exceptions to the principle of absolute majority of votes cast are as follows: the European Parliament may set up a committee of inquiry to investigate alleged contraventions or maladministration in the implementation of EC law at the request of only a quarter of its members; it must act by a majority of its members to adopt its own rules of procedure; and, finally, a motion of censure against the Commission can only be carried by a two-thirds majority of votes cast which also represents a majority of the European Parliament's members.

(v) Committees

The majority of the European Parliament's work is carried out by the parliamentary standing Committees. There are 20 such Committees composed of MEPs broadly representing the strength of the political groups in the European Parliament. Sub-committees and temporary Committees have also been set up to deal with specific issues such as drugs, racism and human rights. Each Committee has a specific area of responsibility.

European Parliamentary Committees

C1	Foreign Affairs, Security and Defence Policy
C2	Agriculture and Rural Development
C3	Budgets
C4	Economic and Monetary Affairs and Industrial Policy
C5	Research, Technological Development and Energy
C6	External Economic Relations
C7	Legal Affairs and Citizens' Rights
C8	Social Affairs and Employment
C9	Regional Policy
C10	Transport and Tourism
C11	Environment, Public Health and Consumer Protection
C12	Culture, Youth, Education and the Media
C13	Development and Co-operation
C14	Civil Liberties and Internal Affairs
C15	Budgetary Control
C16	Institutional Affairs
C17	Fisheries
C18	Rules of Procedure, the Verification of Credentials and Immunities
C19	Women's Rights
C20	Petitions
	Unemployment (temporary Committee until July 1995)

There is no reason to believe that these Committees will not continue to exist in largely the same form when the newly elected European Parliament convenes. A *Rapporteur* is appointed from the appropriate Committee for each proposal and is responsible for producing a report and draft resolutions on the proposal. These are then debated by the European Parliament in plenary session. In practice, however, unless the proposal is particularly sensitive, the European Parliament will merely adopt the *Rapporteur's* opinion with little debate.

(vi) The Committee on Petitions and the Ombudsman

It has long been the case that anyone with a grievance against the EC may petition the European Parliament to investigate the matter on his behalf. The **Committee on Petitions** was responsible for reporting to the European Parliament in such cases. This *ad hoc* right of petition was formally incorporated into the Treaty of Rome by the Maastricht Treaty. The Committee on Petitions has dealt with, in particular, problems encountered by individuals in exercising the four freedoms (free movement of goods, services, capital and persons), for example, in relation to customs formalities and border controls.

In addition, the Maastricht Treaty also created a **Community Ombudsman** to consider complaints of maladministration by the EC institutions and other bodies (with the exception of the ECJ and CFI in the exercise of their judicial capacity). The Ombudsman is to be appointed by the European Parliament in consultation with the other institutions, with the first Ombudsman to be appointed after the European Parliamentary elections in June 1994. The Ombudsman is completely independent of the other EC institutions and will have the power to conduct inquiries either following complaints by individuals, MEPs or on its own initiative. The Council and the Commission have agreed that the Ombudsman must be granted access to all information and files that he requests, including documentation held by national authorities, unless a refusal can be justified on the grounds of secrecy. Where the Ombudsman finds that there has been maladministration, the relevant institution or body is required to respond to the Ombudsman's findings within three months.

However, neither the Committee on Petitions nor the Ombudsman has any formal powers to ensure compliance with their findings as they have, for example, no right to bring proceedings before the ECJ. It will be the European Parliament itself which takes any necessary action on their behalf, either in the form of political pressure or, in extreme cases, by bringing proceedings before the ECJ. However, the European Parliament's right to bring action is limited to protecting its own prerogatives so its ability to correct maladministration is very restricted.

5. THE COURT OF JUSTICE OF THE EUROPEAN COMMUNITIES ("ECJ")

(i) Introduction

The ECJ, which is located in Luxembourg, is the final arbiter on issues of European Community law. It should not be confused with the European Court of Human Rights set up under the European Convention on Human Rights (ECHR), which is entirely separate and is located in Strasbourg (see Chapter 9 on the Council of Europe's activities). There are two distinct classes of action before the ECJ. The first consists of actions begun in the ECJ itself which are known as direct actions. These include cases brought by the Commission against Member States for failure to fulfil EC Treaty obligations (Article 169); by Member States against fellow Member States for failure to fulfil Treaty obligations (Article 170); by Member States, EC institutions or individuals to review the legality of acts by EC institutions (Article 173); and actions by Member States, EC institutions or individuals against EC institutions for failure to act (Article 175). In addition, the Court has an advisory role, delivering, in particular, opinions on agreements entered into by the Community with third countries or other international organisations. If the ECJ issues an adverse opinion, the agreement will usually be amended to meet the ECJ's objections. For instance, as a result of the ECJ's first opinion on the European Economic Area Agreement that it was incompatible with European Community law, the Agreement was amended to take into account the ECJ's concerns. The second type of actions are ones begun in a national court or tribunal from which references for a preliminary ruling are made to the ECJ on issues of validity or interpretation of EC law (Article 177) (see Chapter 8).

(ii) Composition

The ECJ consists of 15 Judges and nine Advocates-General who are appointed by common agreement between the 15 Member States for a renewable term of six years. In practice, each Member

State appoints a Judge of its nationality to the Court. Now that there is an odd number of Member States there is no longer any need to appoint an extra Judge from one of the larger Member States. The Judges and Advocates-General have varied backgrounds: academics, national judges and lawyers from private practice or from governmental bodies.

The ECJ may either sit in plenary session of all 15 Judges, a small plenum (comprising an odd number of Judges from nine to 11), or in chambers of either three or five (or seven, after accession) Judges. Plenary sessions are required in cases brought by Member States or Community institutions or when a Member State or a Community institution which is party to the proceedings so requests. The Advocates-General advise the Court on cases coming before it, one being appointed for each case. The Advocate-General produces an Opinion in each case which he presents to the Court.

(iii) Court of First Instance

Attached to the ECJ is the Court of First Instance of the European Communities ("CFI"). It was established under the provisions of the Single European Act 1986, in particular to reduce the backlog of cases awaiting decision at ECJ level. It is composed of 15 Judges (in practice one from each Member State) and sits in Chambers of three or five Judges (or in plenary session). There are no Advocates-General.

Prior to the entry into force of the Maastricht Treaty the CFI only had limited jurisdiction, namely to hear cases brought by private parties in the fields of anti-trust and coal and steel and in employment cases brought by Community officials and actions for damages connected with such cases. The Maastricht Treaty gave the Court of Justice the right to request the Council to make a reallocation of jurisdiction (after consulting the Commission and European Parliament). Accordingly, now, the CFI also hears cases brought by private parties in all fields. Its jurisdiction in anti-dumping and anti-subsidy cases was introduced as from 1 March 1994. However, the CFI cannot hear Article 177 references. Appeals from the CFI are heard by the ECJ.

As an institution, the CFI is still relatively young. In competition cases, however, the CFI has already demonstrated a greater willing-

Actions before the ECJ*

ECJ
- All 177 cases
- All other actions not within CFI jurisdiction
- Appeals from CFI

Article 177
References from national courts for preliminary rulings on any question of EC law arising in national proceedings.

Article 169
Actions by the Commission against Member States for failure to fulfil EC obligations.

Article 173
Actions by Member States, EC institutions or individuals to review the legality of acts by EC institutions.

Article 170
Actions by Member States against Member States for failure to fulfil EC obligations.

Article 178
Actions for compensation against the EC for damage caused by EC institutions or its servants.

Article 175
Actions by Member States, EC institutions or individuals against EC institutions for failure to act.

CFI
Hears cases brought by private parties in all fields.

* Chapter 8 contains further details of these actions. In addition, the ECJ also has jurisdiction in a number of other instances. For example, it may hear cases pursuant to arbitration clauses contained in contracts concluded by or on behalf of the EC, and, under the agreement for the creation of the European Economic Area ("EEA Agreement"), the ECJ will have, in certain circumstances, jurisdiction in relation to the interpretation and application of the EEA Agreement.

ness than the ECJ to enter into the details of acts of the Commission and to criticise actions of the Commission. It still remains to be seen whether the CFI's more combative approach will be supported by the ECJ.

(iv) Role

As the constitutional court of the Community and the court of last resort, the ECJ has the ultimate responsibility for ensuring that the fundamental principles of the Treaty of Rome are applied and, in particular, that individual interests are judicially protected. Over the last three decades, the ECJ has issued many landmark judgments. The doctrines of direct effect and primacy of EC law have, as a result of ECJ case law, become fundamental in ensuring the application of EC law at national level (see Chapter 8). In ensuring the uniform interpretation of EC law throughout the Community, the ECJ has also proved to be one of the driving forces towards European integration and, in particular, towards the completion of the internal market. In certain areas, its interpretation of the Treaty has allowed the Commission to exercise its powers in such a way as to overcome opposition or inertia at the political level of the Council of Ministers. It has the power to award interim measures and damages and can now, as a result of the Maastricht Treaty, also impose fines on Member States who have failed to comply with an earlier ECJ judgment against them.

The Maastricht Treaty expressly excluded the CFSP and home affairs and judicial co-operation from the ECJ's jurisdiction. It remains to be seen whether, despite this express exclusion, the ECJ will develop a role which impacts on these areas. In particular, certain cases, for example those relating to immigration and border controls, may well fall within both the ECJ's jurisdiction under the EC Treaty as well as the excluded areas of home affairs and judicial co-operation. The Maastricht Treaty does however extend the ECJ's jurisdiction to cover acts of and disputes concerning the European Parliament and the ECB.

6. OTHER COMMUNITY BODIES

(i) Introduction

In addition to the Council, the Commission, the European Parliament and the ECJ, the EC Treaty also provides for a Court of Auditors and an Economic and Social Committee. The Treaty of Maastricht establishes two further Community institutions, the Committee of the Regions and the European Monetary Institute, and gives Treaty status to a third, the European Investment Bank. These are discussed below.

The Member States have established a number of other bodies in specialised fields under various Regulations and Directives which have a role to play in the Community's activities, but which are not formally institutions of the Community. These include the Task Force for Human Resources, Education Training and Youth (Brussels); the European Community Humanitarian Office (Brussels); the European Foundation for the Improvement of Living and Working Conditions (Dublin); the European Centre for the Development of Vocational Training (Thessaloniki); a number of research and development units in Ispra (Italy), Geel (Belgium), Karlsruhe (Germany) and Petten (the Netherlands); and the more recent European Environment Agency (Copenhagen), the European Training Foundation (Turin), the European Agency for the Evaluation of Medicinal Products (London), the Office for Veterinary and Plant Health Inspection and Control (Dublin), the Trade Marks Office (Alicante), the European Monitoring Centre for Drugs and Drug Addiction (Lisbon) and the Agency for Health and Safety at Work (Bilbao). These are also discussed below.

(ii) The Court of Auditors

The Court of Auditors was established as a formal Community institution in 1977 and is the Community's financial watchdog. It is based in Luxembourg and has the task of auditing the Community's revenue and expenditure, working closely with national governments. It consists of 15 members, one from each Member State, appointed for a six-year term by mutual consent of the Council after consulting the European Parliament.

Like Commissioners, members of the Court of Auditors must act in the Community's interest and be completely independent. The Court of Auditors has extensive investigative powers and produces an annual report on the EU budget at the end of each financial year as well as opinions on proposed funding programmes and legislation.

(iii) The Economic and Social Committee (EcoSoC)

EcoSoC is a consultative body of 222 members who are appointed by the Council in consultation with the Commission for a renewable term of four years. A new Committee was appointed in September 1994. EcoSoC members must act independently in the best interests of the Community. Each Member State is allocated a number of members.

EcoSoC members			
Austria	12	Finland	9
France	24	Greece	12
Germany	24	Netherlands	12
Italy	24	Portugal	12
UK	24	Denmark	9
Spain	21	Ireland	9
Belgium	12	Luxembourg	6
		Sweden	12

EcoSoC is divided into three interest groups: "employers", made up of representatives of employers' organisations and chambers of commerce; "workers", made up of trade union representatives; and various interests such as representatives of small businesses, consumer organisations, farmers, the professions and environmentalists. The Commission or the Council are required to consult EcoSoC in respect of proposals involving, for example, social, regional and environmental policy including internal market legislation. In other cases, consultation is optional, although EcoSoC can adopt opinions on its own initiative. EcoSoC is divided into nine sections, each dealing with the main areas covered by the Treaty of Rome such as external relations, economic and monetary questions and protection of the environment. It is within these sections that EcoSoC's opinions are drafted before being adopted by a majority vote in EcoSoC's plenary sessions. Although EcoSoC has no right to amend draft legislation and its opinions are not binding, they can, nonetheless, be influential since they represent the views of those whose interests are likely to be affected by proposed legislation. The Commission and EcoSoC have tended to work closely together whilst relations with the Council have not traditionally been very close. However, in the last few years, co-operation has improved with the President of the Council addressing EcoSoC on matters to be considered at forthcoming European Councils.

(iv) The Committee of the Regions

The Committee of the Regions, like EcoSoC, whose organisational and membership structure it mirrors, is an advisory body. It was set up under the Maastricht Treaty to give the regions and local authorities a bigger say in the legislative process. While its role in the legislative process is similar to that of EcoSoC, the consultation of the Committee of the Regions is mandatory in far fewer areas. The Council and the Commission are required to consult the Committee on proposals in certain specified areas named in the EC Treaty, for example, public health, culture and education, and it may do so on a voluntary basis in other areas. Nonetheless, any failure to consult the Committee in areas where the EC Treaty requires it, could result in legislation being annulled in the ECJ in Article 173 proceedings. Further, the Committee is also entitled to issue opinions on its own initiative.

Each Member State is required to appoint an allocated number of representatives of regional and local bodies in the same proportions as EcoSoC (see Section (iii) above). Members are appointed for a renewable period of four years with a president appointed by the Committee every two years. Although the Committee should have commenced work on the coming into force of the Maastricht Treaty in November 1993, some Member States were late in submitting their lists of representatives to the Council (due in part to differences as to whether the representatives should be elected) and so appointments were not made until the end of January 1994. Given its shaky start, it remains to be seen how influential the Committee will become in the legislative process and, in particular, how often the Council and the Commission will consult it and take its opinions into account.

(v) The European Monetary Institute (EMI)

The European Monetary Institute was established in January 1994 as the body responsible for preparing for full economic and monetary union. The EMI is to be directed and managed by a president and the governors of the national central banks. The President, appointed by the Member States under recommendation of the Committee of Governors of the national central banks after consultation with the European Parliament and Council, is Baron Alexandre Lamfalussy. His Vice-President is Maurice Doyle, Governor of the Irish Central Bank. The EMI is now up and running in Frankfurt.

Economic and monetary union is examined in Chapter 1 Section (iii) *supra*.

(vi) The European Investment Bank (EIB)

The aim of the EIB, based in Luxembourg, is to promote economic and social cohesion by providing finance for public and private projects in all economic sectors both within and outside the Community. Such projects include loans for trans-European transport and telecommunications networks, capital investment by small and medium-sized enterprises and environmental projects. Although it is one of the world's major international financial institutions, with "AAA" rating for its securities, it is a non-profit-making organisation raising capital on the world's money markets. In 1991, it borrowed 13.7 billion ECU (around £9.6 billion approximately) and lent 15.3 billion ECU (around £10.7 billion approximately). The EIB is managed by a board of 15 governors, consisting of the finance ministers of each Member State, who are responsible for overseeing the bank's credit policy. The board of governors appoints a board of 25 directors who are responsible for the bank's day-to-day activities and who have the sole power to grant loans and guarantees and fix interest rates. The EIB works closely with the Commission to ensure that its activities complement the Commission's own funding programmes, some of which are described below.

In May 1994, the Member States ratified a change in the statute of the EIB to allow its governors to set up the European Investment Fund (EIF). The EIF is intended to provide guarantees for the long-term financing of major European infrastructure investment and to assist the realisation of projects by small and medium-sized enterprises.

(vii) The New EC Agencies

With the entry into force of the Maastricht Treaty, the European Council, in October 1993, agreed the location of a number of new bodies essential to the operation of the single market. Political stalemate and bargaining had prevented agreement on siting before now. The new agencies are:

● the European Environment Agency (Copenhagen);

● the European Training Foundation (Turin);

● the Office for Veterinary and Plant Health Inspection and Control (Dublin);

● the European Monitoring Centre for Drugs and Drug Addiction (Lisbon);

● the European Agency for the Evaluation of Medicinal Products (London);

● the Agency for Health and Safety at Work (Bilbao);

● the Office for Harmonisation in the Internal Market (trade marks, designs and models) (the Trade Mark Office), including its Board of Appeal (Alicante); and

● Europol, and the Europol Drugs Unit (The Hague).

Luxembourg is being promoted as the seat of the Common Appeal Court for Community patents as provided for in the Protocol on the Settlement of Litigation concerning the infringement and validity of Community patents annexed to the Community Patent Agreement of December 1989.

Three of the most important of the bodies in this line-up are the European Environment Agency, the Trade Mark Office and the European Agency for Evaluation of Medicinal Products.

The Commission formally launched the **European Environment Agency** in December 1993, three and a half years after the legislation agreeing its creation was adopted. The Agency, and the European environment information and observation network which it will co-ordinate, are intended to provide the Community and Member States with objective and reliable comparable data on the environment. The principal aims of the Agency are to assess the quality of the environment, environmental pressures and sensitivity.

The Community-wide trade mark registration system was only finally agreed in December 1993. The Community trade mark confers a uniform right over the whole EC, in theory removing the need to file separate applications for protection in each Member State. The **Trade Mark Office** will be set up in Alicante, Spain, and is not expected to be in a position to make registrations until mid- to late-1995.

New measures adopted in June 1993 are intended to promote the free circulation of medicinal products within the Community. It is recognised to be impossible, at this stage, to dismantle the existing national regulatory structures and replace them with one centralised structure like the US Food and Drug Administration. Thus, from 1995 onwards, the registration procedures for medicinal products within the Community will involve:

- a centralised Community registration procedure, reserved for innovatory medicinal products, leading to a single Community-wide authorisation, valid for all 15 Member States;

- a decentralised procedure, applicable to most medicinal products, based upon the principle of mutual recognition, and covering a variable number of Member States; and

- a national procedure, limited to applications of local interest concerning a single Member State.

Use of the centralised procedure will be compulsory for medicinal products derived from biotechnology, and optional for other innovatory new products. Applications for authorisation will be submitted directly to the **European Medicines Evaluation Agency**. The Agency consists mainly of the pre-existing Committee for Proprietary Medicinal Products (CPMP) and the Committee for Veterinary Medicinal Products (CVMP), supported by an administrative and technical secretariat and reinforced scientific capability.

(viii) Community Funding Bodies

The Community operates a number of funding programmes of benefit to EU and non-EU countries and, both directly and indirectly, to businesses. The most important programme is composed of three separate funds, collectively known as the Structural Funds, aimed at assisting the less prosperous regions and sectors of the Community. The three funds are the European Social Fund (ESF), the European Regional Development Fund (ERDF) and the European Agricultural Guidance and Guarantee Fund (EAGGF). These are often better known by their French acronyms: FSE, FEDER and FEOGA, respectively. The latter is by far the most important in terms of value. Aid is usually in the form of co-financing for projects with any Community aid having to be matched by funds from national sources. DGV, DGVI and DGXVI are collectively responsible for administering these funds and for drawing up annual framework programmes setting out the Community's priority actions and the amount of funding available. In addition to the Structural Funds, a new Cohesion Fund was agreed at Maastricht to concentrate on co-financing projects relating to the environment and transport infrastructure. This was in operation, under an interim financial instrument from April 1993. The final instrument came into force in May 1994. At present, only Ireland, Greece, Portugal and Spain are eligible for funds although the East German *Länder* and East Berlin are also being considered as potential beneficiaries.

Funding is also available to EU businesses for research and development projects. The majority of such funding is aimed at smaller companies who have difficulty in raising the necessary finance for such projects, in particular in the telecommunications, information technology and energy sectors. Funding is also available to support small and medium-sized enterprises not only for research and development but also to facilitate, among other things, capital investment, technology transfer and training.

The EC has also established a number of programmes to help non-EU developing countries which can be of benefit to businesses operating in the EU. PHARE (Aid and Assistance for the Restructuring of the Economy in Central and Eastern Europe) was established in 1989 with the basic objective of transforming the centralised economies of the recipient states into economies based on market forces. Programmes have included funding for environmental protection, nuclear safety, health care, education and training, agriculture and privatisation programmes. TACIS (Technical Assistance to the CIS and Georgia), set up in 1991, aims to facilitate the recovery and economic reforms within the former Soviet Union. The programme aims to assist in the development of market economies in the CIS and Georgia by providing know-how, training and essential equipment. Areas targeted by TACIS include oil and gas production, nuclear safety, energy-saving projects, training of personnel in the public and private sectors, transport infrastructure, food distribution and the development of banking and financial services. The PHARE and TACIS units within DGI are responsible for selecting projects and for administering the various action programmes in close co-operation with the recipient states. The Commission maintains a register of companies, consultants and experts interested in being considered for the award of contracts under both the PHARE and TACIS programmes. In addition, the EU also provides funding to Asia, Latin America, Africa, the Caribbean, Pacific countries and Mediterranean regions.

7. THE EC LEGISLATIVE PROCESS

(i) Introduction

The changes which have, over the last decade, been made to the Treaty of Rome, in particular by the Single European Act and more recently the Maastricht Treaty, have somewhat modified the balance of influence of the Community institutions in the legislative process. As a result of the extension under the Single European Act of qualified voting by the co-operation procedure and the introduction of the co-decision procedure under the Maastricht Treaty, individual Member States, in many areas, can no longer indefinitely block proposed legislation.

(ii) Types of EC Legislation

EC legislation may take the form of Regulations, Directives, Decisions, Recommendations or Opinions:

- **Regulations** – These have general application and are directly applicable in all Member States. They are immediately binding on Member States and may also bind individuals. No national legislation is required to give effect to Regulations. In the event of a conflict between a Regulation and national law, the Regulation prevails. Regulations are normally issued by the Council, although the Council can empower the Commission to make a Regulation within a prescribed framework. Most competition law Regulations are, for example, Commission Regulations.

- **Directives** – These are binding on Member States as to the result to be achieved, within a stated period, but they leave the method of implementation to the discretion of the national governments. In itself, a Directive does not initially have legal force in the Member States but particular provisions may have direct effect if the Directive is not correctly implemented. Again, most Directives are issued by the Council but in limited areas, for example Article 90, the Commission can and does issue Directives.

- **Decisions** – These are addressed to particular parties and are binding in their entirety on those to whom they are addressed, whether Member States, companies or individuals.

- **Recommendations and Opinions** – These have no binding legal force as such and are merely advisory. Often their aim is to encourage desirable, but not necessarily enforceable, good practices throughout the Community. However, like other forms of EC legislation, national courts are bound to take them into consideration when interpreting national law.

Regulations, Directives addressed to all Member States and Directives and Decisions adopted under the co-decision procedure must be published in the Official Journal of the European Community (OJ). Other Directives and Decisions, Recommendations and Opinions are not required to be published in the OJ, although they generally are for information purposes. Directives and Decisions are, however, required to be notified to those to whom they are addressed and only take effect upon such notification.

(iii) The Decision-Making Process

The term "adopted" tends to be rather overused in an EC context. The Commission "adopts" a proposal when it decides to put it forward to the Council as draft legislation. The Council may "adopt" a common position or consensus in relation to a proposal before it is sent to the European Parliament for consideration. The European Parliament "adopts" its opinion, as does EcoSoC. However, it is only when the Council actually votes to "adopt" the proposal itself that it becomes valid EC legislation. In the case of Directives, the Member States must then adopt national implementing measures.

In brief, the Commission has the right to initiate proposals; EcoSoC, the Committee of the Regions and the European Parliament each express an opinion; and the Council has the ultimate power to adopt, amend or reject the proposed measure. This is an oversimplification of a long process – one that is often referred to as a "negotiation". While this is a curious term for a legislative process, it is revealing of the possibility at all stages for both formal and informal consultation.

Except in certain circumstances, for example when the Commission itself is empowered to legislate, Community legislation is passed using one of three legislative procedures depending upon the Treaty provision being relied upon.

(iv) The Consultation Procedure

The EC Treaty initially provided only for the consultation procedure. It allowed the European Parliament only one reading, and the Council would adopt the proposal either unanimously or by a simple or qualified majority depending on the legal basis for the proposal. Following a constitutional crisis in 1965 and the Luxembourg Accord, the Council tried to reach unanimous agreement on all proposals, whether or not this was strictly required under the Treaty. This desire for unanimity often resulted in proposals needing to be toned down substantially in order to be adopted and many were delayed for a number of years.

(v) The Co-operation Procedure

The changes to the EC Treaty made by the Single European Act extended the circumstances in which a qualified majority vote is sufficient, thereby reducing the need for unanimity and speeding up the process of legislation. This applied principally to harmonisation measures for the completion of the single market and which now have been transferred by the Treaty of Maastricht to the co-decision procedure. Under the co-operation procedure the Council, on a proposal from the Commission and after obtaining the opinion of the Parliament (the First Reading) seeks to achieve a "common position" (essentially, a political consensus). The text of the common position is then referred to the Parliament (the Second Reading). The Parliament has three months in which to endorse the common position (either expressly or implicitly) or to reject or amend it. If the Parliament endorses the common position, the legislation is then adopted by the Council in accordance with that position; if the Parliament has rejected the Council's common position, unanimity is required for its adoption by the Council. If the Parliament proposes amendments, the Commission has one month in which to decide whether or not to accept these; it may adopt all or any of the Parliament's proposed amendments but is not obliged to do so. It then forwards the proposal to the Council, and if it has not accepted amendments of the Parliament, it must express its opinion on them. The Council proceeds to a Second Reading. It votes by qualified majority where the Commission has endorsed the Parliament's amendments, and unanimously where the Commission has not done so. If the proposal is substantially amended, the Parliament has to be re-consulted. Majority voting under the co-operation procedure does not apply to certain sensitive areas such as tax harmonisation, the free movement of persons, and the rights and interests of employed persons; in these areas the Council continues to act by unanimous vote. The operation of the procedure is illustrated by Appendix C which details the various stages that the Utilities Directive went through.

(vi) The Co-Decision Procedure

The Maastricht Treaty introduced a third legislative procedure known as "co-decision". It is required to be used mainly in relation to harmonisation measures for the completion of the internal market, general action programmes relating to the environment, research and development and proposals dealing with the free movement of workers and the right of establishment. It is a variant of the co-operation procedure but gives the European Parliament more say if its amendments are not adopted after its Second Reading.

If the European Parliament is minded to reject a common position of the Council, or if the Council does not approve the European Parliament's amendments to a common position, a Conciliation Committee (consisting of members of the Council or their representatives, and an equal number of Parliamentary representatives) will try to reach an agreed joint text. The Commission "takes part" in the Conciliation Committee's work and is required to try to reconcile the views of the two sides. If the Committee agrees on a joint text, it must be approved by the European Parliament (acting by absolute majority) and the Council (by qualified majority) within six weeks. If no joint text can be agreed, the Council may confirm by qualified majority its original common position, with or without the amendments proposed by the

European Parliament, but this confirmation can be overridden (ie the legislation can be vetoed) by the European Parliament acting by absolute majority within a further six weeks.

(vii) Delegated Legislation

Certain articles of the EC Treaty and Council Regulations empower the Commission to legislate of its own accord. Thus, for example, the Commission has been empowered by Council Regulation 19/65 to adopt its own Regulations exempting certain agreements from the competition provisions contained in Article 85 of the Treaty (these Commission regulations are commonly referred to as "block exemptions"). Once power to legislate is given to the Commission, the Commission need not consult either the Council, the European Parliament, EcoSoC or any other body although this will depend on the precise terms of the empowering legislation. In the present example, the Commission is, however, required to consult the Advisory Committee on Restrictive Practices and Monopolies which has special responsibility for competition matters. In practice, this involves consultation with the Member States, since the Committee is made up of officials appointed by the Member States. The method of working, role and effect of such Advisory Committees are unclear. More recently formed Advisory Committees, such as the Advisory Committee on Concentrations, publish their opinions. Others do not.

(viii) EEA Legislative Process

The EEA and its legislative process are described in Chapter 9 *infra*. New decision-making bodies have been created which exist alongside the EC legislative process. Although independent, the EEA legislative mechanism interrelates with that of the EC. Legislation can only be proposed for the EEA by the European Commission. Since the EFTA states only have the right to be consulted on new EC legislation, new EC legislation does not automatically become part of EEA law. It will only do so after a positive decision of the EEA Joint Committee.

Consultation Procedure

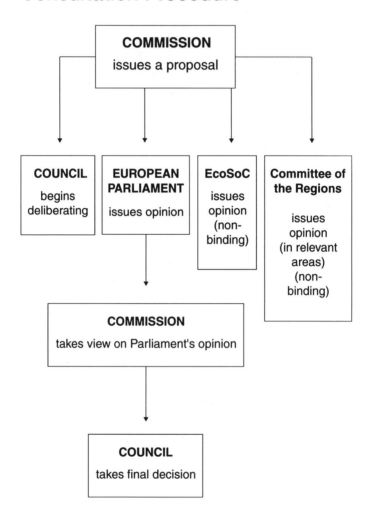

Co-Operation Procedure

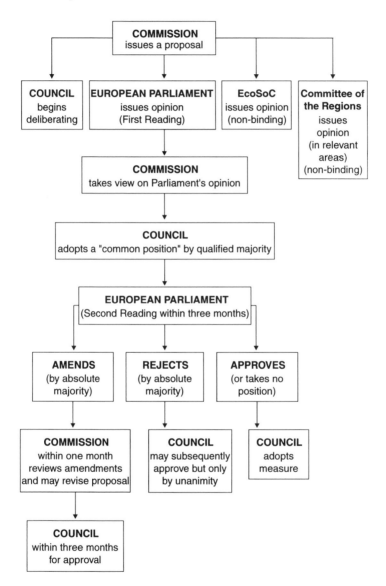

New Co-Decision Procedure

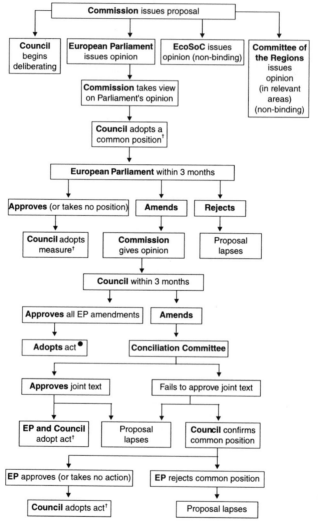

† Council acts by qualified majority voting.
● Unanimity is required if the Council wishes to adopt an EP amendment on which
  the Commission gave a negative opinion. Otherwise qualified majority voting applies.

Delegated Legislation*

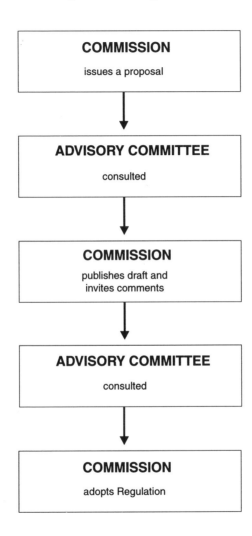

* The example given is based on the procedure for adopting (or amending) Block Exemptions pursuant to Council Regulation 19/65.

New Co-Decision Procedure (including EEA)

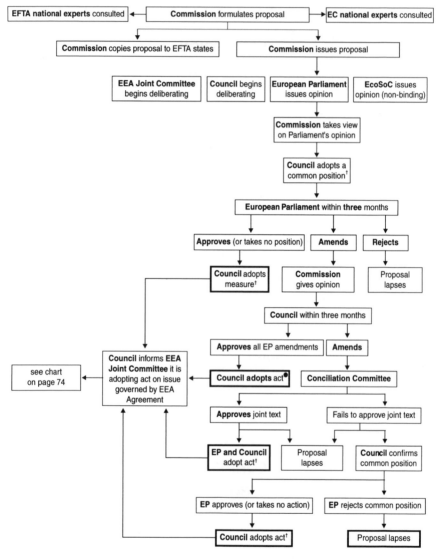

† Council acts by qualified majority voting.
● Unanimity is required if the Council wishes to adopt an EP amendment on which
  the Commission gave a negative opinion. Otherwise qualified majority voting applies.

8. ENFORCING EC RIGHTS

(i) Introduction

Recent developments in the case law of the ECJ have substantially improved the position of individuals, companies and interest groups relying on EC law in national courts, by developing the extent and way in which EC rights can be enforced.

(ii) Principles of EC Law

Two fundamental principles lie at the heart of the Community's legal order: **the primacy of EC law** and **direct effect**.

The ECJ has said that, in signing the Treaty of Rome, Member States definitively transferred their sovereign rights (albeit in limited fields) to the Community. This transfer of sovereignty cannot be reversed by Member States adopting national measures which are inconsistent with Community law. Community law is therefore not only an integral part of national law but also has priority over any conflicting law of the Member States. As a result, national courts are not only bound to apply Community law but may not give effect to any national law which is inconsistent with applicable EC rules. This is the principle of primacy (or supremacy). Those EC Member States with written constitutions, and especially Germany, continue to struggle with this issue.

In addition, Community law confers rights and imposes obligations not only on the Community institutions and the Member States but also on their citizens. In certain circumstances, the case law of the ECJ allows individuals and companies to rely on Community provisions against Member States before national courts and to give remedies in the event of a breach. This is the principle of direct effect. The basic requirements which must be fulfilled in order for a provision to be directly effective are that the provision must be clear and precise, unconditional and unqualified and not subject to any further measures on the part of the Member State. It must not therefore leave any substantial latitude or discretion to the Member State in its implementation. Those seeking to enforce obligations under Directives may, however, only invoke the provisions of a Directive (as opposed to a Regulation or Treaty provision) against the state, as an issue of "vertical direct effect" and not private individuals or undertakings as an issue of "horizontal direct effect", and only once the Directive's deadline for implementation has passed.

The concept of direct effect is one that has progressively been extended by the ECJ and is one, together with the principle of primacy, which can be used by companies and individuals to enforce their substantive EC rights. For example, national courts have the power, and may be required in certain circumstances, to grant interim relief, even against the State, to ensure that EC rights are protected pending the outcome of proceedings. Furthermore, in a landmark judgment, the ECJ held that an individual may be entitled to compensation from the State for damage caused to it by a Member State's failure to implement EC Directives or other infringement of EC law. Such a development is clearly of central importance for both individuals seeking to invoke their EC law rights and the governments of Member States carrying out the difficult task of implementing EC legislation. In the ECJ's most recent ruling on direct effect the Court has, however, refused to accept the possibility that individuals may rely on the "horizontal" direct effect of Directives. In other words, a private party may not rely on the provisions of Directives in national court proceedings as against other private parties. Nevertheless, the ruling does not detract from a private party's right to compensation from the State.

It is worth noting in this context that "the State" can include not only central and local government but also public agencies, nationalised industries and, in certain circumstances, private companies that are heavily regulated.

(iii) Challenging Community Acts

Article 169 of the Treaty is the most important means at the Commission's disposal to ensure that Community law is observed by the Member States. Article 169 empowers the Commission to bring proceedings in the ECJ against Member States which fail to comply with their Treaty obligations. Prior to bringing an action, the Commission must inform the Member State concerned of the alleged breach and give it the opportunity either to answer the allegation or to take any necessary corrective action. If the Member State then fails to act the Commission will issue a reasoned opinion. It is only after the Member State has had the opportunity to submit observations on the Commission's opinion that the Commission can commence proceedings. Infringement proceedings are brought by the Commission at the behest of the relevant Directorates-General and in conjunction with the Commission Legal Service.

As originally drafted, the Treaty did not provide for sanctions to be imposed against a Member State which had been found to be in breach of its EC obligations. The Maastricht Treaty amended the Treaty of Rome to allow the ECJ, on an application by the Commission, to be able to fine Member States for failure to comply with an ECJ judgment.

The Commission often brings such proceedings following a complaint by private parties or pressure groups. The making of a complaint to the Commission is the simplest way for an individual to ensure the application of Community law. Such complaints should at first be addressed to the relevant DG. It is often possible to push forward the progress of the complaint by contacting a member of the *Cabinet* of the Commissioner responsible for the area concerned. Some complainants have been known to write directly to the President of the Commission! However, if the Commission takes proceedings against the Member State, the complainant has no right to be represented in the procedure. Furthermore, although a complainant can require the Commission to make a decision whether or not to pursue an action following a complaint, the complainant cannot force the Commission to bring proceedings.

Under Article 173 of the Treaty, EC institutions and Member States and the ECB (when it is established) can institute proceedings in the ECJ against a Community institution (or the ECB) to review the legality of its acts. Private parties cannot, however, challenge the legality of EC legislation directly before the ECJ (although a private party may do so indirectly in the national courts – see Chapter 8 Section (iv)). A private party can only have an act reviewed if it was addressed to him or, if it was addressed to another person or a Member State, if he can show that it is of direct and individual concern to him. This effectively means that an applicant has to establish that he has been singled out for operation of the decision or is legally affected by it. Article 173 proceedings are usually initiated by private parties in the context of competition law or anti-dumping investigations by the Commission.

Article 175 deals with inaction by a Community institution and the ECB. As under Article 173, Member States, the Community institutions and the ECB have the power to bring such actions but individuals may only do so if an EC institution or the ECB has failed to address an act to that person or to define its position when called upon to do so.

Article 178 confers competence on the ECJ to deal with damages claims under Article 215. Article 215 confers a remedy in damages on individuals who are directly affected by illegal acts of Community institutions. Article 185 grants the ECJ the power to suspend the application of a contested act; and by Article 186 it may prescribe interim measures in any case before it.

(iv) Preliminary Rulings by the European Court of Justice

One of the ECJ's main duties is to ensure the uniform interpretation of Community law. National courts, in cases where any question of Community law arises, may request the ECJ to clarify any such points by means of a reference for a preliminary ruling under Article 177. These preliminary rulings are legally binding. National courts presented with a question involving the interpretation of the Treaty of Rome, or the validity or interpretation of EC law, may submit a number of abstract questions for the ECJ's determination. When the ECJ has considered the questions, it will reply to the national court, again in the abstract, and it will be for the national court to apply the ruling to the facts and give its judgment. The ECJ does not determine the application of EC law to the particular facts. A national court has a discretion whether to refer a question to the ECJ, unless it is acting as a court of last instance within the Member State and determination of the EC point is necessary for its decision, in which case it is obliged to refer such questions. However, only the ECJ has authority to rule that an EC measure is invalid. In contrast to a somewhat reluctant attitude in the past, lower national courts in the EU have in recent years demonstrated an increasing willingness to refer questions of EC law to the ECJ.

It is not the parties who make the reference for a preliminary ruling but the national court itself. Therefore, the ECJ's duty is towards the national court and not the parties, and it is for the national court to formulate its own questions when making its reference. However, the parties to the national proceedings, the Commission, the Council and the Member States have the right to submit to the Court written statements of the case or comments and may subsequently be heard in oral argument. In addition, the ECJ has indicated that references for preliminary rulings should only be made once both parties to the national proceedings have been heard before the national court.

Even since the delegation of part of its jurisdiction to the CFI, the procedure of the ECJ (which alone has jurisdiction over Article 177 references) still often appears to have all the speed and sense of urgency of a glacier. Following a reference by a national court (which may itself be the culmination of many years of national proceedings) it may take up to two to three years before the ECJ gives a ruling, during which time national proceedings are usually stayed. The case must then be referred back to the national courts for definitive judgment. The Article 177 procedure is often used as a stalling tactic in national proceedings.

Significant Article 177 judgments by the ECJ 1990–94

Case	Country	Topic
Marleasing (1990)	Spain	Company law
Francovich (1991)	Italy	Company insolvency/damages
Keck (1993)	France	Free movement of goods
Corbeau (1993)	Belgium	Postal monopoly/competition
Gallaher (1993)	United Kingdom	Tobacco advertising
Ten Oever (1993)	Netherlands	Sex discrimination/pensions
Phil Collins (1993)	Germany	Copyright
Marshall (1993)	United Kingdom	Sex discrimination
TWD (1994)	Germany	State aids
Coloroll (1994)	various	Sex discrimination/pensions
Webb (1994)	United Kingdom	Sex discrimination/pregnancy
Faccini Dori (1994)	Italy	Direct effect

9. THE COUNCIL OF EUROPE

(i) Introduction

The Council of Europe is an international inter-governmental organisation whose main aims are to:

- protect human rights and pluralist democracy;

- promote awareness of a European cultural identity and encourage its development;

- seek solutions to problems facing European society (minorities, xenophobia, intolerance, environmental protection, bioethics, drugs etc);

- provide a political anchor and serve as a guardian of human rights for Europe's post-communist democracies; and

- assist the central and eastern European countries with their political, legislative and constitutional reforms.

The Council of Europe should not be confused with the Council of the European Union. Nor should it be regarded as part of the EC or EU. The two organisations are quite distinct. The 15 Member States of the EU are, however, all members of the Council of Europe. A full list of the 34 member countries at the time of going to press is contained in the table on page 14. Any European state can become a member provided it accepts the principle of the rule of law and guarantees everyone under its jurisdiction the enjoyment of human rights and fundamental freedoms by signing the European Convention on Human Rights. The following countries have officially applied for membership: Albania, Andorra, Belarus, Croatia, Former Yugoslav Republic of Macedonia, Latvia, Moldova, Russia and the Ukraine.

(ii) Institutions

The **Committee of Ministers** is the decision-making body of the Council of Europe. It is composed of the Ministers for Foreign Affairs of the 32 member countries or their permanent representatives. The Committee decides what action to take on recommendations from the **Parliamentary Assembly** and the **Congress of Local and Regional Authorities of Europe**, and on proposals from various inter-governmental committees and conferences of specialised ministers.

The Committee of Ministers meets at least twice a year; their permanent representatives meet at least twice a month to discuss issues of mutual political interest (except defence issues). Most decisions require a two-thirds majority of the votes cast. Certain important decisions, such as the adoption of Recommendations addressed to governments, must be taken unanimously. On questions of procedure, a simple majority is sufficient.

Decisions of the Committee of Ministers are transmitted to member governments as Recommendations or as European Conventions or agreements which are binding on the states which ratify them. The Committee also adopts Declarations or Resolutions on political questions and international issues. Over 150 Conventions have been drawn up to date, notably, the European Convention on Human Rights and the European Social Charter. Others include Conventions on the prevention of torture, terrorism, spectator violence, transfrontier television and data protection.

The **Parliamentary Assembly** comprises representatives of the member countries who have been elected or appointed by their national parliaments. Each country has between two and 18 representatives proportionate to the size of its population. Five political groups have been created. It meets four times a year in Strasbourg and once in one of the member countries.

The Parliamentary Assembly is free to choose its own agenda. Its deliberations play an advisory role: the texts adopted by the Assembly provide guidelines for the Committee of Ministers and national governments. Special guest status has been created by the Parliamentary Assembly to allow delegations from Central and Eastern Europe to attend its plenary sessions. The Assembly also provides a discussion forum for other international organisations such as the OECD, the EBRD and the European Space Agency. The Assembly has been the instigator of many international treaties, including the European Convention on Human Rights.

The **Congress of Local and Regional Authorities of Europe** is a consultative body representing the local and regional authorities of the member countries. It works in two chambers: the Chamber of Local Authorities and the Chamber of Regions. Each works by setting up small *ad hoc* working groups to tackle specific issues. The main purpose of the Congress is to ensure the participation of local and regional authorities in the process of European unity and in the work of the Council of Europe. One of its most important tasks is to promote the functioning of local and regional democracy in the larger Europe and to strengthen transfrontier regional planning, economic development and environmental protection.

(iii) Human Rights

One of the landmark achievements of the Council of Europe is the **European Convention on Human Rights**. It sets out the inalienable rights and freedoms of each individual and obliges states to guarantee their enjoyment by everyone within their jurisdiction. It has established an enforcement machinery whereby states, and, on certain conditions, individuals, may refer alleged violations of the Convention to the **European Commission of Human Rights**.

The **European Commission of Human Rights** is composed of a number of lawyers equal to the number of member countries who are elected by the Committee of Ministers from a list of names submitted by each state's delegation to the Parliamentary Assembly. They hold office for six years. Members of the Commission are expected to act independently and not to represent the state which put forward their name for election.

Complaints are first examined by the Commission as to their admissibility. Most complaints are by individuals although companies can complain. The principles in the Convention are increasingly being applied in commercial situations. If the Commission finds them admissible, they will try to secure a friendly settlement, failing that, they will establish the facts and express an opinion as to whether there has been a violation. The case may then be referred for a final decision to the **European Court of Human Rights**. The Court delivers final judgments which are binding on the member countries concerned and may award compensation and costs to a successful applicant. The judgments are not directly effective in the same way as judgments of the ECJ. They are binding in international law.

The Court consists of one judge from each member country. The judges are elected for nine years by the Parliamentary Assembly. Like members of the Commission, the judges sit in their individual capacity, do not represent the states which proposed them, and enjoy complete independence in the performance of their duties. The Court is renewed one-third at a time and judges can be re-elected.

In the majority of cases the Court will sit in chambers of 13 judges (comprising nine full members and four non-voting substitute members); and decisions on cases which are to be declared inadmissible will be taken by the unanimous decision of a committee of three judges. The Court will only sit in Grand Chamber as 19 judges to decide exceptional cases and in even more exceptional cases a Plenary Session of all 32 judges (Romania and Andorra have yet to have a judge appointed).

Cases not referred to the Court are decided on by the Committee of Ministers, whose decisions are final and binding. The Committee of Ministers is also responsible for supervising the implementation of the Court's judgments.

A new Protocol 11 to the Convention, signed by the Member States on 11 May 1994, will set up a single permanent Court in place of the existing two-tier system of a Commission and a Court. The new single Court should ensure better access to the system for the individual and cases should be resolved more quickly and more efficiently. The Committee of Ministers will no longer have competence to deal with the merits of cases, although it will maintain its enforcement role. The new arrangements will come into force one year after the Protocol has been ratified by the national Parliament of the member countries.

The Community has been discussing the possibility of acceding to the European Convention on Human Rights. There are conflicting views about the usefulness of accession. While the EC Treaty already provides for the protection of fundamental rights, some believe that accession would bring greater clarity to the relationship between the systems of protection offered by the Community and the Convention and fill the deficiencies which arguably exist in the protection of those involved in EC law proceedings (most notably, proceedings relating to alleged infringements of the competition rules). In any event, Article F(2) of the Maastricht Treaty requires the EU to respect the fundamental rights guaranteed by the Convention as general principles of Community law.

10. THE NEW EUROPE

(i) The European Economic Area

The European Economic Area (EEA), which entered into force on 1 January 1994, aims to create a common market based on the four fundamental freedoms of people, goods, capital and services within its territory (see Chapter 1 Section (v) above for a general introduction). These are supported by so-called "flanking" policies on competition, where the EC rules are more or less entirely transposed to the EEA, and in other fields, such as environmental and social policy, in which there is to be closer co-operation. Essentially, the single European market has been extended to cover the territory of the participating EFTA countries, with these EFTA countries being given very little time to adapt their laws to EC laws. Although the EEA greatly extends the links between the EC and EFTA, it does not establish a customs union; there is no common external trade policy, nor any common agricultural, fisheries or taxation policies.

The participating EFTA states in the relevant fields accepted almost the entirety of EC legislation up to 31 July 1991, the date of substantive agreement. This is referred to as the "*acquis communautaire*" and is largely contained in extensive annexes to the EEA Agreement. The EFTA states have also accepted that the parts of the Agreement which are in substance identical to the EC/ECSC treaties or derived legislation will be interpreted in accordance with ECJ rulings given prior to the date of the Agreement. The EEA states have also now adopted an additional package of legislation covering EC measures which were adopted after July 1991 and before the EEA Agreement came into force on 1 January 1994. The legislation contained in that package came into force in the EEA states on 1 July 1994 (subject to individual derogations). Procedures have been put in place which aim to ensure that any further amendments to the annexes take effect contemporaneously with the adoption of any new EC legislation.

The Agreement provides for a number of new institutions: an EEA Council, an EEA Joint Committee, an EFTA Surveillance Authority and an EFTA Court. This institutional structure reflects amendments needed to accommodate concerns expressed by the

ECJ when it was consulted on the original draft of the EEA Agreement. There is also to be an EEA Joint Parliamentary Committee, made up of delegations from the European Parliament and from EFTA national parliaments, and an EEA Consultative Committee composed of delegations from the Community's Economic and Social Committee and from the EFTA Consultative Committee. Neither of these joint bodies will have any real power.

The EEA Council comprises all the members of the EC Council and of the EC Commission, and one member from the Government of each participating EFTA state. Presidency of the EEA Council will alternate every six months between the EC Council and the EFTA Governments. Like the EC Council, the EEA Council will not be a fixed body; it will be formed by the appropriate ministers and Commission officials according to the topic under discussion. It is to meet at least twice a year. The Community and EFTA will each have to speak with one voice. This requires the EFTA states to agree their negotiating position before EEA Council meetings, which in turn will put pressure on the presently limited EFTA infrastructure. A Standing Committee of EFTA states has, therefore, been created by separate agreement amongst the EFTA States, for the purpose of co-ordinating their views.

The EEA Council is responsible for giving the political impetus in the implementation of the EEA Agreement and laying down general guidelines for the EEA Joint Committee. It is to assess the overall functioning and development of the Agreement and also to take the political decisions leading to amendment of the Agreement.

Despite the similarity in names, the EEA Council and the EC Council are very different bodies. The EEA Council has the political functions described, but no legislative authority. The EC Council, in contrast, is the forum in which EC Member States vote to adopt new legislation, in addition to more general political functions.

The EEA Joint Committee comprises representatives of the Contracting Parties, with Presidency alternating between the EC Commission and EFTA representatives. The Joint Committee can set up sub-committees and working groups. The Joint Committee, like the EEA Council, is to take decisions by agreement between the Community on the one hand and the EFTA States "speaking with one voice" on the other. It is to meet at least monthly and to report annually on the operation of the Agreement. The Joint Committee will be in charge of the daily operation of the EEA.

Its role is to "ensure the effective implementation and operation of this Agreement" and to "carry out exchanges of views and information and take decisions in the cases provided for". There are three principal elements to that role. First, the Joint Committee is the filter for the transposition of new EC law into EEA law, by means of amendments to the annexes and protocols to the EEA Agreement. Secondly, it is required to act so as to preserve the homogeneous interpretation of the Agreement in the light of future judgments rendered by the EC and EFTA courts. Thirdly, it has a major role in the disputes resolution procedure.

By separate agreement between themselves, the EFTA states have set up an EFTA Surveillance Authority and an EFTA Court. The EFTA Surveillance Authority is an independent body having some of the functions of the Commission, namely monitoring the compliance by the EFTA states with their obligations under the Agreement and responsibility for competition matters. The EFTA Surveillance Authority has already announced that it intends to bring infringement proceedings against Austria and Norway for failure to implement the Directive on Environmental Impact Assessments and against Sweden for its failure to implement the Acquired Rights Directive (workers' rights). That said, the EFTA Surveillance Authority has a relatively limited role, compared with that of the Commission, reflecting the lack of standing of the EFTA states in the legislative process.

There are provisions for co-operation, exchange of information and consultation. Disputes between the Commission and EFTA Surveillance Authority on a particular subject can be referred to the EEA Joint Committee under a dispute procedure.

As a parallel to the role played in the EC by the ECJ, the EFTA States have created the EFTA Court which has jurisdiction to deal with disputes over EFTA surveillance procedures, appeals against decisions of the EFTA Surveillance Authority in competition matters, and disputes between EFTA states. The EFTA Court has, within EFTA participating states, equivalent powers to those of the ECJ in the Community as regards enforcement proceedings (Articles 169 and 171 Treaty of Rome) and judicial review (Article 173). It will also be able to give advisory opinions on EEA law.

The separate agreement also sets out detailed rules on the composition and structure of the EFTA Court and the EFTA Surveillance Authority. There is a declaration by the EFTA states that

Transposition of new EC law into EEA law

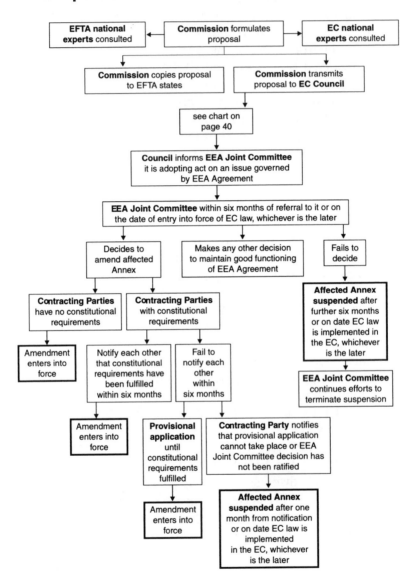

see chart on
page 40

they will set up a court of first instance to hear appeals in EEA/ EFTA competition cases should the need arise.

Although the EFTA states will wish to influence the development of future EC legislation, their role, as envisaged in the Agreement, is rather limited. The counterpart of this limited role is that such legislation does not automatically become part of EEA law.

One of the terms most frequently used to describe the EEA is homogeneous, *i.e.* the fact that provisions are given the same meaning and effect across both EC and EFTA territories. In order to fulfil the requirement of an homogeneous EEA, it is necessary for the Contracting Parties to be able to achieve a joint, parallel development of the legal orders of the EC and EFTA in areas covered by the Agreement. In doing so, it was necessary to take into account the requirement of the Community that its decision-making autonomy concerning the development of internal Community law not be jeopardised and the desire of the EFTA states to participate in the decision-making process and thus not have to take over new EC legislation as a *"fait accompli"*. The close association of EFTA states to the legislative process in the Community was accepted only as regards the preparatory phase, *i.e.* before the establishment of formal Commission proposals.

When drawing up proposals for legislation in fields covered by the Agreement, the EC Commission is to seek the views of EFTA experts in the same way as it obtains the views of EC national experts. Its proposal is to be transmitted to the EFTA states at the same time as it is sent to the EC Council. Discussions then begin in the Joint Committee. The intention is that the amendment of annexes to the EEA Agreement should take place "as closely as possible" to the corresponding introduction of new EC legislation. If no agreement can be reached within six months the "affected part" of the relevant annex is regarded as provisionally suspended at the end of a further period of six months, provided that "the corresponding EC Act is implemented in the Community". These provisions are exceptionally complex: it is not at all clear where an annex should be regarded as "affected"; how far suspension would go; nor what constitutes implementation within the Community.

Now that Austria, Finland and Sweden have become full members of the EU, the question remains as to what will happen to the EEA. It seems unlikely that such burdensome institutional structures and complex procedures will be retained for the benefit of Iceland and Norway, and possibly also Liechtenstein (if it does eventually resolve the problems caused by its customs union with Switzerland and join the EEA). One possibility is that a similar but simplified structure may be retained to cater for other countries, such as Poland and Hungary, as a transitional phase before full EU membership. Slovenia has applied for EFTA membership and others may follow. Whether this flows through to EEA membership remains to be seen.

(ii) The Europe Agreements

On 1 February 1994, enhanced association agreements, known as "Europe Agreements", between the European Community and Poland and Hungary entered into force. Interim agreements, containing the trade aspects of the association accords, had been in operation since March 1992. Europe Agreements have also been entered into with Romania, the Czech and Slovak Republics and Bulgaria, although so far only interim trade agreements are in operation in these other states. Although the Europe Agreements were negotiated bilaterally, and are not therefore identical, their contents are broadly similar. All Agreements entered into after those with Poland and Hungary include provisions stating that respect for democratic principles and human rights is an essential part of the association and provides for unilateral suspension of an Agreement in the case of "special urgency", *i.e.* if a reform process goes drastically wrong. One of the express aims of the Europe Agreements is to provide a framework for gradual integration into the Community.

The Europe Agreements go beyond the precedents of previous association agreements concluded with countries such as Malta, Cyprus and Turkey, which focus purely on economic and trade aspects essentially in relation to goods. The Europe Agreements have an express political, as well as economic, character and deal with services, people and capital as well as goods. The Agreements do not, however, seek to mirror the four freedoms found in the Treaty of Rome. Thus, for example, there is no right of establishment.

The Europe Agreements each have a transitional period of a maximum of 10 years, divided into two successive stages each lasting, in principle, five years, although transition from one to the other depends upon economic development and the progress of reform. The primary aim of the Europe Agreements is the creation of separate free trade areas between the European Community and each associated country. A timetable for the elimination of customs duties, tariffs, quantitative restrictions and measures of equivalent effect is provided on an asymmetrical basis, *i.e.* with the EC making concessions earlier than the associated countries. The provisions on free movement of goods have been in force since March 1992 via the interim agreements.

The Europe Agreements contain competition and state aid rules equivalent to those in the Treaty of Rome, already in force via the interim arrangements. The Europe Agreements, unlike the EEA Agreement, do not, however, provide for any notification or exemption procedure comparable to that in the EC Treaty.

The rules necessary to implement the competition provisions have yet to be established, so in the meantime the parties remain free to apply appropriate measures in cases of incompatible practices. As regards mergers which fall within the scope of the European Community Merger Regulation and which have a significant impact on the economy of the applicable central/east European state, there are arrangements for an exchange of views.

Europe Agreement provisions on cross-border services merely set out the parties' undertaking to take necessary steps to allow progressively the supply of services by EU/central and eastern European companies or nationals. There are also provisions allowing for the liberalisation of capital movements but, again, no firm timetable for achievement of this is set.

As far as the EU is concerned, companies and nationals of the associated States are entitled to equal treatment with EU nationals from the date of entry into force of the applicable Europe Agreement. Equal treatment is to apply immediately for EU companies and nationals already established in the associated country, as well as to most industrial and construction sectors, and to be introduced during the transitional period for other sectors, including financial services. There are special temporary provisions allowing only the associated states (reflecting the asymmetrical nature of the Agreements) to take exceptional safeguard measures in order to protect emerging industries or certain sectors undergoing restructuring or facing serious difficulties. This cannot, however, affect EC undertakings or nationals already established in the associated States.

(iii)   Trade and Economic Co-operation Agreements

In May 1992, the EC signed 10-year conventional trade and economic co-operation agreements with Estonia, Latvia and Lithuania. These provided, amongst other things, for most-favoured nation treatment regarding customs duties and internal taxes; the removal of quotas on imports; and exchange of information to assist transition to market economics. At the same time, joint declarations calling for closer political co-operation were adopted. Similar agreements were also signed with Albania and Slovenia.

In July 1994, the agreements with Estonia, Latvia and Lithuania were replaced by Free Trade Agreements which came into force on 1 January 1995.

These Free Trade Agreements provide for the reciprocal abolition of obstacles to trade and the removal of barriers and restrictions to trade in industrial goods. Trade in sensitive sectors, for example textiles, steel and agriculture, are to be covered under special separate regimes. While the EC will abolish all trade restrictions immediately upon each of the Agreement's entry into force, Latvia has been granted a transitional period of two to four years and Lithuania of six years. In each case, concessions have been negotiated for agricultural and fisheries products. The Agreement negotiated with Estonia is the most ambitious of the three in that there is no transitional period and the sensitive textiles sector is included within the general liberalisation. Exceptions to the free movement provisions allow the Baltic States to impose increased customs duties for the protection of infant industries on certain sectors undergoing restructuring in the face of serious difficulties.

Other provisions in the Free Trade Agreements are modelled on the interim trade agreements concluded with the Central and Eastern European countries: these include provisions on payments, competition rules, monopolies, customs co-operation and approximation of laws on trade and customs matters. Services are excluded from the Trade Agreement and there are no provisions dealing specifically with intellectual property rights.

The Free Trade Agreements will in time undoubtedly be replaced by the Europe Agreement framework, as the Baltic States want to follow the same paths to closer relations which the EU has taken with Poland, Hungary, the Czech Republic and Slovakia, and, eventually, by EU membership.

(iv) Partnership Agreements

A 10-year general trade and economic co-operation agreement between the EEC and the USSR was signed in December 1989. After the disintegration of the USSR and its replacement in December 1991 by the Commonwealth of Independent States (CIS), formed by 12 former Republics of the Union, with the exception of Georgia, the European Commission began to consider a new type of agreement, somewhere between the trade and economic co-operation agreement of the past and the Europe Agreements already signed with Poland, Hungary and the Czech Republic and Slovakia.

As a result, partnership agreements with the Ukraine, Kazakhstan, Russia, Belarus, Kyrgyzstan and Moldova have been signed. The agreements contain the conditions for the establishment and operation of companies, trade and services between the parties, investment and capital flows, protection of intellectual property, legislative co-operation, economic, cultural and financial co-operation as well as institutional arrangements. Exploratory talks with other Republics may lead to other such agreements. The Commission has stated that it has no intention of differentiating between "European" and "Asian" Republics.

The Partnership and Co-operation Agreement between Russia and the EU was signed in June 1994. The Agreement aims to boost economic and political links. The principal features of the Agreement are as follows:

- the parties have agreed to hold discussions in 1998 on prospects for creating a free trade area;

- the parties will have regular political dialogue at all levels;

- the parties have agreed to uphold human rights and democracy and to safeguard ethnic minorities and the rule of law;

- the EU supports Russia's future accession to the World Trade Organisation;

- the Agreement regulates the nuclear fuels trade: a safeguard clause protects EU uranium producers against surges of Russian imports;

- EU firms and individuals will be able to invest freely in Russia and to repatriate investments and profits;

- Russia will scrap (by 1996) a decree limiting the activities of foreign banks (the five European banks already operating in Russia will be immediately "grandfathered" by way of exemption);

- all quotas on Russian exports to the EU (apart from certain textile and steel products) will be removed except for temporary limited Russian quotas on EU imports where industries face grave social problems or where Russian companies risk near total loss of markets;

- the Agreement does not seek immediate removal of all current tariffs since Russian tariffs are much higher than those in the EU; and

- the Agreement fosters economic co-operation and promotes Russian nuclear safety and the restructuring of state-owned companies.

Appendix A

The Commissioners

The 15 Member States nominated their new Commission candidates to take up their posts during January 1995 following their collective investiture by the European Parliament. The new Commission's term of office will run for five years (to bring it into line with the term of office of the European Parliament). The list of new Commissioners and their portfolios is as follows:

Luxembourg

Jacques Santer

Portfolio: President; Secretariat General; Legal Service; Security Office; Forward Studies Unit; Inspectorate General; Joint Interpreting and Conference Service (SCIC); Spokesman's Service; Monetary matters (with Mr de Silguy); Common Foreign and Security Policy (with Mr Van Den Broek); and Institutional questions and the 1996 Inter-governmental Conference (with Mr Oreja).

Formerly Luxembourg Prime Minister, Minister of State for the Treasury and Minister for Cultural Affairs since July 1989; Governor of the International Monetary Fund since August 1989; Governor of the European Bank for Reconstruction and Development (EBRD) since 1991; Chairman of the European People's Party of the European Parliament from April 1987 to May 1990; and Governor of the World Bank between 1984 and 1989.

France

Edith Cresson

Portfolio: Science, Research and Development; Joint Research Centre; and Human Resources, Education, Training and Youth.

Elected member of the European Parliament in 1979; Minister for Industrial Redeployment and Foreign Trade from 1984–86; Minister for European Affairs from 1988–90; and French Prime Minister from 1991–92.

Yves-Thibault de Silguy

Portfolio: Economic and financial affairs; Monetary matters (in agreement with the President); Credit and investments; and Statistical Office.

French Ministry of Foreign Affairs until mid-1976 and Ministry of Economic and Financial Affairs until mid-1977; former Advisor to Mr Ortoli, Vice-President of the Commission from 1981–84. French Prime Minister's office from 1986–88 and Director of Usinor Sacilor until March 1993.

Germany

Martin Bangemann

Portfolio: Industrial affairs; and Information technologies and telecommunications.

German Federal Minister of Economics from June 1984 to the end of 1988; MEP from 1973–84; Member of the German Bundestag from 1972–80 (re-elected in 1987); Vice-President of the Commission, responsible for the internal market, industrial affairs and relations with the European Parliament from 1989 until 31 October 1993.

Monika Wulf-Mathies

Portfolio: Vice-President of the Commission; Regional policy; Relations with the Committee of the Regions; and the Cohesion Fund (in agreement with Mr Kinnock and Mrs Bjerregaard).

Elected to OTV managing executive Committee; re-elected in 1980; and appointed chairperson of OTV in September 1982; re-elected again in 1984, 1988 and 1992.

UK

Sir Leon Brittan

Portfolio: Vice-President of the Commission; External relations with North America, Australia, New Zealand, Japan, China, South Korea, Hong Kong, Macao and Taiwan; Common commercial policy; and relations with the OECD and WTO.

UK Secretary of State for Trade and Industry from 1985–86; former Vice-President of the Commission from 1989–93.

Neil Kinnock

Portfolio: Transport (including trans-European net-works).

Former leader of the UK Labour Party from 1983–92.

Spain

Manuel Marin

Portfolio: Vice-President of the Commission; External relations with the Southern Mediterranean, Middle and Near East, Latin America and Asia (except Japan, China, South Korea, Hong Kong, Macao and Taiwan).

Vice-President of the Commission of the EC; member responsible for social affairs, education and employment from 1986–88; continued as Vice-President (member responsible for Development Co-operation (Africa, Caribbean and Pacific countries within the Lomé Convention) and Fisheries policy) – from January 1989 to December 1992.

Marcelino Oreja

Portfolio: Institutional questions and preparation of the Inter-Governmental Conference in 1996 (in agreement with the President); Relations with the European Parliament; Relations with the Member States on openness, communication and information; Cultural and Audiovisual Policy; and Publications Office.

Member of the Commission since 28 April 1994, responsible for energy, the Euratom Supply Agency and transport policy; former MEP (elected in 1989, resigning in June 1993 when elected in 1993 as a member of the Congress of Alava).

Italy

Emma Bonino

Portfolio: Consumer Policy; and the European Community Humanitarian Office (ECHO); and Fisheries.

Elected Member of the European Parliament in 1979 and elected Member of the Italian Parliament in 1976.

Mario Monti

Portfolio: Internal Market; Financial services; Customs and indirect taxation; and Direct taxation.

Elected President of Bocconi University in 1994; former MEP and Member of the Committee for Competition law from 1987–88.

Denmark

Ritt Bjerregaard

Portfolio: Environment; and Nuclear security.

Appointed Minister for Education in 1973; Minister for Social Affairs from 1979–81; and Member of the Parliamentary Assembly of the Council of Europe since 1990.

Belgium

Karel Van Miert

Portfolio: Competition policy.

Member of the Commission since January 1989, first in charge of transport, credit and investment and consumer policy affairs and justice (also responsible for environment as from 1 July 1992).

Netherlands

Hans Van Den Broek

Portfolio: External relations with the countries of Central and
             Eastern Europe and the countries of the former Soviet
             Union, Turkey, Cyprus, Malta and other European
             countries; Common Foreign and Security Policy (in
             agreement with the President); and External Service.

Appointed Member of the Commission in charge of External Political Relations, Common Foreign and Security Policy and Enlargement negotiations in January 1993; and Secretary of State for
Foreign Affairs from September 1981 until May 1982.

Portugal

Joao De Deus Pinheiro

Portfolio: External relations with the countries of Africa, the Car-
             ibbean and Pacific (including the Lomé Convention)
             and South Africa.

Member of the Commission since 1993, responsible for relations
with the European Parliament, transparency, communication and
information and cultural and audiovisual policy; Secretary of State
for Education and School Administration from 1981–82; Minister
of Education and Culture from 1984–86 respectively, and Minister
for Foreign Affairs from 1987; expert on science policy at
UNESCO and the OECD; and Vice-President of the National
Board for Scientific and Technological Research in 1983–84.

Ireland

Padraig Flynn

Portfolio: Employment and Social affairs; and Relations with the
             Economic and Social Committee (EcoSoC).

Member of the Commission since January 1993, responsible for
social affairs and employment, immigration, home affairs and

justice; Minister for Justice since February 1992; Minister for the Environment from March 1987 until November 1991; and Minister of State at the Department of Transport and Power from 1980–81.

Greece

Christos Papoutsis

Portfolio: Energy and Euratom Supply Agency; Small and Medium-sized Enterprises; and Tourism.

Vice-President of the Socialist Group of the European Parliament since 1987.

Austria

Franz Fischler

Portfolio: Agriculture and rural development.

Appointed Federal Minister for Agriculture and Forestry in April 1989; responsible for culture and education, land use planning, environmental protection and various other matters at the Tyrol Chamber of Agriculture from 1979–89.

Sweden

Anita Gradin

Portfolio: Immigration and home and judicial affairs; Relations with the ombudsman; Financial control; and Anti-fraud measures.

Appointed Ambassador of Sweden to Austria and Slovenia as well as to the IAEA and UN in 1992; Minister with responsibility for Foreign Trade at the Ministry for Foreign Affairs from 1986–91.

Finland

Erkki Liikanen

Portfolio: Budget; Personnel and Administration; and Translation
             and Information technology.

Ambassador at the Finnish Mission to the European Union since
1990.

Appendix B

Directorate-General III

Industry

Commissioner: Martin Bangemann

Director-General: Ricardo Perissich

Directorate A	Directorate B	Directorate C
Industrial Policy	**Legislation, Standardisation and Telematics Networks**	**Industrial Affairs I: basic industries**
Head: François Lamoreux	**Head:** Evangelos Vardakas	**Head:** Pedro Ortún Silván
Subject areas:	**Subject areas:**	**Subject areas:**
Industrial and technological relations. Industrial co-operation. Competitiveness and policy questions. Industrial aspects of structural assistance. Information technology and telecommunications.	Technical legislation. Standardisation. Quality and certification policy. Environmental questions. European telematics networks and systems.	Steel: internal market. Steel: external questions. Raw and advanced materials. Chemicals, plastic and rubber.

Directorate D	Directorate E	Directorate F
Industrial Affairs II: capital goods industries	**Industrial Affairs III: consumer goods industries**	**RDT: Information Technologies**
Head: Daniele Verdiani	**Head:** Guy Crauser	**Head:** George Metakides
Subject areas:	**Subject areas:**	**Subject areas:**
Mechanical and electrical engineering. Pressure vessels, medical equipment and metrology. Construction. Transport equipment.	Foodstuffs - legislation and technical aspects. Foodstuffs-industry and biotechnology. Pharmaceutical industry. Textiles, clothing, furniture. Automobiles and other road vehicles, tractors. Consumer electronics.	Basic research and scientific relations. Microelectronics. Software and advanced information processing. High performance computing and networking. Peripheral and business systems, house automation. Computer-integrated manufacturing (CIM)

Directorate-General IV

Competition

Commissioner: Karel Van Miert

Director-General: Claus-Dieter Ehlermann

Directorate A	Directorate B	Directorate C
General competition policy	**Restrictive practices, abuse of dominant positions and other distortions of competition I**	**Restrictive practices, abuse of dominant positions and other distortions of competition II**
Head: Rafael Garcia-Cebrian Palencia	**Head:** Humbert Drabbe	**Head:** Gianfranco Rocca
Subject Areas:	**Subject Areas:**	**Subject Areas:**
General policy and international aspects. Relations with the European Parliament and EcoSoC. Legal and procedural problems. Infringement procedures. Intra-Community dumping. Economic questions and studies. Co-ordination of decisions. Public enterprises and state monopolies. Implementation of Articles 101 and 102.	Electrical and electronic manufactured products. Information industries and telecommunications. Mechanical manufactured products and manufacturing industries. Service industries. Media, consumer electronics and music publishing.	Non-ferrous metals, non-metallic mineral products. Construction. Timber, paper, glass and rubber industries. Energy (except coal). Processed chemicals. Agricultural products. Foodstuffs.

Directorate D	Directorate E	Merger Task Force
Restrictive practices, abuse of dominant positions and other distortions of competition III	**State aids**	**Concentrations**
Head: John Temple Lang	**Head:** Asger Petersen	**Acting Head:** Goetz Drauz
Subject Areas:	**Subject Areas:**	3 operational units.
Steel and coal. ECSC inspection. Transport. Tourist industry. Motor vehicles.	General aid schemes. Aids to research and development. Regional aids. Industry aids. Inventory and analysis.	

Directorate-General XIII

Telecommunications Information Market and Exploitation of Research

Commissioner: Martin Bangemann

Director-General: Michel Carpentier

Directorate A	Directorate B	Directorate C
Telecommunications and postal services	**Advanced communications technologies and services**	**Technological developments relating to telematics applications**
Head: Nicholas Argyris	**Head:** Roland Hüber	**Head:** Michael Richonnier
Subject areas:	**Subject areas:**	**Subject areas:**
Telecommunications market. Regulatory aspects of network access, satellite and mobile communications and frequencies. Relations between telecommunications and broadcasting. Transeuropean telecommunications networks. Postal services. International aspects. Structural intervention.	Programmes: preparation and monitoring. Advanced networks and integrated broadband communications. Advanced communications technologies and digital transmission. Mobile communications. Engineering of services. Security of telecommunications and information systems.	Programmes: preparation and monitoring. Telematics networks and services (TNS) applied to administrations, R&TD and urban and rural areas. TNS applied to flexible distance learning. TNS applied to health. TNS applied to the integration of the disabled and elderly. TNS applied to transport.

Directorate D	Directorate E
Dissemination and exploitation of results of R&D, technology transfer and innovation	**Industry and Information Market**
Head: Giulio Grata	**Head:** Frans De Bruine
Subject areas:	**Subject areas:**
Strategic aspects of innovation and exploitation of R&D. Evaluation and exploitation of results of Community R&D. Dissemination of scientific and technical knowledge. Innovation and technology transfer.	Information services market policy. Pilot projects and demonstrations. Library networks and services. Language processing and applications. Basic studies in linguistics.

Directorate-General XV

Internal Market and Financial Services

Commissioner: Mario Monti

Director-General: John Mogg

Directorate A	Directorate B	Directorate C
General Affairs and Co-ordination	**Free Movement of Goods and Public Procurement**	**Financial Institutions**
Head: Thierry Stoll	**Head:** Alfonso Mattera Rigigliano	**Head:** Jean-Pierre Fèvre
Subject areas:	**Subject areas:**	**Subject areas:**
Operation and Completion of the Internal Market. External Aspects of the Internal Market and Financial Services. Free Movement of People and Citizens' Rights. Services and Economic Aspects.	Removal of Trade Barriers and Safeguard Measures. Public Procurement in National Administrations. Public Procurement in the Telecommunications, Transport, Energy, Water and Services Sectors. Policy and Interpretation concerning Free Movement of Goods.	Banks and Financial Establishments. Insurance and Pension Funds. Stock Exchanges and Securities. Cross-Border Payment - systems and Application of Legislation.

Directorate D	Directorate E
Company Law, and Direct Taxation	**Intellectual and Industrial Property**
Head: Hans Claudius Tascher	**Head:** Paul Waterschoot
Subject areas:	**Subject areas:**
Company Taxation and other Direct Taxation; Capital Duty; Taxes on Transactions in Securities. Company Law, Industrial Democracy and Accounting Standards. Multinationals, Groups of Companies and the European Company.	Freedom of Establishment. Freedom to Provide Services. The Regulated Professions. Patents, Trade Marks, Designs and Models and Indications of Origin. Copyright and Neighbouring Rights. Unfair Competition. Media and Data Protection. Civil Law and Access to Justice.

APPENDIX C

The Adoption of a Directive

Introduction

Perhaps the best way of explaining the basic elements of the legislative process, and the lobbying opportunities presented during its course, is to describe how a particular directive came to be adopted. The **Utilities Directive** is a good example since it was adopted under the co-operation procedure in 1990 with the majority of Member States due to implement it by 1 January 1993.

1. Developing a formal proposal

In March 1987, as part of the EC's push for the completion of the internal market, the Commission included in the White Paper on the completion of the internal market an action programme and timetable for opening up the public procurement markets in the telecommunications, transport, water and energy sectors. In October 1988, the Commission submitted two formal proposals to the Council, the first dealing with public procurement in the water, energy and transport sectors and the second dealing with the telecommunications sector. Both proposed Directives were based on Article 100a, thus using the co-operation procedure.

From the beginning of the 1980s, the Commission had been considering extending the existing public procurement rules to the utilities sector and had, therefore, been in discussion with interested parties. Before the proposals were formally submitted to the Council, they would have gone through a fair number of Commission internal drafts. Comments, to be most effective, should be submitted at an early stage in the life of a proposal and this formative time is the best time to do so. However, the Commission drafts proposals in relative secrecy and it can be difficult for third parties and even the

European Parliament to ascertain from the Commission the details of its thinking until it formally adopts a proposal and submits it to the Council. Internal drafts are not generally made available to outside bodies, though they may be circulated to certain interested parties for consultation purposes and the Commission is generally keen to obtain the comments of the pan-European trade associations. At this stage it is important to be in contact with officials in the relevant government departments and officials at the Permanent Representations in Brussels, as Member States are generally represented on advisory committees consulted by the Commission in preparing draft legislation. It is only once the proposal has been adopted by the Commission and sent to the Council that it will be translated into the 11 official languages of the EC and published in the Official Journal.

2. Referral to EcoSoC

The Council of Ministers referred both proposals to EcoSoC for their opinion on 24 October 1988. The proposals were first considered by the Committee for Industry, Commerce, Craft and Services and then in plenary sessions. The Opinions of the Committee's Rapporteurs on the two proposals were adopted at the end of March 1989 approving both proposed Directives but making a number of recommendations.

Although the potential impact of approaching EcoSoC may seem somewhat limited given its purely advisory role, members can be very helpful and influential. In particular, contact with the *Rapporteur* responsible for preparing the Committee's opinion may ensure that your views are raised at this early stage.

3. First Reading by the European Parliament

The proposals were then sent to the European Parliament for its first reading. They were reported on by the Committee on Economic and Monetary Affairs and Industrial Policy and the

European Parliament then debated the proposals and Committee reports, in plenary session, on 25 May 1989. It suggested a large number of individual amendments, and passed two resolutions embodying its general opinion on the proposals. In particular, the European Parliament requested that the two proposals should be incorporated into one single Directive. The European Parliament then referred the proposals back to the Commission and the Council for consideration and amendment in accordance with its opinion.

Approaching your local MEP, an MEP who has links with your business sector, or a member of the Committee which will consider the proposal can be useful in raising the profile of the proposal. The choice of MEP will obviously depend on the influence of the MEP involved. Since the Parliamentary Committee to which the proposal is referred considers the proposal in detail, it is important to ensure that your view is considered by the Committee and is not simply raised in the final Parliamentary debate.

4. Common Position adopted by the Council

The proposals together with EcoSoC's and the European Parliament's opinions were then considered by the Commission. Between May 1989 and March 1990 the Commission and the Council entered into consultations with a view to the Council adopting a common position which would satisfy the concerns of the European Parliament, EcoSoC and the Commission. On 29 March 1990 the Council adopted its common position incorporating, either in full or slightly amended form, 25 of the European Parliament's amendments including combining the two proposals into one.

Contact should be made, at this stage, with national ministers and the permanent representatives to the EU, for it is at this time that real negotiation of proposals at both the political and legislative level takes place.

5. Second Reading by the European Parliament

At the beginning of April 1990 the Council's common position was referred back to the same Parliamentary Committee which had considered the Commission's initial proposal on the European Parliament's first reading. The European Parliament adopted the Council's common position at the end of May 1990 but requested a number of new amendments (as a result of amendments made by the Council and the Commission subsequent to the European Parliament's first reading) and retabled two of its initial amendments.

Obviously, there is normally much less scope to influence the contents of a proposal once it has reached this stage than at the time of the European Parliament's first reading, though it may still be possible if the proposal has undergone substantial amendment between the European Parliament's first and second readings.

6. Revision of the proposal by the Commission

Since the European Parliament approved the Council's common position with amendments, the Commission was obliged to review the proposal. The Commission produced a re-examined proposal in July 1990 which incorporated 11 out of the 21 amendments adopted by the European Parliament in its second reading.

7. Adoption by the Council

The Commission's re-examined proposal was finally adopted by the Council on 17 September 1990 without any further recourse to the European Parliament or EcoSoC.

Member States, with the exception of Spain, Portugal and Greece, were required to implement the Directive by 1 January 1993. Spain has an extension until 1 January 1996 whilst Portugal and Greece have until 1 January 1998.

APPENDIX D

The EC Treaty (the Treaty of Rome as amended by the Single European Act and the Maastricht Treaty)

Preface

The Treaty on European Union was signed at Maastricht on 1 February 1992 and came into force on 1 November 1993 ("Maastricht Treaty").

The Maastricht Treaty will establish a "European Union" between the 12 Member States. The Union is based on the three European Communities (ECSC, EEC and Euratom, as modified by the Maastricht Treaty) to which is added a Common Foreign and Security Policy (CFSP), and co-operation between the Member States "in the spheres of justice and home affairs".

The Maastricht Treaty is made up as follows:

- Common Provisions

- Amendments to the EEC Treaty

- Amendments to the ECSC Treaty

- Amendments to the Euratom Treaty

- Provisions on CFSP

- Provisions on home affairs co-operation

- Final Provisions

- Protocols and Declarations. (There will also be an agreement between 11 states on social policy)

The following text deals only with the amendments made by the Maastricht Treaty to the EEC Treaty (renamed the EC Treaty) and sets out the provisions of the EC Treaty as amended and consolidated by the Maastricht Treaty.

These amendments are wide ranging and of relevance to all practitioners. An example of the importance of some changes introduced by the Maastricht Treaty is the incorporation into the new EC Treaty of the provisions relating to Economic and Monetary Union.

The Maastricht Treaty has given rise to a confusion of terminology. Following Maastricht, the Commission of the European Communities is to be known as the European Commission, the Council of the European Communities is to be known as the Council of the European Union and the Court of Justice of the European Communities is still known as such. The European Economic Community is renamed the European Community. The European Union is a term describing all of the EC, ECSC, Euratom, CSFP and home affairs co-operation.

A number of Protocols were agreed at Maastricht. Reproduced here are those dealing with convergence criteria on monetary union and UK opt outs on social policy and monetary union. Special provisions also exist for other countries.

For ease of reference, text inserted by the Maastricht Treaty has been highlighted and the [] symbol has been inserted to indicate where text has been omitted from the original text.

Treaty establishing the European Community (previously the European Economic Community)

ADOPTED BY THE EC MEMBER STATES

(Done at Rome)	25 March 1957
(as amended at Maastricht by the Treaty on European Union)	7 February 1992
Entry into force (in amended form):	1 November 1993
(as amended at Corfu by the Treaty of Accession for Austria, Finland, Norway and Sweden)	24 June 1994
(as amended most recently by Council Decision 95/1/EC, Euratom, ECSC)	1 January 1995
Entry into force (in amended form)	1 January 1995

Arrangement of Articles

Part One
Principles

Part Two
Citizenship of the Union

Part Three
Community Policies

103

Part Four
Association of the Overseas Countries and Territories

Part Five
Institutions of the Community

Title II
Financial provisions

Part Six
General and Final Provisions

Selected Protocols and Agreement agreed at Maastricht

Protocol on the excessive deficit procedure
Protocol on the convergence criteria referred to in Article 109j of the Treaty establishing the European Community
Protocol on the transition to the third stage of Economic and Monetary Union
Protocol on certain provisions relating to the United Kingdom of Great Britain and Northern Ireland
Protocol on social policy
Agreement on social policy concluded between the Member States of the European Community with the exception of the United Kingdom of Great Britain and Northern Ireland
Protocol on economic and social cohesion
Protocol on the Economic and Social Committee and the Committee of the Regions
Protocol annexed to the Treaty on European Union and to the Treaties establishing the European Communities.

The amended EC Treaty

NB: *Text which is printed in* **bold** *indicates text which has changed since the Maastricht Treaty.*
Text which is printed in **bold italics** *indicates text which has changed since the Treaty of Accession for Austria, Finland, Norway and Sweden, as amended by Council Decision 95/1/EC, Euratom, ECSC on the failure to ratify the Treaty by Norway.*
[] indicates where text has been omitted from the original Treaty of Rome, due to changes made at Maastricht.

Preamble

[THE HEADS OF STATE]

DETERMINED to lay the foundations of an ever closer union among the peoples of Europe,

RESOLVED to ensure the economic and social progress of their countries by common action to eliminate the barriers which divide Europe,

AFFIRMING as the essential objective of their efforts the constant improvement of the living and working conditions of their peoples,

RECOGNISING that the removal of existing obstacles calls for concerted action in order to guarantee steady expansion, balanced trade and fair competition,

ANXIOUS to strengthen the unity of their economies and to ensure their harmonious development by reducing the differences existing between the various regions and the backwardness of the less favoured regions,

DESIRING to contribute, by means of a common commercial policy, to the progressive abolition of restrictions on international trade,

INTENDING to confirm the solidarity which binds Europe and the overseas countries and desiring to ensure the development of their prosperity, in accordance with the principles of the Charter of the United Nations,

RESOLVED by thus pooling their resources to preserve and strengthen peace and liberty, and calling upon the other peoples of Europe who share their ideal to join in their efforts,

HAVE DECIDED to create a **European Community** and to this end ... have agreed as follows.

Part One
Principles

Article 1

By this Treaty, the HIGH CON-TRACTING PARTIES establish among themselves a **EUROPEAN [] COMMUNITY**.

Article 2

The Community shall have as its task, by establishing a common market [] **and an economic and monetary union and by implementing the common policies or activities referred to in Articles 3 and 3a**, to promote throughout the Community a harmonious **and balanced** development of economic activities [], **sustainable and non-inflationary growth respecting the environment, a high degree of convergence of economic performance, a high level of employment and of social protection, the** [] raising of the **standard of living** [] **and quality of life, and economic and social cohesion and solidarity among Member States.**

Article 3

For the purposes set out in Article 2, the activities of the Community shall include, as provided in this Treaty and in accordance with the timetable set out therein:

(a)   the elimination, as between Member States, of customs duties and [] quantitative restrictions on the import and export of goods, and of all other measures having equivalent effect;

(b)   **a common commercial policy;**

(c)   **an internal market charac-terised by** the abolition, as between Member States, of obstacles to the free movement of goods, persons, services and capital;

(d)   **measures concerning the entry and movement of persons in the internal market as provided for in Article 100c;**

(e)   [] **a common policy in the** sphere of agriculture **and fisheries;**

(f)   [] **a common policy in the** sphere of transport;

(g)   [] **a system ensuring that com-**petition in the [] **internal** market is not distorted;

(h)   the approximation of the laws of Member States to the extent required for the [] functioning of the common market;

(i)   **a policy in the social sphere comprising a** European Social Fund;

(j)   **the strengthening of economic and social cohesion;**

(k)   **a policy in the sphere of the environment;**

(l)   **the strengthening of the com-petitiveness of Community industry;**

(m)   **the promotion of research and technological development;**

(n)   **encouragement for the estab-lishment and development of trans-European networks;**

(o)   **a contribution to the attain-ment of a high level of health protection;**

(p)   **a contribution to education and training of quality and to the** flowering of the cultures of the Member States;

(q) a policy in the sphere of development co-operation;

(r) the association of the overseas countries and territories in order to increase trade and promote jointly economic and social development;

(s) a contribution to the strengthening of consumer protection;

(t) measures in the spheres of energy, civil protection and tourism.

Article 3a

1 For the purposes set out in Article 2, the activities of the Member States and the Community shall include, as provided in this Treaty and in accordance with the timetable set out therein, the adoption of an economic policy which is based on the close co-ordination of Member States' economic policies, on the internal market and on the definition of common objectives, and conducted in accordance with the principle of an open market economy with free competition.

2 Concurrently with the foregoing, and as provided in this Treaty and in accordance with the timetable and the procedures set out therein, these activities shall include the irrevocable fixing of exchange rates leading to the introduction of a single currency, the ECU, and the definition and conduct of a single monetary policy and exchange rate policy the primary objective of both of which shall be to maintain price stability and, without prejudice to this objective, to support the general economic policies in the Community, in accordance with the principle of an open market economy with free competition.

3 The activities of the Member States and the Community shall entail compliance with the following guiding principles: stable prices, sound public finances and monetary conditions and a sustainable balance of payments.

Article 3b

The Community shall act within the limits of the powers conferred upon it by this Treaty and of the objectives assigned to it therein.

In areas which do not fall within its exclusive competence, the Community shall take action, in accordance with the principle of subsidiarity, only if and in so far as the objectives of the proposed action cannot be sufficiently achieved by the Member States and can therefore, by reason of the scale or effects of the proposed action, be better achieved by the Community.

Any action by the Community shall not go beyond what is necessary to achieve the objectives of this Treaty.

Article 4

1 The tasks entrusted to the Community shall be carried out by the following institutions:

a EUROPEAN PARLIAMENT
a COUNCIL
a COMMISSION
a COURT OF JUSTICE
a COURT OF AUDITORS

Each institution shall act within the limits of the powers conferred upon it by this Treaty.

2 The Council and the Commission shall be assisted by an Economic and Social Committee and a Committee of the Regions

acting in an advisory capacity.
[]

Article 4a

A European System of Central Banks (hereinafter referred to as "ESCB") and a European Central Bank (hereinafter referred to as "ECB") shall be established in accordance with the procedures laid down in this Treaty; they shall act within the limits of the powers conferred upon them by this Treaty and by the Statute of the ESCB and of the ECB (hereinafter referred to as "Statute of the ESCB") annexed thereto.

Article 4b

A European Investment Bank is hereby established, which shall act within the limits of the powers conferred upon it by this Treaty and the Statute annexed thereto.

Article 5

Member States shall take all appropriate measures, whether general or particular, to ensure fulfilment of the obligations arising out of this Treaty or resulting from action taken by the institutions of the Community. They shall facilitate the achievement of the Community's tasks.

They shall abstain from any measure which could jeopardise the attainment of the objectives of this Treaty.

Article 6 (prior to Maastricht, Article 7; old Article 6 repealed)

Within the scope of application of this Treaty, and without prejudice to any special provisions contained therein, any discrimination on grounds of nationality shall be prohibited.

The Council, **acting in accordance with the procedure referred to in Article 189c**, may [] adopt [] rules designed to prohibit such discrimination.

Article 7 (prior to Maastricht, Article 8)

1 The common market shall be progressively established during a transitional period of 12 years.

This transitional period shall be divided into three stages of four years each; the length of each stage may be altered in accordance with the provisions set out below.

2 To each stage there shall be assigned a set of actions to be initiated and carried through concurrently.

3 Transition from the first to the second stage shall be conditional upon a finding that the objectives specifically laid down in this Treaty for the first stage have in fact been attained in substance and that, subject to the exceptions and procedures provided for in this Treaty, the obligations have been fulfilled.

This finding shall be made at the end of the fourth year by the Council, acting unanimously on a report from the Commission. A Member State may not, however, prevent unanimity by relying upon the non-fulfilment of its own obligations. Failing unanimity, the first stage shall automatically be extended for one year.

At the end of the fifth year, the Council shall make its finding under the same conditions. Failing unanimity, the first stage shall automatically be extended for a further year.

At the end of the sixth year, the Council shall make its finding, acting by a qualified majority on a report from the Commission.

4 Within one month of the last-mentioned vote any Member State which voted with the minority or, if the required majority was not obtained, any Member State shall be entitled to call upon the Council to appoint an arbitration board whose decision shall be binding upon all Member States and upon the institutions of the Community. The arbitration board shall consist of three members appointed by the Council acting unanimously on a proposal from the Commission.

If the Council has not appointed the members of the arbitration board within one month of being called upon to do so, they shall be appointed by the Court of Justice within a further period of one month.

The arbitration board shall elect its own Chairman.

The board shall make its award within six months of the date of the Council vote referred to in the last sub-paragraph of paragraph 3.

5 The second and third stages may not be extended or curtailed except by a decision of the Council, acting unanimously on a proposal from the Commission.

6 Nothing in the preceding paragraphs shall cause the transitional period to last more than 15 years after the entry into force of this Treaty.

7 Save for the exceptions or derogations provided for in this Treaty, the expiry of the transitional period shall constitute the latest date by which all the rules laid down must enter into force and all the measures required for establishing the common market must be implemented.

Article 7a (prior to Maastricht, Article 8a)

The Community shall adopt measures with the aim of progressively establishing the internal market over a period expiring on 31 December 1992, in accordance with the provisions of this Article and of Articles 7b, 7c, 28, 57(2), 59, 70(1), 84, 99, 100a and 100b and without prejudice to the other provisions of this Treaty.

The internal market shall comprise an area without internal frontiers in which the free movement of goods, persons, services and capital is ensured in accordance with the provisions of this Treaty.

Article 7b (prior to Maastricht, Article 8b)

The Commission shall report to the Council before 31 December 1988 and again before 31 December 1990 on the progress made towards achieving the internal market within the time limit fixed in Article 7a.

The Council, acting by a qualified majority on a proposal from the Commission, shall determine the guidelines and conditions necessary to ensure balanced progress in all the sectors concerned.

Article 7c (prior to Maastricht, Article 8c)

When drawing up its proposals with a view to achieving the objectives set out in Article 7a, the Commission shall take into account the extent of the effort that certain economies showing differences in development will have to sustain during the period of establishment of the internal market and it may propose appropriate provisions.

If these provisions take the form of derogations, they must be of a temporary nature and must cause the least possible disturbance to the functioning of the common market.

Part Two
Citizenship of the Union

Article 8

1 Citizenship of the Union is hereby established.

Every person holding the nationality of a Member State shall be a citizen of the Union.

2 Citizens of the Union shall enjoy the rights conferred by this Treaty and shall be subject to the duties imposed thereby.

Article 8a

1 Every citizen of the Union shall have the right to move and reside freely within the territory of the Member States, subject to the limitations and conditions laid down in this Treaty and by the measures adopted to give it effect.

2 The Council may adopt provisions with a view to facilitating the exercise of the rights referred to in paragraph 1; save as otherwise provided in this Treaty, the Council shall act unanimously on a proposal from the Commission and after obtaining the assent of the European Parliament.

Article 8b

1 Every citizen of the Union residing in a Member State of which he is not a national shall have the right to vote and to stand as a candidate at municipal elections in the Member State in which he resides, under the same conditions as nationals of that State. This right shall be exercised subject to detailed arrangements to be adopted before 31 December 1994 by the Council, acting unanimously on a proposal from the Commission and after consulting the European Parliament; these arrangements may provide for derogations where warranted by problems specific to a Member State.

2 Without prejudice to Article 138(3) and to the provisions adopted for its implementation, every citizen of the Union residing in a Member State of which he is not a national shall have the right to vote and to stand as a candidate in elections to the European Parliament in the Member State in which he resides, under the same conditions as nationals of that State. This right shall be exercised subject to detailed arrangements to be adopted before 31 December 1993 by the Council, acting unanimously on a proposal from the Commission and after consulting the European Parliament; these arrangements may provide for derogations where warranted by problems specific to a Member State.

Article 8c

Every citizen of the Union shall, in the territory of a third country in which the Member State of which he is a national is not represented, be entitled to protection by the diplomatic or consular authorities of any Member State, on the same conditions as the nationals of that State.

Before 31 December 1993, Member States shall establish the necessary rules among themselves and start the international negotiations required to secure this protection.

Article 8d

Every citizen of the Union shall have the right to petition the European Parliament in accordance with Article 138d.

Every citizen of the Union may apply to the Ombudsman established in accordance with Article 138e.

Article 8e

The Commission shall report to the European Parliament, to the Council and to the Economic and Social Committee before 31 December 1993 and then every three years on the application of the provisions of this Part. This report shall take account of the development of the Union.

On this basis, and without prejudice to the other provisions of this Treaty, the Council, acting unanimously on a proposal from the Commission and after consulting the European Parliament, may adopt provisions to strengthen or to add to the rights laid down in this Part, which it shall recommend to the Member States for adoption in accordance with their respective constitutional requirements.

Part Three
Community Policies

Title I
Free movement of goods

Article 9

1 The Community shall be based upon a customs union which shall cover all trade in goods and which shall involve the prohibition between Member States of customs duties on imports and exports and of all charges having equivalent effect, and the adoption of a common customs tariff in their relations with third countries.

2 The provisions of Chapter 1, Section 1, and of Chapter 2 of this Title shall apply to products originating in Member States and to products coming from third countries which are in free circulation in Member States.

Article 10

1 Products coming from a third country shall be considered to be in free circulation in a Member State if the import formalities have been complied with and any customs duties or charges having equivalent effect which are payable have been levied in that Member State, and if they have not benefited from a total or partial drawback of such duties or charges.

2 The Commission shall, before the end of the first year after the entry into force of this Treaty, determine the methods of administrative co-operation to be adopted for the purpose of applying Article 9(2), taking into account the need to reduce as much as possible formalities imposed on trade.

Before the end of the first year after the entry into force of this Treaty, the Commission shall lay down the provisions applicable, as regards trade between Member States, to goods originating in another Member State in whose manufacture products have been used on which the exporting Member State has not levied the appropriate customs duties or charges having equivalent effect, or which have benefited from a total or partial drawback of such duties or charges.

In adopting these provisions, the Commission shall take into account the rules for the elimination of customs duties within the Community and for the progressive application of the common customs tariff.

Article 11

Member States shall take all appropriate measures to enable Governments to carry out, within the periods of time laid down, the obligations with regard to customs duties which devolve upon them pursuant to this Treaty.

Chapter 1
The Customs Union

SECTION 1
ELIMINATION OF CUSTOMS DUTIES
BETWEEN MEMBER STATES

Article 12

Member States shall refrain from introducing between themselves any new customs duties on imports or exports or any charges having equivalent effect, and from increasing those which they already apply in their trade with each other.

Article 13

1 Customs duties on imports in force between Member States shall be progressively abolished by them during the transitional period in accordance with Articles 14 and 15.
2 Charges having an effect equivalent to customs duties on imports, in force between Member States, shall be progressively abolished by them during the transitional period. The Commission shall determine by means of directives the timetable for such abolition. It shall be guided by the rules contained in Article 14(2) and (3) and by the directives issued by the Council pursuant to Article 14(2).

Article 14

1 For each product, the basic duty to which the successive reductions shall be applied shall be the duty applied on 1 January 1957.
2 The timetable for the reductions shall be determined as follows:
(a) during the first stage, the first reduction shall be made one year after the date when this Treaty enters into force; the second reduction, 18 months later; the third reduction, at the end of the fourth year after the date when this Treaty enters into force;
(b) during the second stage, a reduction shall be made 18 months after that stage begins; a second reduction, 18 months after the preceding one; a third reduction, one year later;
(c) any remaining reductions shall be made during the third stage; the Council shall, acting by a qualified majority on a proposal from the Commission, determine the timetable therefor by means of directives.
3 At the time of the first reduction, Member States shall introduce between themselves a duty on each

product equal to the basic duty minus 10 per cent.

At the time of each subsequent reduction, each Member State shall reduce its customs duties as a whole in such manner as to lower by 10 per cent its total customs receipts as defined in paragraph 4 and to reduce the duty on each product by at least 5 per cent of the basic duty.

In the case, however, of products on which the duty is still in excess of 30 per cent, each reduction must be at least 10 per cent of the basic duty.

4 The total customs receipts of each Member State, as referred to in paragraph 3, shall be calculated by multiplying the value of its imports from other Member States during 1956 by the basic duties.

5 Any special problems raised in applying paragraphs 1 to 4 shall be settled by directives issued by the Council acting by a qualified majority on a proposal from the Commission.

6 Member States shall report to the Commission on the manner in which effect has been given to the preceding rules for the reduction of duties. They shall endeavour to ensure that the reduction made in the duties on each product shall amount:

- at the end of the first stage, to at least 25 per cent of the basic duty;

- at the end of the second stage, to at least 50 per cent of the basic duty.

If the Commission finds that there is a risk that the objectives laid down in Article 13, and the percentages laid down in this paragraph,

cannot be attained, it shall make all appropriate recommendations to Member States.

7 The provisions of this Article may be amended by the Council, acting unanimously on a proposal from the Commission and after consulting the European Parliament.

Article 15

1 Irrespective of the provisions of Article 14, any Member State may, in the course of the transitional period, suspend in whole or in part the collection of duties applied by it to products imported from other Member States. It shall inform the other Member States and the Commission thereof.

2 The Member States declare their readiness to reduce customs duties against the other Member States more rapidly than is provided for in Article 14 if their general economic situation and the situation of the economic sector concerned so permit.

To this end, the Commission shall make recommendations to the Member States concerned.

Article 16

Member States shall abolish between themselves customs duties on exports and charges having equivalent effect by the end of the first stage at the latest.

Article 17

1 The provisions of Articles 9 to 15(1) shall also apply to customs duties of a fiscal nature. Such duties shall not, however, be taken into consideration for the purpose of calculating either total customs receipts or the reduction of

customs duties as a whole as referred to in Article 14(3) and (4).

Such duties shall, at each reduction, be lowered by not less than 10 per cent of the basic duty. Member States may reduce such duties more rapidly than is provided for in Article 14.

2 Member States shall, before the end of the first year after the entry into force of this Treaty, inform the Commission of their customs duties of a fiscal nature.

3 Member States shall retain the right to substitute for these duties an internal tax which complies with the provisions of Article 95.

4 If the Commission finds that substitution for any customs duty of a fiscal nature meets with serious difficulties in a Member State, it shall authorise that State to retain the duty on condition that it shall abolish it not later than six years after the entry into force of this Treaty. Such authorisation must be applied for before the end of the first year after the entry into force of this Treaty.

SECTION 2
SETTING UP OF THE COMMON
CUSTOMS TARIFF

Article 18

The Member States declare their readiness to contribute to the development of international trade and the lowering of barriers to trade by entering into agreements designed, on a basis of reciprocity and mutual advantage, to reduce customs duties below the general level of which they could avail themselves as a result of the establishment of a customs union between them.

Article 19

1 Subject to the conditions and within the limits provided for hereinafter, duties in the common customs tariff shall be at the level of the arithmetical average of the duties applied in the four customs territories comprised in the Community.

2 The duties taken as the basis for calculating this average shall be those applied by Member States on 1 January 1957.

In the case of the Italian tariff, however, the duty applied shall be that without the temporary 10 per cent reduction. Furthermore, with respect to items on which the Italian tariff contains a conventional duty, this duty shall be substituted for the duty applied as defined above, provided that it does not exceed that latter by more than 10 per cent. Where the conventional duty exceeds the duty applied as defined above by more than 10 per cent, the latter duty plus 10 per cent shall be taken as the basis for calculating the arithmetical average.

With regard to the tariff headings in List A, the duties shown in that List shall, for the purpose of calculating the arithmetical average, be substituted for the duties applied.

3 The duties in the common customs tariff shall not exceed:

(a) 3 per cent for products within the tariff headings in List B;

(b) 10 per cent for products within the tariff headings in List C;

(c) 15 per cent for products within the tariff headings in List D;

(d) 25 per cent for products within the tariff headings in List E;

where in respect of such products, the tariff of the Benelux countries contains a duty not exceeding 3 per cent, such duty shall, for the purpose of calculating the arithmetical average, be raised to 12 per cent.

4 List F prescribes the duties applicable to the products listed therein.

5 The Lists of tariff headings referred to in this Article and in Article 20 are set out in Annex I to this Treaty.

Article 20

The duties applicable to the products in List G shall be determined by negotiation between the Member States. Each Member State may add further products to this List to a value not exceeding 2 per cent of the total value of its imports from third countries in the course of the year 1956.

The Commission shall take all appropriate steps to ensure that such negotiations shall be undertaken before the end of the second year after the entry into force of this Treaty and be concluded before the end of the first stage.

If, for certain products, no agreement can be reached within these periods, the Council shall, on a proposal from the Commission, acting unanimously until the end of the second stage and by a qualified majority thereafter, determine the duties in the common customs tariff.

Article 21

1 Technical difficulties which may arise in applying Articles 19 and 20 shall be resolved, within two years of the entry into force of this Treaty, by directives issued by the Council acting by a qualified majority on a proposal from the Commission.

2 Before the end of the first stage, or at latest when the duties are determined, the Council shall, acting by a qualified majority on a proposal from the Commission, decide on any adjustments required in the interests of the internal consistency of the common customs tariff as a result of applying the rules set out in Articles 19 and 20, taking account in particular of the degree of processing undergone by the various goods to which the common tariff applies.

Article 22

The Commission shall, within two years of the entry into force of this Treaty, determine the extent to which the customs duties of a fiscal nature referred to in Article 17(2) shall be taken into account in calculating the arithmetical average provided for in Article 19(1). The Commission shall take account of any protective character which such duties may have.

Within six months of such determination, any Member State may request that the procedure provided for in Article 20 should be applied to the product in question, but in this event the percentage limit provided in that Article shall not be applicable to that State.

Article 23

1 For the purpose of the progressive introduction of the common customs tariff, Member States shall amend their tariffs applicable to third countries as follows:

(a) in the case of tariff headings on which the duties applied in practice on 1 January 1957 do not differ by more than 15 per cent in either direction from the duties in the common customs tariff, the latter duties shall be applied at the end of the fourth year after the entry into force of this Treaty;

(b) in any other case, each Member State shall, as from the same date, apply a duty reducing by 30 per cent the difference between the duty applied in practice on 1 January 1957 and the duty in the common customs tariff;

(c) at the end of the second stage this difference shall again be reduced by 30 per cent;

(d) in the case of tariff headings for which the duties in the common customs tariff are not yet available at the end of the first stage, each Member State shall, within six months of the Council's action in accordance with Article 20, apply such duties as would result from application of the rules contained in this paragraph.

2 Where a Member State has been granted an authorisation under Article 17(4), it need not, for as long as that authorisation remains valid, apply the preceding provisions to the tariff headings to which the authorisation applies. When such authorisation expires, the Member State concerned shall apply such duty as would have resulted from application of the rules contained in paragraph 1.

3 The common customs tariff shall be applied in its entirety by the end of the transitional period at the latest.

Article 24

Member States shall remain free to change their duties more rapidly than is provided for in Article 23 in order to bring them into line with the common customs tariff.

Article 25

1 If the Commission finds that the production in Member States of particular products contained in Lists B, C and D is insufficient to supply the demands of one of the Member States, and that such supply traditionally depends to a considerable extent on imports from third countries, the Council shall, acting by a qualified majority on a proposal from the Commission, grant the Member State concerned tariff quotas at a reduced rate of duty or duty free.

Such quotas may not exceed the limits beyond which the risk might arise of activities being transferred to the detriment of other Member States.

2 In the case of the products in List E, and of those in List G for which the rates of duty have been determined in accordance with the procedure provided for in the third paragraph of Article 20, the Commission shall, where a change in sources of supply or shortage of supplies within the Community is such as to entail harmful consequences for the processing industries of a Member State, at the request of that Member State, grant it tariff quotas at a reduced rate of duty or duty free.

Such quotas may not exceed the limits beyond which the risk might arise of activities being transferred to the detriment of other Member States.

3 In the case of the products listed in Annex II to this Treaty, the Commission may authorise any Member State to suspend, in whole or in part, collection of the duties

applicable or may grant such Member State tariff quotas at a reduced rate of duty or duty free, provided that no serious disturbance of the market of the products concerned results therefrom.

4 The Commission shall periodically examine tariff quotas granted pursuant to this Article.

Article 26

The Commission may authorise any Member State encountering special difficulties to postpone the lowering or raising of duties provided for in Article 23 in respect of particular headings in its tariff.

Such authorisation may only be granted for a limited period and in respect of tariff headings which, taken together, represent for such State not more than 5 per cent of the value of its imports from third countries in the course of the latest year for which statistical data are available.

Article 27

Before the end of the first stage, Member States shall, in so far as may be necessary, take steps to approximate their provisions laid down by law, regulation or administrative action in respect of customs matters. To this end, the Commission shall make all appropriate recommendations to Member States.

Article 28

Any autonomous alteration or suspension of duties in the common customs tariff shall be decided by the Council acting by a qualified majority on a proposal from the Commission.

Article 29

In carrying out the tasks entrusted to it under this Section the Commission shall be guided by:
(a) the need to promote trade between Member States and third countries;
(b) developments in conditions of competition within the Community insofar as they lead to an improvement in the competitive capacity of undertakings;
(c) the requirements of the Community as regards the supply of raw materials and semi-finished goods; in this connection the Commission shall take care to avoid distorting conditions of competition between Member States in respect of finished goods;
(d) the need to avoid serious disturbances in the economies of Member States and to ensure rational development of production and an expansion of consumption within the Community.

Chapter 2
Elimination of Quantitative Restrictions between Member States

Article 30

Quantitative restrictions on imports and all measures having equivalent effect shall, without prejudice to the following provisions, be prohibited between Member States.

Article 31

Member States shall refrain from introducing between themselves any new quantitative restrictions or measures having equivalent effect.

This obligation shall, however, relate only to the degree of liberalisation attained in pursuance of the decisions of the Council of the Organisation for European Economic Co-operation of 14 January 1955. Member States shall supply the Commission, not later than six months after the entry into force of this Treaty, with lists of the products liberalised by them in pursuance of these decisions. These lists shall be consolidated between Member States.

Article 32

In their trade with one another Member States shall refrain from making more restrictive the quotas and measures having equivalent effect existing at the date of the entry into force of this Treaty.

These quotas shall be abolished by the end of the transitional period at the latest. During that period, they shall be progressively abolished in accordance with the following provisions.

Article 33

1 One year after the entry into force of this Treaty, each Member State shall convert any bilateral quotas open to any other Member States into global quotas open without discrimination to all other Member States.

On the same date, Member States shall increase the aggregate of the global quotas so established in such a manner as to bring about an increase of not less than 20 per cent in their total value as compared with the preceding year. The global quota for each product, however, shall be increased by not less than 10 per cent.

The quotas shall be increased annually in accordance with the same rules and in the same proportions in relation to the preceding year.

The fourth increase shall take place at the end of the fourth year after the entry into force of this Treaty; the fifth, one year after the beginning of the second stage.

2 Where, in the case of a product which has not been liberalised, the global quota does not amount to 3 per cent of the national production of the State concerned, a quota equal to not less than 3 per cent of such national production shall be introduced not later than one year after the entry into force of this Treaty. This quota shall be raised to 4 per cent at the end of the second year, and to 5 per cent at the end of the third. Thereafter, the Member State concerned shall increase the quota by not less than 15 per cent annually.

Where there is no such national production, the Commission shall take a decision establishing an appropriate quota.

3 At the end of the tenth year, each quota shall be equal to not less than 20 per cent of the national production.

4 If the Commission finds by means of a decision that during two successive years the imports of any product have been below the level of the quota opened, this global quota shall not be taken into account in calculating the total value of the global quotas. In such case, the Member State shall abolish quota restrictions on the product concerned.

5 In the case of quotas representing more than 20 per cent of the national production of the product concerned, the Council may, acting

by a qualified majority on a proposal from the Commission, reduce the minimum percentage of 10 per cent laid down in paragraph 1. This alteration shall not, however, affect the obligation to increase the total value of global quotas by 20 per cent annually.

6 Member States which have exceeded their obligations as regards the degree of liberalisation attained in pursuance of the decisions of the Council of the Organisation for European Economic Co-operation of 14 January 1955 shall be entitled, when calculating the annual total increase of 20 per cent provided for in paragraph 1, to take into account the amount of imports liberalised by autonomous action. Such calculation shall be submitted to the Commission for its prior approval.

7 The Commission shall issue directives establishing the procedure and timetable in accordance with which Member States shall abolish, as between themselves, any measures in existence when this Treaty enters into force which have an effect equivalent to quotas.

8 If the Commission finds that the application of the provisions of this Article, and in particular of the provisions concerning percentages, makes it impossible to ensure that the abolition of quotas provided for in the second paragraph of Article 32 is carried out progressively, the Council may, on a proposal from the Commission, acting unanimously during the first stage and by a qualified majority thereafter, amend the procedure laid down in this Article and may, in particular, increase the percentages fixed.

Article 34

1 Quantitative restrictions on exports, and all measures having equivalent effect, shall be prohibited between Member States.

2 Member States shall, by the end of the first stage at the latest, abolish all quantitative restrictions on exports and any measures having equivalent effect which are in existence when this Treaty enters into force.

Article 35

The Member States declare their readiness to abolish quantitative restrictions on imports from and exports to other Member States more rapidly than is provided for in the preceding Articles, if their general economic situation and the situation of the economic sector concerned so permit.

To this end, the Commission shall make recommendations to the Member States concerned.

Article 36

The provisions of Articles 30 to 34 shall not preclude prohibitions or restrictions on imports, exports or goods in transit justified on grounds of public morality, public policy or public security; the protection of health and life of humans, animals or plants; the protection of national treasures possessing artistic, historic or archaeological value; or the protection of industrial and commercial property. Such prohibitions or restrictions shall not, however, constitute a means of arbitrary discrimination or a disguised restriction on trade between Member States.

Article 37

1 Member States shall progressively adjust any State monopolies of a commercial character so as to ensure that when the transitional period has ended no discrimination regarding the conditions under which goods are procured and marketed exists between nationals of Member States.

The provisions of this Article shall apply to any body through which a Member State, in law or in fact, either directly or indirectly supervises, determines or appreciably influences imports or exports between Member States. These provisions shall likewise apply to monopolies delegated by the State to others.

2 Member States shall refrain from introducing any new measure which is contrary to the principles laid down in paragraph 1 or which restricts the scope of the Articles dealing with the abolition of customs duties and quantitative restrictions between Member States.

3 The timetable for the measures referred to in paragraph 1 shall be harmonised with the abolition of quantitative restrictions on the same products provided for in Articles 30 to 34.

If a product is subject to a State monopoly of a commercial character in only one or some Member States, the Commission may authorise the other Member States to apply protective measures until the adjustment provided for in paragraph 1 has been effected; the Commission shall determine the conditions and details of such measures.

4 If a State monopoly of a commercial character has rules which are designed to make it easier to dispose of agricultural products or obtain for them the best return, steps should be taken in applying the rules contained in this Article to ensure equivalent safeguards for the employment and standard of living of the producers concerned, account being taken of the adjustments that will be possible and the specialisation that will be needed with the passage of time.

5 The obligations on Member States shall be binding only insofar as they are compatible with existing international agreements.

6 With effect from the first stage the Commission shall make recommendations as to the manner in which and the timetable according to which the adjustment provided for in this Article shall be carried out.

Title II
Agriculture

Article 38

1 The common market shall extend to agriculture and trade in agricultural products. "Agricultural products" means the products of the soil, of stockfarming and of fisheries and products of first-stage processing directly related to these products.

2 Save as otherwise provided in Articles 39 to 46, the rules laid down for the establishment of the common market shall apply to agricultural products.

3 The products subject to the provisions of Articles 39 to 46 are listed in Annex II to this Treaty. Within two years of the entry into force of this Treaty, however, the Council shall, acting by a qualified majority on a proposal from the

Commission, decide what products are to be added to this list.

4 The operation and development of the common market for agricultural products must be accompanied by the establishment of a common agricultural policy among the Member States.

Article 39

1 The objectives of the common agricultural policy shall be:
(a) to increase agricultural productivity by promoting technical progress and by ensuring the rational development of agricultural production and the optimum utilisation of the factors of production, in particular labour;
(b) thus to ensure a fair standard of living for the agricultural community, in particular by increasing the individual earnings of persons engaged in agriculture;
(c) to stabilise markets;
(d) to assure the availability of supplies;
(e) to ensure that supplies reach consumers at reasonable prices.

2 In working out the common agricultural policy and the special methods for its application, account shall be taken of:
(a) the particular nature of agricultural activity, which results from the social structure of agriculture and from structural and natural disparities between the various agricultural regions;
(b) the need to effect the appropriate adjustments by degrees;
(c) the fact that in the Member States agriculture constitutes a sector closely linked with the economy as a whole.

Article 40

1 Member States shall develop the common agricultural policy by degrees during the transitional period and shall bring it into force by the end of that period at the latest.

2 In order to attain the objectives set out in Article 39 a common organisation of agricultural markets shall be established.

This organisation shall take one of the following forms, depending on the product concerned:
(a) common rules on competition;
(b) compulsory co-ordination of the various national market organisations;
(c) a European market organisation.

3 The common organisation established in accordance with paragraph 2 may include all measures required to attain the objectives set out in Article 39, in particular regulation of prices, aids for the production and marketing of the various products, storage and carryover arrangements and common machinery for stabilising imports or exports.

The common organisation shall be limited to pursuit of the objectives set out in Article 39 and shall exclude any discrimination between producers or consumers within the Community.

Any common price policy shall be based on common criteria and uniform methods of calculation.

4 In order to enable the common organisation referred to in paragraph 2 to attain its objectives, one or more agricultural guidance and guarantee funds may be set up.

Article 41

To enable the objectives set out in Article 39 to be attained, provision may be made within the framework of the common agricultural policy for measures such as:
(a) an effective co-ordination of efforts in the spheres of vocational training, of research and of the dissemination of agricultural knowledge; this may include joint financing of projects or institutions;
(b) joint measures to promote consumption of certain products.

Article 42

The provisions of the Chapter relating to rules on competition shall apply to production of and trade in agricultural products only to the extent determined by the Council within the framework of Article 43(2) and (3) and in accordance with the procedure laid down therein, account being taken of the objectives set out in Article 39.

The Council may, in particular, authorise the granting of aid:
(a) for the protection of enterprises handicapped by structural or natural conditions;
(b) within the framework of economic development programmes.

Article 43

1 In order to evolve the broad lines of a common agricultural policy, the Commmission shall, immediately this Treaty enters into force, convene a conference of the Member States with a view to making a comparison of their agricultural policies, in particular by producing a statement of their resources and needs.

2 Having taken into account the work of the conference provided for in paragraph 1, after consulting the Economic and Social Committee and within two years of the entry into force of this Treaty, the Commission shall submit proposals for working out and implementing the common agricultural policy, including the replacement of the national organisations by one of the forms of common organisation provided for in Article 40(2), and for implementing the measures specified in this Title.

These proposals shall take account of the interdependence of the agricultural matters mentioned in this Title.

The Council shall, on a proposal from the Commission and after consulting the European Parliament, acting unanimously during the first two stages and by a qualified majority thereafter, make regulations, issue directives, or take decisions, without prejudice to any recommendations it may also make.

3 The Council may, acting by a qualified majority and in accordance with paragraph 2, replace the national market organisations by the common organisation provided for in Article 40(2) if:
(a) the common organisation offers Member States which are opposed to this measure and which have an organisation of their own for the product in question equivalent safeguards for the employment and standard of living of the producers concerned, account being taken of the adjustments that will be possible and the specialisation that will be needed with the passage of time;

(b) such an organisation ensures conditions for trade within the Community similar to those existing in a national market.

4 If a common organisation for certain raw materials is established before a common organisation exists for the corresponding processed products, such raw materials as are used for processed products intended for export to third countries may be imported from outside the Community.

Article 44

1 Insofar as progressive abolition of customs duties and quantitative restrictions between Member States may result in prices likely to jeopardise the attainment of the objectives set out in Article 39, each Member State shall, during the transitional period, be entitled to apply to particular products, in a non-discriminatory manner and in substitution for quotas and to such an extent as shall not impede the expansion of the volume of trade provided for in Article 45(2), a system of minimum prices below which imports may be either:

- temporarily suspended or reduced; or
- allowed, but subjected to the condition that they are made at a price higher than the minimum price for the product concerned.

In the latter case the minimum prices shall not include customs duties.

2 Minimum prices shall neither cause a reduction of the trade existing between Member States when this Treaty enters into force nor form an obstacle to progressive expansion of this trade. Minimum prices shall not be applied so as to form an obstacle to the development of a natural preference between Member States.

3 As soon as this Treaty enters into force the Council shall, on a proposal from the Commission, determine objective criteria for the establishment of minimum price systems and for the fixing of such prices.

These criteria shall in particular take account of the average national production costs in the Member State applying the minimum price, of the position of the various undertakings concerned in relation to such average production costs, and of the need to promote both the progressive improvement of agricultural practice and the adjustments and specialisation needed within the common market.

The Commission shall further propose a procedure for revising these criteria in order to allow for and speed up technical progress and to approximate prices progressively within the common market.

These criteria and the procedure for revising them shall be determined by the Council acting unanimously within three years of the entry into force of this Treaty.

4 Until the decision of the Council takes effect, Member States may fix minimum prices on condition that these are communicated beforehand to the Commission and to the other Member States so that they may submit their comments.

Once the Council has taken its decision, Member States shall fix minimum prices on the basis of the criteria determined as above.

The Council may, acting by a qualified majority on a proposal from the Commission, rectify any decisions taken by Member States which do not conform to the criteria defined above.

5 If it does not prove possible to determine the said objective criteria for certain products by the beginning of the third stage, the Council may, acting by a qualified majority on a proposal from the Commission, vary the minimum prices applied to these products.

6 At the end of the transitional period, a table of minimum prices still in force shall be drawn up. The Council shall, acting on a proposal from the Commission and by a majority of nine votes in accordance with the weighting laid down in the first subparagraph of Article 148(2), determine the system to be applied within the framework of the common agricultural policy.

Article 45

1 Until national market organisations have been replaced by one of the forms of common organisation referred to in Article 40(2), trade in products in respect of which certain Member States:

- have arrangements designed to guarantee national producers a market for their products; and
- are in need of imports,

shall be developed by the conclusion of long-term agreements or contracts between importing and exporting Member States.

These agreements or contracts shall be directed towards the progressive abolition of any discrimination in the application of these arrangements to the various producers within the Community.

Such agreements or contracts shall be concluded during the first stage; account shall be taken of the principle of reciprocity.

2 As regards quantities, these agreements or contracts shall be based on the average volume of trade between Member States in the products concerned during the three years before the entry into force of this Treaty and shall provide for an increase in the volume of trade within the limits of existing requirements, account being taken of traditional patterns of trade.

As regards prices, these agreements or contracts shall enable producers to dispose of the agreed quantities at prices which shall be progressively approximated to those paid to national producers on the domestic market of the purchasing country.

This approximation shall proceed as steadily as possible and shall be completed by the end of the transitional period at the latest.

Prices shall be negotiated between the parties concerned within the framework of directives issued by the Commission for the purpose of implementing the two preceding subparagraphs.

If the first stage is extended, these agreements or contracts shall continue to be carried out in accordance with the conditions applicable at the end of the fourth year after the entry into force of this Treaty, the obligation to increase quantities and to approximate prices being suspended until transition to the second stage.

Member States shall avail themselves of any opportunity open to them under their legislation, particularly in respect of import policy, to ensure the conclusion and carrying out of these agreements or contracts.

3 To the extent that Member States require raw materials for the

manufacture of products to be exported outside the Community in competition with products of third countries, the above agreements or contracts shall not form an obstacle to the importation of raw materials for this purpose from third countries. This provision shall not, however, apply if the Council unanimously decides to make provision for payments required to compensate for the higher price paid on goods imported for this purpose on the basis of these agreements or contracts in relation to the delivered price of the same goods purchased on the world market.

Article 46

Where in a Member State a product is subject to a national market organisation or to internal rules having equivalent effect which affect the competitive position of similar production in another Member State, a countervailing charge shall be applied by Member States to imports of this product coming from the Member State where such organisation or rules exist, unless the State applies a countervailing charge on export.

The Commission shall fix the amount of these charges at the level required to redress the balance; it may also authorise other measures, the conditions and details of which it shall determine.

Article 47

As to the functions to be performed by the Economic and Social Committee in pursuance of this Title, its agricultural section shall hold itself at the disposal of the Commission to prepare, in accordance with the provisions of Articles 197 and 198, the deliberations of the Committee.

Title III
Free movement of persons, services and capital

Chapter 1
Workers

Article 48

1 Freedom of movement for workers shall be secured within the Community by the end of the transitional period at the latest.
2 Such freedom of movement shall entail the abolition of any discrimination based on nationality between workers of the Member States as regards employment, remuneration and other conditions of work and employment.
3 It shall entail the right, subject to limitations justified on grounds of public policy, public security or public health:

(a) to accept offers of employment actually made;

(b) to move freely within the territory of Member States for this purpose;

(c) to stay in a Member State for the purpose of employment in accordance with the provisions governing the employment of nationals of that State laid down by law, regulation or administrative action;

(d) to remain in the territory of a Member State after having been employed in that State, subject to conditions which shall be embodied in implementing regulations to be drawn up by the Commission.

4 The provisions of this Article shall not apply to employment in the public service.

Article 49

As soon as this Treaty enters into force, the Council shall, [] **acting in accordance with the procedure referred to in Article 189b** and after consulting the Economic and Social Committee, issue directives or make regulations setting out the measures required to bring about, by progressive stages, freedom of movement for workers, as defined in Article 48, in particular:

(a) by ensuring close co-operation between national employment services;

(b) by systematically and progressively abolishing those administrative procedures and practices and those qualifying periods in respect of eligibility for available employment, whether resulting from national legislation or from agreements previously concluded between Member States, the maintenance of which would form an obstacle to liberalisation of the movement of workers;

(c) by systematically and progressively abolishing all such qualifying periods and other restrictions provided for either under national legislation or under agreements previously concluded between Member States as imposed on workers of other Member States conditions regarding the free choice of employment other than those imposed on workers of the State concerned;

(d) by setting up appropriate machinery to bring offers of employment into touch with applications for employment and to facilitate the achievement of a balance between supply and demand in the employment market in such a way as to avoid serious threats to the standard of living and level of employment in the various regions and industries.

Article 50

Member States shall, within the framework of a joint programme, encourage the exchange of young workers.

Article 51

The Council shall, acting unanimously on a proposal from the Commission, adopt such measures in the field of social security as are necessary to provide freedom of movement for workers; to this end, it shall make arrangements to secure for migrant workers and their dependants:

(a) aggregation, for the purpose of acquiring and retaining the right to benefit and of calculating the amount of benefit, of all periods taken into account under the laws of the several countries;

(b) payment of benefits to persons resident in the territories of Member States.

Chapter 2
Right of Establishment

Article 52

Within the framework of the provisions set out below, restrictions on the freedom of establishment of nationals of a Member State in the territory of another Member State shall be abolished by progressive stages in the course of the transitional period. Such progressive abolition shall also apply to restrictions on the setting up of agencies, branches or subsidiaries by nationals of any Member State established in the territory of any Member State.

Freedom of establishment shall include the right to take up and pursue activities as self-employed persons and to set up and manage undertakings, in particular companies or firms within the meaning of the second paragraph of Article 58, under the conditions laid down for its own nationals by the law of the country where such establishment is effected, subject to the provisions of the Chapter relating to capital.

Article 53

Member States shall not introduce any new restrictions on the right of establishment in their territories of nationals of other Member States, save as otherwise provided in this Treaty.

Article 54

1 Before the end of the first stage, the Council shall, acting unanimously on a proposal from the Commission and after consulting the Economic and Social Committee and the European Parliament, draw up a general programme for the abolition of existing restrictions on freedom of establishment within the Community. The Commission shall submit its proposal to the Council during the first two years of the first stage.

The programme shall set out the general conditions under which freedom of establishment is to be attained in the case of each type of activity and in particular the stages by which it is to be attained.

2 In order to implement this general programme or, in the absence of such programme, in order to achieve a stage in attaining freedom of establishment as regards a particular activity, the Council [], **acting in accordance with the procedure referred to in Article 189b** and after consulting the Economic and Social Committee, [] **shall act by means of directives.**

3 The Council and the Commission shall carry out the duties devolving upon them under the preceding provisions, in particular:

(a) by according, as a general rule, priority treatment to activities where freedom of establishment makes a particularly valuable contribution to the development of production and trade;

(b) by ensuring close co-operation between the competent authorities in the Member States in order to ascertain the particular situation within the Community of the various activities concerned;

(c) by abolishing those administrative procedures and practices, whether resulting from national legislation or from agreements previously concluded between Member States, the maintenance of which would form an obstacle to freedom of establishment;

(d) by ensuring that workers of one Member State employed in the territory of another Member State may remain in that territory for the purpose of taking up activities therein as self-employed persons, where they satisfy the conditions which they would be required to satisfy if they were entering that State at the time when they intended to take up such activities;

(e) by enabling a national of one Member State to acquire and use land and buildings situated in the territory of another Member State, insofar as this does not conflict with the principles laid down in Article 39(2);

(f) by effecting the progressive abolition of restrictions on freedom of establishment in every branch of activity under consideration, both as regards the conditions for setting up agencies, branches or subsidiaries in the territory of a Member State and as regards the subsidiaries in the territory of a Member State and as regards the conditions governing the entry of personnel belonging to the main establishment into managerial or supervisory posts in such agencies, branches or subsidiaries;

(g) by co-ordinating to the necessary extent the safeguards which, for the protection of the interests of members and others, are required by Member States of companies or firms within the meaning of the second paragraph of Article 58 with a view to making such safeguards equivalent throughout the Community;

(h) by satisfying themselves that the conditions of establishment are not distorted by aids granted by Member States.

Article 55

The provisions of this Chapter shall not apply, so far as any given Member State is concerned, to activities which in that State are connected, even occasionally, with the exercise of official authority.

The Council may, acting by a qualified majority on a proposal from the Commission, rule that the provisions of this Chapter shall not apply to certain activities.

Article 56

1 The provisions of this Chapter and measures taken in pursuance thereof shall not prejudice the applicability of provisions laid down by law, regulation or administrative action providing for special treatment for foreign nationals on grounds of public policy, public security or public health.

2 Before the end of the transitional period, the Council shall, acting unanimously on a proposal from the Commission and after consulting the European Parliament, issue directives for the co-ordination of the **above mentioned** provisions laid down by law, regulation or administrative action. After the end of the second stage, however, the Council shall, acting [] **in accordance with the procedure referred to in Article 189b**, issue directives for the co-ordination of such provisions as, in each Member State, are a matter for regulation or administrative action.

Article 57

1 In order to make it easier for persons to take up and pursue activities as self-employed persons, the Council shall, [] **acting in**

accordance with the procedure referred to in Article 189b, issue directives for the mutual recognition of diplomas, certificates and other evidence of formal qualifications.

2 For the same purpose, the Council shall, before the end of the transitional period, [] issue directives for the co-ordination of the provisions laid down by law, regulation or administrative action in Member States concerning the taking up and pursuit of activities as self-employed persons. [] **The Council, acting unanimously on a proposal from the Commission and after consulting the European Parliament, shall decide on directives** the implementation of which involves in at least one Member State amendment of the existing principles laid down by law governing the professions with respect to training and conditions of access for natural persons. In other cases the Council shall act [] **in accordance with the procedure referred to in Article 189b**.

3 In the case of the medical and allied and pharmaceutical professions, the progressive abolition of restrictions shall be dependent upon co-ordination of the conditions for their exercise in the various Member States.

Article 58

Companies or firms formed in accordance with the law of a Member State and having their registered office, central administration or principal place of business within the Community shall, for the purposes of this Chapter, be treated in the same way as natural persons who are nationals of Member States.

"Companies or firms" means companies or firms constituted under civil or commercial law, including co-operative societies, and other legal persons governed by public or private law, save for those which are non-profit-making.

Chapter 3
Services

Article 59

Within the framework of the provisions set out below, restrictions on freedom to provide services within the Community shall be progressively abolished during the transitional period in respect of nationals of Member States who are established in a State of the Community other than that of the person for whom the services are intended.

The Council may, acting by a qualified majority on a proposal from the Commission, extend the provisions of the Chapter to nationals of a third country who provide services and who are established within the Community.

Article 60

Services shall be considered to be "services" within the meaning of this Treaty where they are normally provided for remuneration, insofar as they are not governed by the provisions relating to freedom of movement for goods, capital and persons.

"Services" shall in particular include:

(a) activities of an industrial character;

(b) activities of a commercial character;

(c) activities of craftsmen;

(d) activities of the professions.

Without prejudice to the provisions of the Chapter relating to the right of establishment, the person providing a service may, in order to do so, temporarily pursue his activity in the State where the service is provided, under the same conditions as are imposed by that State on its own nationals.

Article 61

1 Freedom to provide services in the field of transport shall be governed by the provisions of the Title relating to transport.
2 The liberalisation of banking and insurance services connected with movements of capital shall be effected in step with the progressive liberalisation of movement of capital.

Article 62

Save as otherwise provided in this Treaty, Member States shall not introduce any new restrictions on the freedom to provide services which have in fact been attained at the date of the entry into force of this Treaty.

Article 63

1 Before the end of the first stage, the Council shall, acting unanimously on a proposal from the Commission and after consulting the Economic and Social Committee and the European Parliament, draw up a general programme for the abolition of existing restrictions on freedom to provide services within the Community. The Commission shall submit its proposal to the Council during the first two years of the first stage.
   The programme shall set out the general conditions under which and the stages by which each type of service is to be liberalised.
2 In order to implement this general programme or, in the absence of such programme, in order to achieve a stage in the liberalisation of a specific service, the Council shall, on a proposal from the Commission and after consulting the Economic and Social Committee and the European Parliament, issue directives, acting unanimously until the end of the first stage and by a qualified majority thereafter.
3 As regards the proposals and decisions referred to in paragraphs 1 and 2, priority shall as a general rule be given to those services which directly affect production costs or the liberalisation of which helps to promote trade in goods.

Article 64

The Member States declare their readiness to undertake the liberalisation of services beyond the extent required by the directives issued pursuant to Article 63(2), if their general economic situation and the situation of the economic sector concerned so permit.
   To this end, the Commission shall make recommendations to the Member States concerned.

Article 65

As long as restrictions on freedom to provide services have not been abolished, each Member State shall apply such restrictions without distinction on grounds of nationality or residence to all persons providing services within the meaning of the first paragraph of Article 59.

Article 66

The provisions of Articles 55 to 58 shall apply to the matters covered by this Chapter.

Chapter 4
Capital and Payments

(As from 1 January 1994, Articles 67 to 73 were replaced by Articles 73b, c, d, e, f and g.)

Article 73b

1 Within the framework of the provisions set out in this Chapter, all restrictions on the movement of capital between Member States and between Member States and third countries shall be prohibited.
2 Within the framework of the provisions set out in this Chapter, all restrictions on payments between Member States and between Member States and third countries shall be prohibited.

Article 73c

1 The provisions of Article 73b shall be without prejudice to the application to third countries of any restrictions which exist on 31 December 1993 under national or Community law adopted in respect of the movement of capital to or from third countries involving direct investment – including investment in real estate – establishment, the provision of financial services or the admission of securities to capital markets.
2 Whilst endeavouring to achieve the objective of free movement of capital between Member States and third countries to the greatest extent possible and without prejudice to the other Chapters of this Treaty, the Council may, acting by a qualified majority on a proposal from the Commission, adopt measures on the movement of capital to or from third countries involving direct investment – including investment in real estate – establishment, the provision of financial services or the admission of securities to capital markets. Unanimity shall be required for measures under this paragraph which constitute a step back in Community law as regards the liberalisation of the movement of capital to or from third countries.

Article 73d

1 The provisions of Article 73b shall be without prejudice to the right of Member States:
(a) to apply the relevant provisions of their tax law which distinguish between tax-payers who are not in the same situation with regard to their place of residence or with regard to the place where their capital is invested;
(b) to take all requisite measures to prevent infringements of national law and regulations, in particular in the field of taxation and the prudential supervision of financial institutions, or to lay down procedures for the declaration of capital movements for purposes of administrative or statistical information, or to take measures which are justified on grounds of public policy or public security.
2 The provisions of this Chapter shall be without prejudice to the applicability of restrictions on the right of establishment which are compatible with this Treaty.
3 The measures and procedures

referred to in paragraphs 1 and 2 shall not constitute a means of arbitrary discrimination or a disguised restriction on the free movement of capital and payments as defined in Article 73b.

Article 73e

By way of derogation from Article 73b, Member States which, on 31 December 1993, enjoy a derogation on the basis of existing Community law, shall be entitled to maintain, until 31 December 1995 at the latest, restrictions on movements of capital authorised by such derogations as exist on that date.

Article 73f

Where, in exceptional circumstances, movements of capital to or from third countries cause, or threaten to cause, serious difficulties for the operation of economic and monetary union, the Council, acting by a qualified majority on a proposal from the Commission and after consulting the ECB, may take safeguard measures with regard to third countries for a period not exceeding six months if such measures are strictly necessary.

Article 73g

1 If, in the cases envisaged in Article 228a, action by the Community is deemed necessary, the Council may, in accordance with the procedure provided for in Article 228a, take the necessary urgent measures on the movement of capital and on payments as regards the third countries concerned.
2 Without prejudice to Article 224 and as long as the Council has not taken measures pursuant to paragraph 1, a Member State may, for

serious political reasons and on grounds of urgency, take unilateral measures against a third country with regard to capital movements and payments. The Commission and the other Member States shall be informed of such measures by the date of their entry into force at the latest.
The Council may, acting by a qualified majority on a proposal from the Commission, decide that the Member State concerned shall amend or abolish such measures. The President of the Council shall inform the European Parliament of any such decision taken by the Council.

Article 73h

Until 1 January 1994, the following provisions shall be applicable:
(1) Each Member State undertakes to authorise, in the currency of the Member State in which the creditor or the beneficiary resides, any payments connected with the movement of goods, services or capital, and any transfers of capital and earnings, to the extent that the movement of goods, services, capital and persons between Member States has been liberalised pursuant to this Treaty.
The Member States declare their readiness to undertake the liberalisation of payments beyond the extent provided in the preceding sub-paragraph, in so far as their economic situation in general and the state of their balance of payments in particular so permit.
(2) In so far as movements of goods, services and capital are limited only by restrictions on payments connected therewith,

these restrictions shall be progressively abolished by applying, *mutatis mutandis*, the provisions of this Chapter and the Chapters relating to the abolition of quantitative restrictions and to the liberalisation of services.

(3) Member States undertake not to introduce between themselves any new restrictions on transfers connected with the invisible transactions listed in Annex III to this Treaty.

The progressive abolition of existing restrictions shall be effected in accordance with the provisions of Articles 63 to 65, in so far as such abolition is not governed by the provisions contained in paragraphs 1 and 2 or by the other provisions of this Chapter.

(4) If need be, Member States shall consult each other on the measures to be taken to enable the payments and transfers mentioned in this Article to be effected; such measures shall not prejudice the attainment of the objectives set out in this Treaty.

Title IV
Transport

Article 74

The objectives of this Treaty shall, in matters governed by this Title, be pursued by Member States within the framework of a common transport policy.

Article 75

1 For the purpose of implementing Article 74, and taking into account the distinctive features of transport, the Council shall, acting [] in accordance with the procedure referred to in Article 189c and after consulting the Economic and Social Committee [], lay down:

(a) common rules applicable to international transport to or from the territory of a Member State or passing across the territory of one or more Member States;

(b) the conditions under which non-resident carriers may operate transport services within a Member State;

(c) measures to improve transport safety;

(d) any other appropriate provisions.

2 The provisions referred to in (a) and (b) of paragraph 1 shall be laid down during the transitional period.

3 By way of derogation from the procedure provided for in paragraph 1, where the application of provisions concerning the principles of the regulatory system for transport would be liable to have a serious effect on the standard of living and on employment in certain areas and on the operation of transport facilities, they shall be laid down by the Council acting unanimously on a proposal from the Commission, after consulting the European Parliament and the Economic and Social Committee. In so doing, the Council shall take into account the need for adaptation to the economic development which will result from establishing the common market.

Article 76

Until the provisions referred to in Article 75(1) have been laid down, no Member State may, without the unanimous approval of the Council, make the various provisions governing the subject when this Treaty enters into force less favourable in their direct or indirect effect on carriers of other Member States as compared with carriers who are nationals of that State.

Article 77

Aids shall be compatible with this Treaty if they meet the needs of co-ordination of transport or if they represent reimbursement for the discharge of certain obligations inherent in the concept of a public service.

Article 78

Any measures taken within the framework of this Treaty in respect of transport rates and conditions shall take account of the economic circumstances of carriers.

Article 79

1 In the case of transport within the Community, discrimination which takes the form of carriers charging different rates and imposing different conditions for the carriage of the same goods over the same transport links on grounds of the country of origin or of destination of the goods in question, shall be abolished, at the latest, before the end of the second stage.

2 Paragraph 1 shall not prevent the Council from adopting other measures in pursuance of Article 75(1).

3 Within two years of the entry into force of this Treaty, the Council shall, acting by a qualified majority on a proposal from the Commission and after consulting the Economic and Social Committee, lay down rules for implementing the provisions of paragraph 1.

The Council may in particular lay down the provisions needed to enable the institutions of the Community to secure compliance with the rule laid down in paragraph 1 and to ensure that users benefit from it to the full.

4 The Commission shall, acting on its own initiative or on application by a Member State, investigate any cases of discrimination falling within paragraph 1 and, after consulting any Member State concerned, shall take the necessary decisions within the framework of the rules laid down in accordance with the provisions of paragraph 3.

Article 80

1 The imposition by a Member State, in respect of transport operations carried out within the Community, of rates and conditions involving any element of support or protection in the interest of one or more particular undertakings or industries shall be prohibited as from the beginning of the second stage, unless authorised by the Commission.

2 The Commission shall, acting on its own initiative or on application by a Member State, examine the rates and conditions referred to in paragraph 1, taking account in particular of the requirements of an appropriate regional economic policy, the needs of underdeveloped areas and the problems of areas seriously affected by political circumstances on the one hand, and of the effects of such rates and conditions on competition between the different modes of transport on the other.

After consulting each Member State concerned, the Commission shall take the necessary decisions.

3   The prohibition provided for in paragraph 1 shall not apply to tariffs fixed to meet competition.

Article 81

Charges or dues in respect of the crossing of frontiers which are charged by a carrier in addition to the transport rates shall not exceed a reasonable level after taking the costs actually incurred thereby into account.

Member States shall endeavour to reduce these costs progressively.

The Commission may make recommendations to Member States for the application of this Article.

Article 82

The provisions of this Title shall not form an obstacle to the application of measures taken in the Federal Republic of Germany to the extent that such measures are required in order to compensate for the economic disadvantages caused by the division of Germany to the economy of certain areas of the Federal Republic affected by that division.

Article 83

An Advisory Committee consisting of experts designated by the Governments of Member States, shall be attached to the Commission. The Commission, whenever it considers it desirable, shall consult the Committee on transport matters without prejudice to the powers of the transport section of the Economic and Social Committee.

Article 84

1   The provisions of this Title shall apply to transport by rail, road and inland waterway.

2   The Council may, acting by a qualified majority, decide whether, to what extent and by what procedure appropriate provisions may be laid down for sea and air transport.

The procedural provisions of Article 75(1) and (3) shall apply.

Title V
Common rules on competition, taxation and approximation of laws

Chapter 1
Rules on Competition

SECTION 1
RULES APPLYING TO
UNDERTAKINGS

Article 85

1   The following shall be prohibited as incompatible with the common market: all agreements between undertakings, decisions by associations of undertakings and concerted practices which may affect trade between Member States and which have as their object or effect the prevention, restriction or distortion of competition within the common market, and in particular those which:

(a)   directly   or   indirectly   fix purchase or selling prices or any other trading conditions;

(b)   limit or control production, markets, technical development, or investment;

(c)   share markets or sources of supply;

(d) apply dissimilar conditions to equivalent transactions with other trading parties, thereby placing them at a competitive disadvantage;

(e) make the conclusion of contracts subject to acceptance by the other parties of supplementary obligations which, by their nature or according to commercial usage, have no connection with the subject of such contracts.

2 Any agreements or decisions prohibited pursuant to this Article shall be automatically void.

3 The provisions of paragraph 1 may, however, be declared inapplicable in the case of:

• any agreement or category of agreements between undertakings;

• any decision or category of decisions by associations of undertakings;

• any concerted practice or category of concerted practices;

which contributes to improving the production or distribution of goods or to promoting technical or economic progress, while allowing consumers a fair share of the resulting benefit, and which does not:

(a) impose on the undertakings concerned restrictions which are not indispensable to the attainment of these objectives;

(b) afford such undertakings the possibility of eliminating competition in respect of a substantial part of the products in question.

Article 86

Any abuse by one or more undertakings of a dominant position within the common market or in a substantial part of it shall be prohibited as incompatible with the common market in so far as it may affect trade between Member States.

Such abuse may, in particular, consist in:

(a) directly or indirectly imposing unfair purchase or selling prices or other unfair trading conditions;

(b) limiting production, markets or technical development to the prejudice of consumers;

(c) applying dissimilar conditions to equivalent transactions with other trading parties, thereby placing them at a competitive disadvantage;

(d) making the conclusion of contracts subject to acceptance by the other parties of supplementary obligations which, by their nature or according to commercial usage, have no connection with the subject of such contracts.

Article 87

1 Within three years of the entry into force of this Treaty the Council shall, acting unanimously on a proposal from the Commission and after consulting the European Parliament, adopt any appropriate regulations or directives to give effect to the principles set out in Articles 85 and 86.

If such provisions have not been adopted within the period mentioned, they shall be laid down by the Council, acting by a qualified majority on a proposal from the Commission and after consulting the European Parliament.

2 The regulations or directives referred to in paragraph 1 shall be designed in particular:

(a) to ensure compliance with the prohibitions laid down in Article 85(1) and in Article 86 by making provision for fines and periodic penalty payments;

(b) to lay down detailed rules for the application of Article 85(3), taking into account the need to ensure effective supervision on the one hand, and to simplify administration to the greatest possible extent on the other;

(c) to define, if need be, in the various branches of the economy, the scope of the provisions of Articles 85 and 86;

(d) to define the respective functions of the Commission and of the Court of Justice in applying the provisions laid down in this paragraph;

(e) to determine the relationship between national laws and the provisions contained in this Section or adopted pursuant to this Article.

Article 88

Until the entry into force of the provisions adopted in pursuance of Article 87, the authorities in Member States shall rule on the admissibility of agreements, decisions and concerted practices and on abuse of a dominant position in the common market in accordance with the law of their country and with the provisions of Article 85, in particular paragraph 3, and of Article 86.

Article 89

1 Without prejudice to Article 88, the Commission shall, as soon as it takes up its duties, ensure the application of the principles laid down in Articles 85 and 86. On application by a Member State or on its own initiative, and in co-operation with the competent authorities in the Member States, who shall give it their assistance, the Commission shall investigate cases of suspected infringement of these principles. If it finds that there has been an infringement, it shall propose appropriate measures to bring it to an end.

2 If the infringement is not brought to an end, the Commission shall record such infringement of the principles in a reasoned decision. The Commission may publish its decision and authorise Member States to take the measures, the conditions and details of which it shall determine, needed to remedy the situation.

Article 90

1 In the case of public undertakings and undertakings to which Member States grant special or exclusive rights, Member States shall neither enact nor maintain in force any measure contrary to the rules contained in this Treaty, in particular to those rules provided for in Article [] 6 and Articles 85 to 94.

2 Undertakings entrusted with the operation of services of general economic interest or having the character of a revenue-producing monopoly shall be subject to the rules contained in this Treaty, in particular to the rules on competition, in so far as the application of such rules does not obstruct the performance, in law or in fact, of the particular tasks assigned to them. The development of trade must not be affected to such an extent as would be contrary to the interests of the Community.

3 The Commission shall ensure the application of the provisions of this Article and shall, where necessary, address appropriate directives or decisions to Member States.

SECTION 2
DUMPING

Article 91

1 If during the transitional period, the Commission, on application by a Member State or by any other interested party, finds that dumping is being practised within the common market, it shall address recommendations to the person or persons with whom such practices originate for the purpose of putting an end to them.

Should the practices continue, the Commission shall authorise the injured Member State to take protective measures, the conditions and details of which the Commission shall determine.

2 As soon as this Treaty enters into force, products which originate in or are in free circulation in one Member State and which have been exported to another Member State shall, on re-importation, be admitted into the territory of the first-mentioned State free of all customs duties, quantitative restrictions or measures having equivalent effect. The Commission shall lay down appropriate rules for the application of this paragraph.

SECTION 3
AIDS GRANTED BY STATES

Article 92

1 Save as otherwise provided in this Treaty, any aid granted by a Member State or through State resources in any form whatsoever which distorts or threatens to distort competition by favouring certain undertakings or the production of certain goods shall, in so far as it affects trade between Member States, be incompatible with the common market.

2 The following shall be compatible with the common market:

(a) aid having a social character, granted to individual consumers, provided that such aid is granted without discrimination related to the origin of the products concerned;

(b) aid to make good the damage caused by natural disasters or exceptional occurrences;

(c) aid granted to the economy of certain areas of the Federal Republic of Germany affected by the division of Germany, in so far as such aid is required in order to compensate for the economic disadvantages caused by that division.

3 The following may be considered to be compatible with the common market:

(a) aid to promote the economic development of areas where the standard of living is abnormally low or where there is serious underemployment;

(b) aid to promote the execution of an important project of common European interest or to remedy a serious disturbance in the economy of a Member State;

(c) aid to facilitate the development of certain economic activities or of certain economic areas, where such aid does not adversely affect trading conditions to an extent contrary to the common interest. However, the aids granted to shipbuilding as of

1 January 1957 shall, in so far as they serve only to compensate for the absence of customs protection, be progressively reduced under the same conditions as apply to the elimination of customs duties, subject to the provisions of this Treaty concerning common commercial policy towards third countries;

(d) **aid to promote culture and heritage conservation where such aid does not affect trading conditions and competition in the Community to an extent that is contrary to the common interest;**

(e) such other categories of aid as may be specified by decision of the Council acting by a qualified majority on a proposal from the Commission.

Article 93

1 The Commission shall, in co-operation with Member States, keep under constant review all systems of aid existing in those States. It shall propose to the latter any appropriate measures required by the progressive development or by the functioning of the common market.

2 If, after giving notice to the parties concerned to submit their comments, the Commission finds that aid granted by a State or through State resources is not compatible with the common market having regard to Article 92, or that such aid is being misused, it shall decide that the State concerned shall abolish or alter such aid within a period of time to be determined by the Commission.

If the State concerned does not comply with this decision within the prescribed time, the Commission or any other interested State may, in derogation from the provisions of Articles 169 and 170, refer the matter to the Court of Justice direct.

On application by a Member State, the Council may, acting unanimously, decide that aid which that State is granting or intends to grant shall be considered to be compatible with the common market, in derogation from the provisions of Article 92 or from the regulations provided for in Article 94, if such a decision is justified by exceptional circumstances. If, as regards the aid in question, the Commission has already initiated the procedure provided for in the first sub-paragraph of this paragraph, the fact that the State concerned has made its application to the Council shall have the effect of suspending that procedure until the Council has made its attitude known.

If, however, the Council has not made its attitude known within three months of the said application being made, the Commission shall give its decision on the case.

3 The Commission shall be informed, in sufficient time to enable it to submit its comments, of any plans to grant or alter aid. If it considers that any such plan is not compatible with the common market having regard to Article 92, it shall without delay initiate the procedure provided for in paragraph 2. The Member State concerned shall not put its proposed measures into effect until this procedure has resulted in a final decision.

Article 94

The Council, acting by a qualified majority on a proposal from the

Commission **and after consulting the European Parliament**, may make any appropriate regulations for the application of Articles 92 and 93 and may in particular determine the conditions in which Article 93(3) shall apply and the categories of aid exempted from this procedure.

Chapter 2
Tax Provisions

Article 95

No Member State shall impose, directly or indirectly, on the products of other Member States any internal taxation of any kind in excess of that imposed directly or indirectly on similar domestic products.

Furthermore, no Member State shall impose on the products of other Member States any internal taxation of such a nature as to afford indirect protection to other products.

Member States shall, not later than at the beginning of the second stage, repeal or amend any provisions existing when this Treaty enters into force which conflict with the preceding rules.

Article 96

Where products are exported to the territory of any Member State, any repayment of internal taxation shall not exceed the internal taxation imposed on them whether directly or indirectly.

Article 97

Member States which levy a turnover tax calculated on a cumu-lative multi-stage tax system may, in the case of internal taxation imposed by them on imported products or of repayments allowed by them on exported products, establish average rates for products or groups of products, provided that there is no infringement of the principles laid down in Articles 95 and 96.

Where the average rates established by a Member State do not conform to these principles, the Commission shall address appropriate directives or decisions to the State concerned.

Article 98

In the case of charges other than turnover taxes, excise duties and other forms of indirect taxation, remissions and repayments in respect of exports to other Member States may not be granted and countervailing charges in respect of imports from Member States may not be imposed unless the measures contemplated have been previously approved for a limited period by the Council acting by a qualified majority on a proposal from the Commission.

Article 99

The Council shall, acting unanimously on a proposal from the Commission and after consulting the European Parliament **and the Economic and Social Committee**, adopt provisions for the harmonisation of legislation concerning turnover taxes, excise duties and other forms of indirect taxation to the extent that such harmonisation is necessary to ensure the establishment and the functioning of the internal market within the time limit laid down in Article 7a.

Chapter 3
Approximation of Laws

Article 100

The Council shall, acting unanimously on a proposal from the Commission **and after consulting the European Parliament and the Economic and Social Committee**, issue directives for the approximation of such [] **laws, regulations or administrative provisions of the** Member States as directly affect the establishment or functioning of the common market.

Article 100a

1 By way of derogation from Article 100 and save where otherwise provided in this Treaty, the following provisions shall apply for the achievement of the objectives set out in Article [] **7a**. The Council shall, acting [] **in accordance with the procedure referred to in Article 189b** and after consulting the Economic and Social Committee, adopt the measures for the approximation of the provisions laid down by law, regulation or administrative action in Member States which have as their object the establishment and functioning of the internal market.

2 Paragraph 1 shall not apply to fiscal provisions, to those relating to the free movement of persons nor to those relating to the rights and interests of employed persons.

3 The Commission, in its proposals envisaged in paragraph 1 concerning health, safety, environmental protection and consumer protection, will take as a base a high level of protection.

4 If, after the adoption of a harmonisation measure by the Council acting by a qualified majority, a Member State deems it necessary to apply national provisions on grounds of major needs referred to in Article 36, or relating to protection of the environment or the working environment, it shall notify the Commission of these provisions.

The Commission shall confirm the provisions involved after having verified that they are not a means of arbitrary discrimination or a disguised restriction on trade between Member States.

By way of derogation from the procedure laid down in Articles 169 and 170, the Commission or any Member State may bring the matter directly before the Court of Justice if it considers that another Member State is making improper use of the powers provided for in this Article.

5 The harmonisation measures referred to above shall, in appropriate cases, include a safeguard clause authorising the Member States to take, for one or more of the non-economic reasons referred to in Article 36, provisional measures subject to a Community control procedure.

Article 100b

1 During 1992, the Commission shall, together with each Member State, draw up an inventory of national laws, regulations and administrative provisions which fall under Article 100a and which have not been harmonised pursuant to that Article.

The Council, acting in accordance with the provisions of Article 100a, may decide that the provisions in force in a Member State must be recognised as being equivalent to those applied by another Member State.

2 The provisions of Article 100a(4) shall apply by analogy.

3 The Commission shall draw up the inventory referred to in the first sub-paragraph of paragraph 1 and shall submit appropriate proposals in good time to allow the Council to act before the end of 1992.

Article 100c

1 The Council, acting unanimously on a proposal from the Commission and after consulting the European Parliament, shall determine the third countries whose nationals must be in possession of a visa when crossing the external borders of the Member States.

2 However, in the event of an emergency situation in a third country posing a threat of a sudden inflow of nationals from that country into the Community, the Council, acting by a qualified majority on a recommendation from the Commission, may introduce, for a period not exceeding six months, a visa requirement for nationals from the country in question. The visa requirement established under this paragraph may be extended in accordance with the procedure referred to in paragraph 1.

3 From 1 January 1996, the Council shall adopt the decisions referred to in paragraph 1 by a qualified majority. The Council shall, before that date, acting by a qualified majority on a proposal from the Commission and after consulting the European Parliament, adopt measures relating to a uniform format for visas.

4 In the areas referred to in this Article, the Commission shall examine any request made by a Member State that it submit a proposal to the Council.

5 This Article shall be without prejudice to the exercise of the responsibilities incumbent upon the Member States with regard to the maintenance of law and order and the safeguarding of internal security.

6 This Article shall apply to other areas if so decided pursuant to Article K.9 of the provisions of the Treaty on European Union which relate to co-operation in the fields of justice and home affairs, subject to the voting conditions determined at the same time.

7 The provisions of the conventions in force between the Member States governing areas covered by this Article shall remain in force until their content has been replaced by directives or measures adopted pursuant to this Article.

Article 100d

The Co-ordinating Committee consisting of senior officials set up by Article K.4 of the Treaty on European Union shall contribute, without prejudice to the provisions of Article 151, to the preparation of the proceedings of the Council in the fields referred to in Article 100c.

Article 101

Where the Commission finds that a difference between the provisions laid down by law, regulation or administrative action in Member States is distorting the conditions of competition in the common market and that the resultant distortion needs to be eliminated, it shall consult the Member States concerned.

If such consultation does not result in an agreement eliminating the distortion in question, the

Council shall, on a proposal from the Commission, acting unanimously during the first stage and by a qualified majority thereafter, issue the necessary directives. The Commission and the Council may take any other appropriate measures provided for in this Treaty.

Article 102

1 Where there is reason to fear that the adoption or amendment of a provision laid down by law, regulation or administrative action may cause distortion within the meaning of Article 101, a Member State desiring to proceed therewith shall consult the Commission. After consulting the Member States, the Commission shall recommend to the States concerned such measures as may be appropriate to avoid the distortion in question.
2 If a State desiring to introduce or amend its own provisions does not comply with the recommendation addressed to it by the Commission, other Member States shall not be required, in pursuance of Article 101, to amend their own provisions in order to eliminate such distortion. If the Member State which has ignored the recommendation of the Commission causes distortion detrimental only to itself, the provisions of Article 101 shall not apply.

[] Title VI
Economic and monetary policy

Chapter 1
Economic Policy

Article 102a

[] Member States shall conduct their economic policies with a view to contributing to the achievement of the objectives of the Community, as defined in Article 2, and in the context of the broad guidelines referred to in Article 103(2).

The Member States and the Community shall act in accordance with the principle of an open market economy with free competition, favouring an efficient allocation of resources, and in compliance with the principles set out in Article 3a.

[] Article 103

1 Member States shall regard their [] economic policies as a matter of common concern and shall co-ordinate them within the Council, in accordance with the provisions of Article 102a. []
2 [] The Council shall, acting by a qualified majority on a recommendation from the Commission, formulate a draft for the broad guidelines of the economic policies of the Member States and of the Community, and shall report its findings to the European Council.

The European Council shall, acting on the basis of the report from the Council, discuss a conclusion on the broad guidelines of the economic policies of the Member States and of the Community.

On the basis of this conclusion, the Council shall, acting by a qualified majority, adopt a recommendation setting out these broad guidelines. The Council shall inform the European Parliament of its recommendation.
3 [] In order to ensure closer co-ordination of economic policies and sustained convergence of the

economic performances of the Member States, the Council shall, on the basis of reports submitted by the Commission, monitor economic developments in each of the Member States and in the Community as well as the consistency of economic policies with the broad guidelines referred to in paragraph 2, and regularly carry out an overall assessment.

For the purpose of this multilateral surveillance, Member States shall forward information to the Commission about important measures taken by them in the field of their economic policy and such other information as they deem necessary.

4 [] Where it is established, under the procedure referred to in paragraph 3, that the economic policies of a Member State are not consistent with the broad guidelines referred to in paragraph 2 or that they risk jeopardising the proper functioning of economic and monetary union, the Council may, acting by a qualified majority on a recommendation from the Commission, make the necessary recommendations to the Member State concerned. The Council may, acting by a qualified majority on a proposal from the Commission, decide to make its recommendations public.

The President of the Council and the Commission shall report to the European Parliament on the results of multilateral surveillance. The President of the Council may be invited to appear before the competent Committee of the European Parliament if the Council has made its recommendations public.

5 The Council, acting in accordance with the procedure referred to in Article 189c, may adopt detailed rules for the multilateral surveillance procedure referred to in paragraphs 3 and 4 of this Article.

Article 103a

1 Without prejudice to any other procedures provided for in this Treaty, the Council may, acting unanimously on a proposal from the Commission, decide upon the measures appropriate to the economic situation, in particular if severe difficulties arise in the supply of certain products.

2 Where a Member State is in difficulties or is seriously threatened with severe difficulties caused by exceptional occurrences beyond its control, the Council may, acting unanimously on a proposal from the Commission, grant, under certain conditions, Community financial assistance to the Member State concerned. Where the severe difficulties are caused by natural disasters, the Council shall act by qualified majority. The President of the Council shall inform the European Parliament of the decision taken.

Article 104
[]

1 Overdraft facilities or any other type of credit facility with the ECB or with the central banks of the Member States (hereinafter referred to as "national central banks") in favour of Community institutions or bodies, central governments, regional, local or other public authorities, other bodies governed by public law or public undertakings of Member States shall be prohibited, as shall the purchase directly from them by the ECB or national central banks of debt instruments.

2 Paragraph 1 shall not apply to publicly-owned credit institutions

which, in the context of the supply of reserves by central banks, shall be given the same treatment by national central banks and the ECB as private credit institutions.

Article 104a

1 Any measure, not based on prudential considerations, establishing privileged access by Community institutions or bodies, central governments, regional, local or other public authorities other bodies governed by public law, or public undertakings of Member States to financial institutions shall be prohibited.

2 The Council, acting in accordance with the procedure referred to in Article 189c, shall, before 1 January 1994, specify definitions for the application of the prohibition referred to in paragraph 1.

Article 104b

1 The Community shall not be liable for or assume the commitments of central governments, regional, local or other public authorities, other bodies governed by public law or public undertakings of any Member State, without prejudice to mutual financial guarantees for the joint execution of a specific project. A Member State shall not be liable for or assume the commitments of central governments, regional, local or other public authorities, other bodies governed by public law or public undertakings of another Member State, without prejudice to mutual financial guarantees for the joint execution of a specific project.

2 If necessary, the Council, acting in accordance with the procedure referred to in Article 189c, may specify definitions for the application of the prohibitions referred to in

Article 104 and in this Article.

Article 104c

1 Member States shall avoid excessive government deficits.

2 The Commission shall monitor the development of the budgetary situation and of the stock of government debt in the Member States with a view to identifying gross errors. In particular it shall examine compliance with budgetary discipline on the basis of the following two criteria:

(a) whether the ratio of the planned or actual government deficit to gross domestic product exceeds a reference value, unless:

- either the ratio has declined substantially and continuously and reached a level that comes close to the reference value;

- or, alternatively, the excess over the reference value is only exceptional and temporary and the ratio remains close to the reference value;

(b) whether the ratio of government debt to gross domestic product exceeds a reference value, unless the ratio is sufficiently diminishing and approaching the reference value at a satisfactory pace.

The reference values are specified in the Protocol on the excessive deficit procedure annexed to this Treaty.

3 If a Member State does not fulfil the requirements under one or both of these criteria, the Commission shall prepare a report. The report of the Commission shall also take into account whether the government deficit exceeds government investment expenditure and take into account all other relevant factors, including the medium term economic

and budgetary position of the Member State.

The Commission may also prepare a report if, notwithstanding the fulfilment of the requirements under the criteria, it is of the opinion that there is a risk of an excessive deficit in a Member State.

4 The Committee provided for in Article 109c shall formulate an opinion on the report of the Commission.

5 If the Commission considers that an excessive deficit in a Member State exists or may occur, the Commission shall address an opinion to the Council.

6 The Council shall, acting by a qualified majority on a recommendation from the Commission, and having considered any observations which the Member State concerned may wish to make, decide after an overall assessment whether an excessive deficit exists.

7 Where the existence of an excessive deficit is decided according to paragraph 6, the Council shall make recommendations to the Member State concerned with a view to bringing that situation to an end within a given period. Subject to the provisions of paragraph 8, these recommendations shall not be made public.

8 Where it establishes that there has been no effective action in response to its recommendations within the period laid down, the Council may make its recommendations public.

9 If a Member State persists in failing to put into practice the recommendations of the Council, the Council may decide to give notice to the Member State to take, within a specified time limit, measures for the deficit reduction which is judged necessary by the Council in order to remedy the situation.

In such a case, the Council may request the Member State concerned to submit reports in accordance with a specific timetable in order to examine the adjustment efforts of that Member State.

10 The rights to bring actions provided for in Articles 169 and 170 may not be exercised within the framework of paragraphs 1 to 9 of this Article.

11 As long as a Member State fails to comply with a decision taken in accordance with paragraph 9, the Council may decide to apply or, as the case may be, intensify one or more of the following measures:

• to require the Member State concerned to publish additional information, to be specified by the Council, before issuing bonds and securities;

• to invite the European Investment Bank to reconsider its lending policy towards the Member State concerned;

• to require the Member State concerned to make a non-interest-bearing deposit of an appropriate size with the Community until the excessive deficit has, in the view of the Council, been corrected;

• to impose fines of an appropriate size.

The President of the Council shall inform the European Parliament of the decisions taken.

12 The Council shall abrogate some or all of its decisions as referred to in paragraphs 6 to 9 and 11 to the extent that the excessive deficit in the Member State concerned has, in the view of the Council, been corrected. If the Council has previously made public recommendations, it shall, as soon as the decision under paragraph 8 has been abrogated, make a public

statement that an excessive deficit in the Member State concerned no longer exists.

13 When taking the decisions referred to in paragraphs 7 to 9, 11 and 12, the Council shall act on a recommendation from the Commission by a majority of two thirds of the votes of its members weighted in accordance with Article 148(2), excluding the votes of the representative of the Member State concerned.

14 Further provisions relating to the implementation of the procedure described in this Article are set out in the Protocol on the excessive deficit procedure annexed to this Treaty.

The Council shall, acting unanimously on a proposal from the Commission and after consulting the European Parliament and the ECB, adopt the appropriate provisions which shall then replace the said Protocol.

Subject to the other provisions of this paragraph the Council shall, before 1 January 1994, acting by a qualified majority on a proposal from the Commission and after consulting the European Parliament, lay down detailed rules and definitions for the application of the provisions of the said Protocol.

Chapter 2
Monetary Policy

Article 105

1 [] The primary objective of the ESCB shall be to maintain price stability. Without prejudice to the objective of price stability, the ESCB shall support the general economic policies in the Community with a view to contributing to the achievement of the objectives of the Community as laid down in Article 2. The ESCB shall act in accordance with the principle of an open market economy with free competition, favouring an efficient allocation of resources, and in compliance with the principles set out in Article 3a.

2 The basic tasks to be carried out through the ESCB shall be:
- to define and implement the monetary policy of the Community;
- to conduct foreign exchange operations consistent with the provisions of Article 109;
- to hold and manage the official foreign reserves of the Member States;
- to promote the smooth operation of payment systems.

3 The third indent of paragraph 2 shall be without prejudice to the holding and management by the governments of Member States of foreign exchange working balances.

4 The ECB shall be consulted:
- on any proposed Community act in its fields of competence;
- by national authorities regarding any draft legislative provision in its fields of competence, but within the limits and under the conditions set out by the Council in accordance with the procedure laid down in Article 106(6).

The ECB may submit opinions to the appropriate Community institutions or bodies or to national authorities on matters in its fields of competence.

5 The ESCB shall contribute to the smooth conduct of policies pursued by the competent authorities relating to the prudential supervision of credit institutions and the stability of the financial system.

6 The Council may, acting unanimously on a proposal from the Com-

mission and after consulting the
ECB and after receiving the assent
of the European Parliament, confer
upon the ECB specific tasks concerning policies relating to the prudential supervision of credit
institutions and other financial institutions with the exception of insurance undertakings.

Article 105a

1 The ECB shall have the exclusive right to authorise the issue of
bank notes within the Community.
The ECB and the national central
banks may issue such notes. The
bank notes issued by the ECB and
the national central banks shall be
the only such notes to have the
status of legal tender within the
Community.
2 Member States may issue coins
subject to approval by the ECB of
the volume of the issue. The Council
may, acting in accordance with the
procedure referred to in Article 189c
and after consulting the ECB, adopt
measures to harmonise the denomi-
nations and technical specifications
of all coins intended for circulation
to the extent necessary to permit
their smooth circulation within the
Community.

Article 106

1 [] The ESCB shall be composed
of the ECB and of the national
central banks.
2 The ECB shall have legal personality.
3 The ESCB shall be governed by
the decision-making bodies of the
ECB which shall be the Governing
Council and the Executive Board.
4 The Statute of the ESCB is laid
down in a Protocol annexed to this
Treaty.
5 Articles 5.1, 5.2, 5.3, 17, 18,

19.1, 22, 23, 24, 26, 32.2, 32.3, 32.4,
32.6, 33.1(a) and 36 of the Statute
of the ESCB may be amended by
the Council, acting either by a qualified majority on a recommendation
from the ECB and after consulting
the Commission or unanimously on
a proposal from the Commission and
after consulting the ECB. In either
case, the assent of the European
Parliament shall be required.
6 The Council, acting by a qualified majority either on a proposal
from the Commission and after consulting the European Parliament and
the ECB or on a recommendation
from the ECB and after consulting
the European Parliament and the
Commission, shall adopt the provisions referred to in Articles 4, 5.4,
19.2, 20, 28.1, 29.2, 30.4 and 34.3
of the Statute of the ESCB.

Article 107

When exercising the powers and
carrying out the tasks and duties
conferred upon them by this Treaty
and the Statute of the ESCB,
neither the ECB, nor a national
central bank, nor any member of
their decision-making bodies shall
seek or take instructions from Community institutions or bodies, from
any government of a Member State
or from any other body. The Community institutions and bodies and
the governments of the Member
States undertake to respect this principle and not to seek to influence the
members of the decision-making
bodies of the ECB or of the national
central banks in the performance of
their tasks.

Article 108

Each Member State shall ensure, at
the latest at the date of the establishment of the ESCB, that its

national legislation including the statutes of its national central bank is compatible with this Treaty and the Statute of the ESCB.

Article 108a

1 In order to carry out the tasks entrusted to the ESCB, the ECB shall, in accordance with the provisions of this Treaty and under the conditions laid down in the Statute of the ESCB:
• make regulations to the extent necessary to implement the tasks defined in Article 3.1, first indent, Articles 19.1, 22 and 25.2 of the Statute of the ESCB and in cases which shall be laid down in the acts of the Council referred to in Article 106(6);
• take decisions necessary for carrying out the tasks entrusted to the ESCB under this Treaty and the Statute of the ESCB;
• make recommendations and deliver opinions.
2 A regulation shall have general application. It shall be binding in its entirety and directly applicable in all Member States.

Recommendations and opinions shall have no binding force.

A decision shall be binding in its entirety upon those to whom it is addressed.

Articles 190 to 192 shall apply to regulations and decisions adopted by the ECB.

The ECB may decide to publish its decisions, recommendations and opinions.
3 Within the limits and under the conditions adopted by the Council under the procedure laid down in Article 106(6), the ECB shall be entitled to impose fines or periodic penalty payments on undertakings for failure to comply with obliga-

tions under its regulations and decisions.

Article 109

1 [] By way of derogation from Article 228, the Council may, acting unanimously on a recommendation from the ECB or from the Commission, and after consulting the ECB in an endeavour to reach a consensus consistent with the objective of price stability, after consulting the European Parliament, in accordance with the procedure in paragraph 3 for determining the arrangements, conclude formal agreements on an exchange rate system for the ECU in relation to non-Community currencies. The Council may, acting by a qualified majority on a recommendation from the ECB or from the Commission, and after consulting the ECB in an endeavour to reach a consensus consistent with the objective of price stability, adopt, adjust or abandon the central rates of the ECU within the exchange rate system. The President of the Council shall inform the European Parliament of the adoption, adjustment or abandonment of the ECU central rates.
2 In the absence of an exchange rate system in relation to one or more non-Community currencies as referred to in paragraph 1, the Council, acting by a qualified majority either on a recommendation from the Commission and after consulting the ECB, or on a recommendation from the ECB, may formulate general orientations for exchange rate policy in relation to these currencies. These general orientations shall be without prejudice to the primary objective of the ESCB to maintain price stability.
3 By way of derogation from

Article 228, where agreements concerning monetary or foreign exchange regime matters need to be negotiated by the Community with one or more States or international organisations, the Council, acting by a qualified majority on a recommendation from the Commission and after consulting the ECB, shall decide the arrangements for the negotiation and for the conclusion of such agreements. These arrangements shall ensure that the Community expresses a single position. The Commission shall be fully associated with the negotiations.

Agreements concluded in accordance with this paragraph shall be binding on the institutions of the Community, on the ECB and on Member States.

4 Subject to paragraph 1, the Council shall, on a proposal from the Commission and after consulting the ECB, acting by a qualified majority decide on the position of the Community at international level as regards issues of particular relevance to economic and monetary union and, acting unanimously, decide its representation in compliance with the allocation of powers laid down in Articles 103 and 105.

5 Without prejudice to Community competence and Community agreements as regards Economic and Monetary Union, Member States may negotiate in international bodies and conclude international agreements.

Chapter 3
Institutional Provisions

Article 109a

1 The Governing Council of the ECB shall comprise the members of the Executive Board of the ECB and the Governors of the national central banks.

2 (a) The Executive Board shall comprise the President, the Vice-President and four other members.

(b) The President, the Vice-President and the other members of the Executive Board shall be appointed from among persons of recognised standing and professional experience in monetary or banking matters by common accord of the Governments of the Member States at the level of Heads of State or of Government, on a recommendation from the Council, after it has consulted the European Parliament and the Governing Council of the ECB.

Their term of office shall be eight years and shall not be renewable.

Only nationals of Member States may be members of the Executive Board.

Article 109b

1 The President of the Council and a member of the Commission may participate, without having the right to vote, in meetings of the Governing Council of the ECB.

The President of the Council may submit a motion for deliberation to the Governing Council of the ECB.

2 The President of the ECB shall be invited to participate in Council meetings when the Council is discussing matters relating to the objectives and tasks of the ESCB.

3 The ECB shall address an annual report on the activities of the ESCB and on the monetary policy of both

the previous and current year to the European Parliament, the Council and the Commission, and also to the European Council. The President of the ECB shall present this report to the Council and to the European Parliament, which may hold a general debate on that basis.

The President of the ECB and the other members of the Executive Board may, at the request of the European Parliament or on their own initiative, be heard by the competent Committees of the European Parliament.

Article 109c

1 In order to promote co-ordination of the policies of Member States to the full extent needed for the functioning of the internal market, a Monetary Committee with advisory status is hereby set up.

It shall have the following tasks:
- to keep under review the monetary and financial situation of the Member States and of the Community and the general payments system of the Member States and to report regularly thereon to the Council and to the Commission;
- to deliver opinions at the request of the Council or of the Commission, or on its own initiative for submission to those institutions;
- without prejudice to Article 151, to contribute to the preparation of the work of the Council referred to in Articles 73f, 73g, 103(2), (3), (4) and (5), 103a, 104a, 104b, 104c, 109e(2), 109f(6), 109h, 109i, 109j(2) and 109k(1);
- to examine, at least once a year, the situation regarding the movement of capital and the freedom of payments, as they

result from the application of this Treaty and of measures adopted by the Council; the examination shall cover all measures relating to capital movements and payments; the Committee shall report to the Commission and to the Council on the outcome of this examination.

The Member States and the Commission shall each appoint two members of the Monetary Committee.

2 At the start of the third stage, an Economic and Financial Committee shall be set up. The Monetary Committee provided for in paragraph 1 shall be dissolved.

The Economic and Financial Committee shall have the following tasks:
- to deliver opinions at the request of the Council or of the Commission, or on its own initiative for submission to those institutions;
- to keep under review the economic and financial situation of the Member States and of the Community and to report regularly thereon to the Council and to the Commission, in particular on financial relations with third countries and international institutions;
- without prejudice to Article 151, to contribute to the preparation of the work of the Council referred to in Articles 73f, 73g, 103(2), (3), (4) and (5), 103a, 104a, 104b, 104c, 105(6), 105a(2), 106(5) and (6), 109, 109h, 109i(2) and (3), 109k(2), 109l(4) and (5), and to carry out other advisory and preparatory tasks assigned to it by the Council;
- to examine, at least once a year, the situation regarding the

movement of capital and the freedom of payments, as they result from the application of this Treaty and of measures adopted by the Council; the examination shall cover all measures relating to capital movements and payments; the Committee shall report to the Commission and to the Council on the outcome of this examination.

The Member States, the Commission and the ECB shall each appoint no more than two members of the Committee.

3 The Council shall, acting by a qualified majority on a proposal from the Commission and after consulting the ECB and the Committee referred to in this Article, lay down detailed provisions concerning the composition of the Economic and Financial Committee. The President of the Council shall inform the European Parliament of such a decision.

4 In addition to the tasks set out in paragraph 2, if and as long as there are Member States with a derogation as referred to in Articles 109k and 109l, the Committee shall keep under review the monetary and financial situation and the general payments system of those Member States and report regularly thereon to the Council and to the Commission.

Article 109d

For matters within the scope of Articles 103(4), 104c with the exception of paragraphs 14, 109, 109j, 109k and 109l(4) and (5), the Council or a Member State may request the Commission to make a recommendation or a proposal, as appropriate. The Commission shall examine this request and submit its conclusions to the Council without delay.

Chapter 4
Transitional Provisions

Article 109e

1 The second stage for achieving economic and monetary union shall begin on 1 January 1994.

2 Before that date:

(a) each Member State shall:

● adopt, where necessary, appropriate measures to comply with the prohibitions laid down in Article 73b, without prejudice to Article 73e, and in Articles 104 and 104a(1);

● adopt, if necessary, with a view to permitting the assessment provided for in subparagraph (b), multiannual programmes intended to ensure the lasting convergence necessary for the achievement of economic and monetary union, in particular with regard to price stability and sound public finances;

(b) the Council shall, on the basis of a report from the Commission, assess the progress made with regard to economic and monetary convergence, in particular with regard to price stability and sound public finances, and the progress made with the implementation of Community law concerning the internal market.

3 The provisions of Articles 104, 104a(1), 104b(1) and 104c with the exception of paragraphs 1, 9, 11 and 14 shall apply from the beginning of the second stage.

The provisions of Articles 103a(2), 104c(1), (9) and (11), 105, 105a, 107, 109, 109a, 109b and 109c(2) and (4) shall apply from the beginning of the third stage.

4 In the second stage, Member States shall endeavour to avoid excessive government deficits.

5 During the second stage, each Member State shall, as appropriate, start the process leading to the independence of its central bank, in accordance with Article 108.

Article 109f

1 At the start of the second stage, a European Monetary Institute (hereinafter referred to as "EMI") shall be established and take up its duties; it shall have legal personality and be directed and managed by a Council, consisting of a President and the Governors of the national central banks, one of whom shall be Vice-President.

The President shall be appointed by common accord of the Governments of the Member States at the level of Heads of State or of Government, on a recommendation from, as the case may be, the Committee of Governors of the central banks of the Member States (hereinafter referred to as "Committee of Governors") or the Council of the EMI, and after consulting the European Parliament and the Council. The President shall be selected from among persons of recognised standing and professional experience in monetary or banking matters. Only nationals of Member States may be President of the EMI. The Council of the EMI shall appoint the Vice-President.

The Statute of the EMI is laid down in a Protocol annexed to this Treaty.

The Committee of Governors shall be dissolved at the start of the second stage.

2 The EMI shall:

- strengthen co-operation between the national central banks;
- strengthen the co-ordination of the monetary policies of the Member States, with the aim of ensuring price stability;
- monitor the functioning of the European Monetary System;
- hold consultations concerning issues falling within the competence of the national central banks and affecting the stability of financial institutions and markets;
- take over the tasks of the European Monetary Co-operation Fund, which shall be dissolved; the modalities of dissolution are laid down in the Statute of the EMI;
- facilitate the use of the ECU and oversee its development, including the smooth functioning of the ECU clearing system.

3 For the preparation of the third stage, the EMI shall:

- prepare the instruments and the procedures necessary for carrying out a single monetary policy in the third stage;
- promote the harmonisation, where necessary, of the rules and practices governing the collection, compilation and distribution of statistics in the areas within its field of competence;
- prepare the rules for operations to be undertaken by the national central banks in the framework of the ESCB;
- promote the efficiency of cross-border payments;
- supervise the technical preparation of ECU bank notes.

At the latest by 31 December 1996, the EMI shall specify the regulatory, organisational and logistical framework necessary for the ESCB to perform its tasks in the third stage. This framework shall be submitted for decision to the ECB at the date of its establishment.

4 The EMI, acting by a majority of two-thirds of the members of its Council may:

• formulate opinions or recommendations on the overall orientation of monetary policy and exchange rate policy as well as on related measures introduced in each Member State;

• submit opinions or recommendations to Governments and to the Council on policies which might affect the internal or external monetary situation in the Community and, in particular, the functioning of the European Monetary System;

• make recommendations to the monetary authorities of the Member States concerning the conduct of their monetary policy.

5 The EMI, acting unanimously, may decide to publish its opinions and its recommendations.

6 The EMI shall be consulted by the Council regarding any proposed Community act within its field of competence.

Within the limits and under the conditions set out by the Council, acting by a qualified majority on a proposal from the Commission and after consulting the European Parliament and the EMI, the EMI shall be consulted by the authorities of the Member States on any draft legislative provision within its field of competence.

7 The Council may, acting unanimously on a proposal from the Commission and after consulting the European Parliament and the EMI, confer upon the EMI other tasks for the preparation of the third stage.

8 Where this Treaty provides for a consultative role for the ECB, references to the ECB shall be read as referring to the EMI before the establishment of the ECB.

Where this Treaty provides for a consultative role for the EMI, references to the EMI shall be read, before 1 January 1994, as referring to the Committee of Governors.

9 During the second stage, the term 'ECB' used in Articles 173, 175, 176, 177, 180 and 215 shall be read as referring to the EMI.

Article 109g

The currency composition of the ECU basket shall not be changed.

From the start of the third stage, the value of the ECU shall be irrevocably fixed in accordance with Article 109l(4).

Article 109h

1 Where a Member State is in difficulties or is seriously threatened with difficulties as regards its balance of payments either as a result of an overall disequilibrium in its balance of payments, or as a result of the type of currency at its disposal, and where such difficulties are liable in particular to jeopardise the functioning of the Common Market or the progressive implementation of the common commercial policy, the Commission shall immediately investigate the position of the State in question and the action which, making use of all the means at its disposal, that State has taken or may take in accordance with the provisions of this Treaty. The Commission shall state what measures it recommends the State concerned to take.

If the action taken by a Member State and the measures suggested by the Commission do not prove sufficient to overcome the difficulties which have arisen or which threaten, the Commission shall, after consulting the Committee referred to in Article 109c, recommend to the Council the granting of mutual assistance and appropriate methods therefor.

The Commission shall keep the Council regularly informed of the situation and of how it is developing.

2 The Council, acting by a qualified majority, shall grant such mutual assistance; it shall adopt directives or decisions laying down the conditions and details of such assistance, which may take such forms as:

(a) a concerted approach to or within any other international organisations to which Member States may have recourse;

(b) measures needed to avoid deflection of trade where the State which is in difficulties maintains or reintroduces quantitative restrictions against third countries;

(c) the granting of limited credits by other Member States, subject to their agreement.

3 If the mutual assistance recommended by the Commission is not granted by the Council or if the mutual assistance granted and the measures taken are insufficient, the Commission shall authorise the State which is in difficulties to take protective measures, the conditions and details of which the Commission shall determine.

Such authorisation may be revoked and such conditions and details may be changed by the Council acting by a qualified majority.

4 Subject to Article 109k(6), this Article shall cease to apply from the beginning of the third stage.

Article 109i

1 Where a sudden crisis in the balance of payments occurs and a decision within the meaning of Article 109h(2) is not immediately taken, the Member State concerned may, as a precaution, take the necessary protective measures. Such measures must cause the least possible disturbance in the functioning of the Common Market and must not be wider in scope than is strictly necessary to remedy the sudden difficulties which have arisen.

2 The Commission and the other Member States shall be informed of such protective measures not later than when they enter into force. The Commission may recommend to the Council the granting of mutual assistance under Article 109h.

3 After the Commission has delivered an opinion and the Committee referred to in Article 109c has been consulted, the Council may, acting by a qualified majority, decide that the State concerned shall amend, suspend or abolish the protective measures referred to above.

4 Subject to Article 109k(6), this Article shall cease to apply from the beginning of the third stage.

Article 109j

1 The Commission and the EMI shall report to the Council on the progress made in the fulfilment by the Member States of their obligations regarding the achievement of economic and monetary union. These reports shall include an examination of the compatibility between each Member State's national legislation, including the statutes of its national central bank, and Articles 107 and 108 of this Treaty and the Statute of the ESCB. The reports shall also

examine the achievement of a high degree of sustainable convergence by reference to the fulfilment by each Member State of the following criteria:

- the achievement of a high degree of price stability; this will be apparent from a rate of inflation which is close to that of, at most, the three best performing Member States in terms of price stability;
- the sustainability of the government financial position; this will be apparent from having achieved a government budgetary position without a deficit that is excessive as determined in accordance with Article 104c(6);
- the observance of the normal fluctuation margins provided for by the Exchange Rate Mechanism of the European Monetary System, for at least two years, without devaluing against the currency of any other Member State;
- the durability of convergence achieved by the Member State and of its participation in the Exchange Rate Mechanism of the European Monetary System being reflected in the long-term interest rate levels.

The four criteria mentioned in this paragraph and the relevant periods over which they are to be respected are developed further in a Protocol annexed to this Treaty. The reports of the Commission and the EMI shall also take account of the development of the ECU, the results of the integration of markets, the situation and development of the balances of payments on current account and an examination of the development of unit labour costs and other price indices.

2 On the basis of these reports, the Council, acting by a qualified majority on a recommendation from the Commission, shall assess:

- for each Member State, whether it fulfils the necessary conditions for the adoption of a single currency;
- whether a majority of the Member States fulfil the necessary conditions for the adoption of a single currency,

and recommend its findings to the Council, meeting in the composition of the Heads of State or of Government. The European Parliament shall be consulted and forward its opinion to the Council, meeting in the composition of the Heads of State or of Government.

3 Taking due account of the reports referred to in paragraph 1 and the opinion of the European Parliament referred to in paragraph 2, the Council, meeting in the composition of Heads of State or of Government, shall, acting by a qualified majority, not later than 31 December 1996:

- decide, on the basis of the recommendations of the Council referred to in paragraph 2, whether a majority of the Member States fulfil the necessary conditions for the adoption of a single currency;
- decide whether it is appropriate for the Community to enter the third stage;

and if so;

- set the date for the beginning of the third stage.

4 If by the end of 1997 the date for the beginning of the third stage has not been set, the third stage shall start on 1 January 1999. Before 1 July 1998, the Council, meeting in the composition of Heads of State or of Government, after a repetition of the procedure provided

for in paragraphs 1 and 2, with the exception of the second indent of paragraph 2, taking into account the reports referred to in paragraph 1 and the opinion of the European Parliament, shall, acting by a qualified majority and on the basis of the recommendations of the Council referred to in paragraph 2, confirm which Member States fulfil the necessary conditions for the adoption of a single currency.

Article 109k

1   If the decision has been taken to set the date in accordance with Article 109j(3), the Council shall, on the basis of its recommendations referred to in Article 109j(2), acting by a qualified majority on a recommendation from the Commission, decide whether any, and if so which, Member States shall have a derogation as defined in paragraph 3 of this Article. Such Member States shall in this Treaty be referred to as "Member States with a derogation".

If the Council has confirmed which Member States fulfil the necessary conditions for the adoption of a single currency, in accordance with Article 109j(4), those Member States which do not fulfil the conditions shall have a derogation as defined in paragraph 3 of this Article. Such Member States shall in this Treaty be referred to as "Member States with a derogation".

2   At least once every two years, or at the request of a Member State with a derogation, the Commission and the ECB shall report to the Council in accordance with the procedure laid down in Article 109j(1). After consulting the European Parliament and after discussion in the Council, meeting in the composition of the Heads of State or of Govern-

ment, the Council shall, acting by a qualified majority on a proposal from the Commission, decide which Member States with a derogation fulfil the necessary conditions on the basis of the criteria set out in Article 109j(1), and abrogate the derogations of the Member States concerned.

3   A derogation referred to in paragraph 1 shall entail that the following Articles do not apply to the Member State concerned: Articles 104c(9) and (11), 105(1), (2), (3) and (5), 105a, 108a, 109 and 109a(2)(b). The exclusion of such a Member State and its national central bank from rights and obligations within the ESCB is laid down in Chapter IX of the Statute of the ESCB.

4   In Articles 105(1), (2) and (3), 105a, 108a, 109 and 109a(2)(b), "Member States" shall be read as "Member States without a derogation".

5   The voting rights of Member States with a derogation shall be suspended for the Council decisions referred to in the Articles of this Treaty mentioned in paragraph 3. In that case, by way of derogation from Articles 148 and 189a(1), a qualified majority shall be defined as two-thirds of the votes of the representatives of the Member States without a derogation weighted in accordance with Article 148(2), and unanimity of those Member States shall be required for an act requiring unanimity.

6   Articles 109h and 109i shall continue to apply to a Member State with a derogation.

Article 109l

1   Immediately after the decision on the date for the beginning of the third stage has been taken in accor-

dance with Article 109j(3), or, as the case may be, immediately after 1 July 1998:

- the Council shall adopt the provisions referred to in Article 106(6);
- the governments of the Member States without a derogation shall appoint, in accordance with the procedure set out in Article 50 of the Statute of the ESCB, the President, the Vice-President and the other members of the Executive Board of the ECB. If there are Member States with a derogation, the number of members of the Executive Board may be smaller than provided for in Article 11.1 of the Statute of the ESCB, but in no circumstances shall it be less than four.

As soon as the Executive Board is appointed, the ESCB and the ECB shall be established and shall prepare for their full operation as described in this Treaty and the Statute of the ESCB. The full exercise of their powers shall start from the first day of the third stage.

2 As soon as the ECB is established, it shall, if necessary, take over the tasks of the EMI. The EMI shall go into liquidation upon the establishment of the ECB; the modalities of liquidation are laid down in the Statute of the EMI.

3 If and as long as there are Member States with a derogation, and without prejudice to Article 106(3) of this Treaty, the General Council of the ECB referred to in Article 45 of the Statute of the ESCB shall be constituted as a third decision-making body of the ECB.

4 At the starting date of the third stage, the Council shall, acting with the unanimity of the Member States without a derogation, on a proposal from the Commission and after consulting the ECB, adopt the conversion rates at which their currencies shall be irrevocably fixed and at which irrevocably fixed rate the ECU shall be substituted for these currencies, and the ECU will become a currency in its own right. This measure shall by itself not modify the external value of the ECU. The Council shall, acting according to the same procedure, also take the other measures necessary for the rapid introduction of the ECU as the single currency of those Member States.

5 If it is decided, according to the procedure set out in Article 109k(2), to abrogate a derogation, the Council shall, acting with the unanimity of the Member States without a derogation and the Member State concerned, on a proposal from the Commission and after consulting the ECB, adopt the rate at which the ECU shall be substituted for the currency of the Member State concerned, and take the other measures necessary for the introduction of the ECU as the single currency in the Member State concerned.

Article 109m

1 Until the beginning of the third stage, each Member State shall treat its exchange rate policy as a matter of common interest. In so doing, Member States shall take account of the experience acquired in co-operation within the framework of the European Monetary System (EMS) and in developing the ECU, and shall respect existing powers in this field.

2 From the beginning of the third stage and for as long as a Member State has a derogation, paragraph 1 shall apply by analogy to the

exchange rate policy of that Member State.

Title VII
Common commercial policy

Article 110

By establishing a customs union between themselves Member States aim to contribute, in the common interest, to the harmonious development of world trade, the progressive abolition of restrictions on international trade and the lowering of customs barriers.

The common commercial policy shall take into account the favourable effect which the abolition of customs duties between Member States may have on the increase in the competitive strength of undertakings in those States.

Article 111 **(Repealed by Maastricht Treaty)**
[]

Article 112

1 Without prejudice to obligations undertaken by them within the framework of other international organisations, Member States shall, before the end of the transitional period, progressively harmonise the systems whereby they grant aid for exports to third countries, to the extent necessary to ensure that competition between undertakings of the Community is not distorted.

On a proposal from the Commission, the Council shall, acting unanimously until the end of the second stage and by a qualified majority thereafter, issue any directives needed for this purpose.

2 The preceding provisions shall not apply to such drawback of customs duties or charges having equivalent effect nor to such repayment of indirect taxation including turnover taxes, excise duties and other indirect taxes as is allowed when goods are exported from a Member State to a third country, in so far as such drawback or repayment does not exceed the amount imposed, directly or indirectly, on the products exported.

Article 113

1 [] **The** common commercial policy shall be based on uniform principles, particularly in regard to changes in tariff rates, the conclusion of tariff and trade agreements, the achievement of uniformity in measures of liberalisation, export policy and measures to protect trade such as those to be taken in [] **the event** of dumping or subsidies.

2 The Commission shall submit proposals to the Council for implementing the common commercial policy.

3 Where agreements with [] **one or more States or international organisations** need to be negotiated, the Commission shall make recommendations to the Council, which shall authorise the Commission to open the necessary negotiations.

The Commission shall conduct these negotiations in consultation with a special committee appointed by the Council to assist the Commission in this task [] within the framework of such directives as the Council may issue to it.

The relevant provisions of Article 228 shall apply.

4   In exercising the powers conferred upon it by this Article, the Council shall act by a qualified majority.

Article 114 (Repealed by Maastricht Treaty)
[]

Article 115

In order to ensure that the execution of measures of commercial policy taken in accordance with this Treaty by any Member State is not obstructed by deflection of trade, or where differences between such measures lead to economic difficulties in one or more [] Member States, the Commission shall recommend the methods for the requisite co-operation between Member States. Failing this, the Commission [] **may** authorise Member States to take the necessary protective measures, the conditions and details of which it shall determine.

In case of urgency, [] Member States [] **shall request authorisation to** take the necessary measures [] **themselves from the Commission, which shall take a decision as soon as possible; the Member States concerned shall then notify the measures to the other Member States. The Commission may decide at any time that the Member States concerned shall amend or abolish the measures in question. In the selection of such measures, priority shall be given to those which cause the least disturbance to the functioning of the common market** [].

Article 116 (Repealed by Maastricht Treaty)
[]

Title VIII
Social policy, education, vocational training and youth

Chapter 1
Social Provisions

Article 117

Member States agree upon the need to promote improved working conditions and an improved standard of living for workers, so as to make possible their harmonisation while the improvement is being maintained.

They believe that such a development will ensue not only from the functioning of the common market, which will favour the harmonisation of social systems, but also from the procedures provided for in this Treaty and from the approximation of provisions laid down by law, regulation or administrative action.

Article 118

Without prejudice to the other provisions of this Treaty and in conformity with its general objectives, the Commission shall have the task of promoting close co-operation between Member States in the social field, particularly in matters relating to:

- employment;
- labour law and working conditions;
- basic and advanced vocational training;
- social security;
- prevention of occupational accidents and diseases;
- occupational hygiene;
- the right of association, and col-

lective bargaining between employers and workers.

To this end, the Commission shall act in close contact with Member States by making studies, delivering opinions and arranging consultations both on problems arising at national level and on those of concern to international organisations.

Before delivering the opinions provided for in this Article, the Commission shall consult the Economic and Social Committee.

Article 118a

1 Member States shall pay particular attention to encouraging improvements, especially in the working environment, as regards the health and safety of workers, and shall set as their objective the harmonisation of conditions in this area, while maintaining the improvements made.

2 In order to help achieve the objective laid down in the first paragraph, the Council, acting [] **in accordance with the procedure referred to in Article 189c** and after consulting the Economic and Social Committee, shall adopt by means of directives, minimum requirements for gradual implementation, having regard to the conditions and technical rules obtaining in each of the Member States.

Such directives shall avoid imposing administrative, financial and legal constraints in a way which would hold back the creation and development of small and medium-sized undertakings.

3 The provisions adopted pursuant to this Article shall not prevent any Member State from maintaining or introducing more stringent measures for the protec-tion of working conditions compatible with this Treaty.

Article 118b

The Commission shall endeavour to develop the dialogue between management and labour at European level which could, if the two sides consider it desirable, lead to relations based on agreement.

Article 119

Each Member State shall during the first stage ensure and subsequently maintain the application of the principle that men and women should receive equal pay for equal work.

For the purpose of this Article, "pay" means the ordinary basic or minimum wage or salary and any other consideration, whether in cash or in kind, which the worker receives, directly or indirectly, in respect of his employment from his employer.

Equal pay without discrimination based on sex means:

(a) that pay for the same work at piece rates shall be calculated on the basis of the same unit of measurement;

(b) that pay for work at time rates shall be the same for the same job.

Article 120

Member States shall endeavour to maintain the existing equivalence between paid holiday schemes.

Article 121

The Council may, acting unanimously and after consulting the Economic and Social Committee, assign to the Commission tasks in connection with the implementation of common measures, particularly as regards social security for the migrant workers referred to in Articles 48 to 51.

Article 122

The Commission shall include a separate chapter on social developments within the Community in its annual report to the European Parliament.

The European Parliament may invite the Commission to draw up reports on any particular problems concerning social conditions.

Chapter 2
The European Social Fund

Article 123

In order to improve employment opportunities for workers in the [] **internal** market and to contribute thereby to raising the standard of living, a European Social Fund is hereby established in accordance with the provisions set out below; it shall [] **aim to render** the employment of workers easier and [] **to increase** their geographical and occupational mobility within the Community, **and to facilitate their adaptation to industrial changes and to changes in production systems, in particular through vocational training and retraining.**

Article 124

The Fund shall be administered by the Commission.

The Commission shall be assisted in this task by a Committee presided over by a member of the Commission and composed of representatives of Governments,

trade unions and employers' organisations.

Article 125

[] **The Council, acting in accordance with the procedure referred to in Article 189c and after consulting the Economic and Social Committee, shall adopt implementing decisions relating to the European Social Fund.**

[] **[Former Articles 125–128]**

Chapter 3
Education, Vocational Training and Youth

Article 126

1 The Community shall contribute to the development of quality education by encouraging co-operation between Member States and, if necessary, by supporting and supplementing their action, while fully respecting the responsibility of the Member States for the content of teaching and the organisation of education systems and their cultural and linguistic diversity.

2 Community action shall be aimed at:

- **developing the European dimension in education, particularly through the teaching and dissemination of the languages of the Member States;**
- **encouraging mobility of students and teachers, inter alia by encouraging the academic recognition of diplomas and periods of study;**
- **promoting co-operation between educational establishments;**
- **developing exchanges of information and experience on issues common to the education systems of the Member States;**

- encouraging the development of youth exchanges and of exchanges of socio-educational instructors;
- encouraging the development of distance education.

3 The Community and the Member States shall foster co-operation with third countries and the competent international organisations in the field of education, in particular the Council of Europe.

4 In order to contribute to the achievement of the objectives referred to in this Article, the Council:

- acting in accordance with the procedure referred to in Article 189b, after consulting the Economic and Social Committee and the Committee of the Regions, shall adopt incentive measures, excluding any harmonisation of the laws and regulations of the Member States;
- acting by a qualified majority on a proposal from the Commission, shall adopt recommendations.

Article 127

1 The Community shall implement a vocational training policy which shall support and supplement the action of the Member States, while fully respecting the responsibility of the Member States for the content and organisation of vocational training.

2 Community action shall aim to:

- facilitate adaptation to industrial changes, in particular through vocational training and retraining;
- improve initial and continuing vocational training in order to facilitate vocational integration and reintegration into the labour market;

- facilitate access to vocational training and encourage mobility of instructors and trainees and particularly young people;
- stimulate co-operation on training between educational or training establishments and firms;
- develop exchanges of information and experience on issues common to the training systems of the Member States.

3 The Community and the Member States shall foster co-operation with third countries and the competent international organisations in the sphere of vocational training.

4 The Council, acting in accordance with the procedure referred to in Article 189c and after consulting the Economic and Social Committee, shall adopt measures to contribute to the achievement of the objectives referred to in this Article, excluding any harmonisation of the laws and regulations of the Member States.

Title IX
Culture

Article 128

1 The Community shall contribute to the flowering of the cultures of the Member States, while respecting their national and regional diversity and at the same time bringing the common cultural heritage to the fore.

2 Action by the Community shall be aimed at encouraging co-operation between Member States and, if necessary, supporting and supplementing their action in the following areas:

- improvement of the knowledge and dissemination of the culture and history of the European peoples;

- conservation and safeguarding of cultural heritage of European significance;
- non-commercial cultural exchanges;
- artistic and literary creation, including in the audiovisual sector.

3 The Community and the Member States shall foster co-operation with third countries and the competent international organisations in the sphere of culture, in particular the Council of Europe.

4 The Community shall take cultural aspects into account in its action under other provisions of this Treaty.

5 In order to contribute to the achievement of the objectives referred to in this Article, the Council:

- acting in accordance with the procedure referred to in Article 189b and after consulting the Committee of the Regions, shall adopt incentive measures, excluding any harmonisation of the laws and regulations of the Member States. The Council shall act unanimously throughout the procedures referred to in Article 189b;
- acting unanimously on a proposal from the Commission, shall adopt recommendations.

Title X
Public health

Article 129

1 [] The Community shall contribute towards ensuring a high level of human health protection by encouraging co-operation between the Member States and, if necessary, lending support to their action. Community action shall be directed towards the prevention of diseases, in particular the major health scourges, including drug dependence, by promoting research into their causes and their transmission, as well as health information and education.

Health protection requirements shall form a constituent part of the Community's other policies.

2 Member States shall, in liaison with the Commission, co-ordinate among themselves their policies and programmes in the areas referred to in paragraph 1. The Commission may, in close contact with the Member States, take any useful initiative to promote such co-ordination.

3 The Community and the Member States shall foster co-operation with third countries and the competent international organisations in the sphere of public health.

4 In order to contribute to the achievement of the objectives referred to in this Article, the Council:

- acting in accordance with the procedure referred to in Article 189b, after consulting the Economic and Social Committee and the Committee of the Regions, shall adopt incentive measures, excluding any harmonisation of the laws and regulations of the Member States;
- acting by a qualified majority on a proposal from the Commission, shall adopt recommendations.

Title XI
Consumer protection

Article 129a

1 The Community shall contribute to the attainment of a high level of

consumer protection through:
(a) measures adopted pursuant to Article 100a in the context of the completion of the internal market;
(b) specific action which supports and supplements the policy pursued by the Member States to protect the health, safety and economic interests of consumers and to provide adequate information to consumers.

2 The Council, acting in accordance with the procedure referred to in Article 189b and after consulting the Economic and Social Committee, shall adopt the specific action referred to in paragraph 1(b).

3 Action adopted pursuant to paragraph 2 shall not prevent any Member State from maintaining or introducing more stringent protective measures. Such measures must be compatible with this Treaty. The Commission shall be notified of them.

Title XII
Trans-European networks

Article 129b

1 To help achieve the objectives referred to in Articles 7a and 130a and to enable citizens of the Union, economic operators and regional and local communities to derive full benefit from the setting up of an area without internal frontiers, the Community shall contribute to the establishment and development of trans-European networks in the areas of transport, telecommunications and energy infrastructures.

2 Within the framework of a system of open and competitive markets, action by the Community shall aim at promoting the interconnection and inter-operability of national networks as well as access to such networks. It shall take account in particular of the need to link island, landlocked and peripheral regions with the central regions of the Community.

Article 129c

1 In order to achieve the objectives referred to in Article 129b, the Community:

• shall establish a series of guidelines covering the objectives, priorities and broad lines of measures envisaged in the sphere of trans-European networks; these guidelines shall identify projects of common interest;

• shall implement any measures that may prove necessary to ensure the inter-operability of the networks, in particular in the field of technical standardisation;

• may support the financial efforts made by the Member States for projects of common interest financed by Member States, which are identified in the framework of the guidelines referred to in the first indent, particularly through feasibility studies, loan guarantees or interest rate subsidies; the Community may also contribute, through the Cohesion Fund to be set up no later than 31 December 1993 pursuant to Article 130d, to the financing of specific projects in Member States in the area of transport infrastructure.

The Community's activities shall take into account the potential economic viability of the projects.

2 Member States shall, in liaison with the Commission, co-ordinate among themselves the policies

pursued at national level which may have a significant impact on the achievement of the objectives referred to in Article 129b. The Commission may, in close co-operation with the Member States, take any useful initiative to promote such co-ordination.

3 The Community may decide to co-operate with third countries to promote projects of mutual interest and to ensure the inter-operability of networks.

Article 129d

The guidelines referred to in Article 129c(1) shall be adopted by the Council, acting in accordance with the procedure referred to in Article 189b and after consulting the Economic and Social Committee and the Committee of the Regions.

Guidelines and projects of common interest which relate to the territory of a Member State shall require the approval of the Member State concerned.

The Council, acting in accordance with the procedure referred to in Article 189c and after consulting the Economic and Social Committee and the Committee of the Regions, shall adopt the other measures provided for in Article 129c(1).

Title XIII
Industry

Article 130

1 [] The Community and the Member States shall ensure that the conditions necessary for the competitiveness of the Community's industry exist.

For that purpose, in accordance with a system of open and competitive markets, their action shall be

aimed at:
- speeding up the adjustment of industry to structural changes;
- encouraging an environment favourable to initiative and to the development of undertakings throughout the Community, particularly small and medium-sized undertakings;
- encouraging an environment favourable to co-operation between undertakings;
- fostering better exploitation of the industrial potential of policies of innovation, research and technological development.

2 The Member States shall consult each other in liaison with the Commission and, where necessary, shall co-ordinate their action. The Commission may take any useful initiative to promote such co-ordination.

3 The Community shall contribute to the achievement of the objectives set out in paragraph 1 through the policies and activities it pursues under other provisions of this Treaty. The Council, acting unanimously on a proposal from the Commission, after consulting the European Parliament and the Economic and Social Committee, may decide on specific measures in support of action taken in the Member States to achieve the objectives set out in paragraph 1.

This Title shall not provide a basis for the introduction by the Community of any measure which could lead to a distortion of competition.

Title XIV
Economic and social
cohesion

Article 130a

In order to promote its overall harmonious development, the Community shall develop and pursue its actions leading to the strengthening of its economic and social cohesion.

In particular, the Community shall aim at reducing disparities between the levels of development of the various regions and the backwardness of the least-favoured regions, including rural areas.

Article 130b

Member States shall conduct their economic policies and shall co-ordinate them in such a way as, in addition, to attain the objectives set out in Article 130a. The **formulation and** implementation of the **Community's** policies and **actions and the implementation** of the internal market shall take into account the objectives set out in Article 130a [] and shall contribute to their achievement. The Community shall **also** support the achievement of these objectives by the action it takes through the Structural Funds (European Agricultural Guidance and Guarantee Fund, Guidance Section; European Social Fund; European Regional Development Fund), the European Investment Bank and the other existing financial instruments.

The Commission shall submit a report to the European Parliament, the Council, the Economic and Social Committee and the Committee of the Regions every three years on the progress made towards achieving economic and social cohesion and on the manner in which the various means provided for in this Article have contributed to it. This report shall, if necessary, be accompanied by appropriate proposals.

If specific actions prove necessary outside the Funds and without preju-

dice to the measures decided upon within the framework of the other Community policies, such actions may be adopted by the Council acting unanimously on a proposal from the Commission and after consulting the European Parliament, the Economic and Social Committee and the Committee of the Regions.

Article 130c

The European Regional Development Fund is intended to help to redress the [] **main** regional imbalances in the Community through **participation** in the development and structural adjustment of regions whose development is lagging behind and in the conversion of declining industrial regions.

Article 130d

[] **Without prejudice to Article 130e, the Council, acting unanimously on a proposal from the Commission and after obtaining the assent of the European Parliament and consulting the Economic and Social Committee and the Committee of the Regions, shall define the tasks, priority objectives and the organisation of the Structural Funds, which may involve grouping the Funds. The Council, acting by the same procedure, shall also define the general rules applicable to them and the provisions necessary to ensure their effectiveness and the co-ordination of the Funds with one another and with the other existing financial instruments.**

The Council, acting in accordance with the same procedure, shall before 31 December 1993 set up a Cohesion Fund to provide a financial contribution to projects in the fields of environment and trans-European networks in the area of transport infrastructure.

Article 130e

[] Implementing decisions relating to the European Regional Development Fund shall be taken by the Council, acting **in accordance with the procedure referred to in Article 189c and after consulting the Economic and Social Committee and the Committee of the Regions.** With regard to the European Agricultural Guidance and Guarantee Fund, Guidance Section, and the European Social Fund, Articles 43 [] **and 125**, respectively, **shall continue to apply.**

Title XV
Research and technological development

Article 130f

1 The Community [] **shall have the objective of strengthening** the scientific and technological **bases** of **Community** industry and **encouraging** it to become more competitive at international level, **while promoting all the research activities deemed necessary by virtue of other Chapters of this Treaty.**
2 [] **For this purpose the Community shall, throughout the Community,** encourage undertakings, including small and medium-sized undertakings, research centres and universities in their research and technological development activities **of high quality**; it shall support their efforts to co-operate with one another, aiming, notably, at enabling undertakings to exploit the [] internal market potential to the full, in particular through the opening up of national public contracts, the definition of common standards and the removal of legal and fiscal [] **obstacles** to that co-operation.
3 **All Community activities under this Treaty in the area of research and technological development, including demonstration projects, shall be decided on and implemented in accordance with the provisions of this Title.**
[]

Article 130g

In pursuing these objectives, the Community shall carry out the following activities, complementing the activities carried out in the Member States:
(a) implementation of research, technological development and demonstration programmes, by promoting co-operation with **and between** undertakings, research centres and universities;
(b) promotion of co-operation in the field of Community research, technological development and demonstration with third countries and international organisations;
(c) dissemination and optimisation of the results of activities in Community research, technological development and demonstration;
(d) stimulation of the training and mobility of researchers in the Community.

Article 130h

1 **The Community and the Member States shall co-ordinate their research and technological development activities so as to ensure that national policies and Community policy are mutually consistent.**
2 [] **In close** [] **co-operation** with

the Member States, the Commission may take any useful initiative to promote the co-ordination referred to in paragraph 1.

Article 130i

1 [] A multi-annual framework programme, setting out all the activities of the Community, shall be adopted by the Council, acting in accordance with the procedure referred to in Article 189b after consulting the Economic and Social Committee. The Council shall act unanimously throughout the procedures referred to in Article 189b.

The framework programme shall:
• establish the scientific and technological objectives to be achieved by the activities provided for in Article 130g and fix the relevant priorities;
• indicate the broad lines of such activities;
• fix the maximum overall amount and the detailed rules for Community financial participation in the framework programme and the respective shares in each of the activities provided for.

2 The framework programme [] shall be adapted or supplemented as the situation changes.

3 The framework programme shall be implemented through specific programmes developed within each activity. Each specific programme shall define the detailed rules for implementing it, fix its duration and provide for the means deemed necessary. The sum of the amounts deemed necessary, fixed in the specific programmes, may not exceed the overall maximum amount fixed for the framework programme and each activity.

4 The Council, acting by a qualified majority on a proposal from the Commission and after consulting the European Parliament and the Economic and Social Committee, shall adopt the specific programmes.

Article 130j (formerly Article 130k)

For the implementation of the multi-annual framework programme the Council shall:
• determine the rules for the participation of undertakings, research centres and universities;
• lay down the rules governing the dissemination of research results.

Article 130k (formerly Article 130l)

In implementing the multi-annual framework programme, supplementary programmes may be decided on involving the participation of certain Member States only, which shall finance them subject to possible Community participation.

The Council shall adopt the rules applicable to supplementary programmes, particularly as regards the dissemination of knowledge and access by other Member States.

Article 130l (formerly Article 130m)

In implementing the multi-annual framework programme the Community may make provision, in agreement with the Member States concerned, for participation in research and development programmes undertaken by several Member States, including participation in the structures created for the execution of those programmes.

Article 130m (formerly Article 130n)

In implementing the multi-annual framework programme the Community may make provision for co-operation in Community research, technological development and demonstration with third countries or international organisations.

The detailed arrangements for such co-operation may be the subject of agreements between the Community and the third parties concerned, which shall be negotiated and concluded in accordance with Article 228.

Article 130n (formerly Article 130o)

The Community may set up joint undertakings or any other structure necessary for the efficient execution of [] Community research, technological development and demonstration **programmes**.
[]

Article 130o (formerly Article 130q)

The Council [], acting unanimously on a proposal from the Commission and after consulting the European Parliament and the Economic and Social Committee, **shall** adopt the provisions referred to in **Article [] 130n**.

The Council [], **acting [] in accordance with the procedure referred to in Article 189c and** after consulting the Economic and Social Committee, [] **shall** adopt the provisions referred to in Articles [] **130j to 130l**. [] Adoption of **the** supplementary programmes shall [] require the agreement of the Member States concerned.

Article 130p

At the beginning of each year the Commission shall send a report to the European Parliament and the Council. The report shall include information on research and technological development activities and the dissemination of results during the previous year, and the work programme for the current year.

Article 130q (**Repealed by Maastricht Treaty**)

Title XVI
Environment

Article 130r

1 [] Community policy on the environment shall contribute to pursuit of the following objectives:
- preserving, protecting and improving the quality of the environment;
- [] protecting human health;
- [] prudent and rational utilisation of natural resources;
- **promoting measures at international level to deal with regional or worldwide environmental problems.**

2 **Community policy on the environment shall aim at a high level of protection taking into account the diversity of situations in the various regions of the Community. It shall be based on the precautionary principle** [] **and on the principles that** preventive action should be taken, that environmental damage should as a priority be rectified at source and that the polluter should pay. Environmental protection requirements [] **must be integrated into the definition and implementation of other Community policies.**

In this context, harmonisation

measures answering these requirements shall include, where appropriate, a safeguard clause allowing Member States to take provisional measures, for non-economic environmental reasons, subject to a Community inspection procedure.

3 In preparing its [] **policy** on the environment, the Community shall take account of:

- available scientific and technical data;
- environmental conditions in the various regions of the Community;
- the potential benefits and costs of action or lack of action;
- the economic and social development of the Community as a whole and the balanced development of its regions.

[]

4 Within their respective spheres of competence, the Community and the Member States shall co-operate with third countries and with the [] **competent** international organisations.

The arrangements for Community co-operation may be the subject of agreements between the Community and the third parties concerned, which shall be negotiated and concluded in accordance with Article 228.

The previous **sub**paragraph shall be without prejudice to Member States' competence to negotiate in international bodies and to conclude international agreements.

Article 130s

1 The Council, acting [] **in accordance with the procedure referred to in Article 189c** and after consulting the [] Economic and Social Committee, shall decide what action is to be taken by the Community **in** order to achieve the objectives referred to in Article 130r.

2 By way of derogation from the decision-making procedure provided for in paragraph 1 and without prejudice to Article 100a, the Council, acting unanimously on a proposal from the Commission and after consulting the European Parliament and the Economic and Social Committee, shall adopt:

- provisions primarily of a fiscal nature;
- measures concerning town and country planning, land use with the exception of waste management and measures of a general nature, and management of water resources;
- measures significantly affecting a Member State's choice between different energy sources and the general structure of its energy supply.

The Council [] **may**, under the conditions laid down in the preceding subparagraph, define those matters **referred to in this paragraph** on which decisions are to be taken by a qualified majority.

3 In other areas, general action programmes setting out priority objectives to be attained shall be adopted by the Council, acting in accordance with the procedure referred to in Article 189b and after consulting the Economic and Social Committee.

The Council, acting under the terms of paragraph 1 or paragraph 2, according to the case, shall adopt the measures necessary for the implementation of these programmes.

4 Without prejudice to certain measures of a Community nature, the Member States shall finance and implement the environment policy.

5 Without prejudice to the princi-

ple that the polluter should pay, if a measure based on the provisions of paragraph 1 involves costs deemed disproportionate for the public authorities of a Member State, the Council shall, in the act adopting that measure, lay down appropriate provisions in the form of:

- temporary derogations; and/or
- financial support from the Cohesion Fund to be set up no later than 31 December 1993 pursuant to Article 130d.

Article 130t

The protective measures adopted [] pursuant to Article 130s shall not prevent any Member State from maintaining or introducing more stringent protective measures. **Such measures must be** compatible with this Treaty. **They shall be notified to the Commission.**

Title XVII
Development co-operation

Article 130u

1 Community policy in the sphere of development co-operation, which shall be complementary to the policies pursued by the Member States, shall foster:

- the sustainable economic and social development of the developing countries, and more particularly the most disadvantaged among them;
- the smooth and gradual integration of the developing countries into the world economy;
- the campaign against poverty in the developing countries.

2 The Community policy in this area shall contribute to the general objective of developing and consolidating democracy and the rule of law, and to that of respecting human rights and fundamental freedoms.

3 The Community and the Member States shall comply with the commitments and take account of the objectives they have approved in the context of the United Nations and other competent international organisations.

Article 130v

The Community shall take account of the objectives referred to in Article 130u in the policies that it implements which are likely to affect developing countries.

Article 130w

1 Without prejudice to the other provisions of this Treaty the Council, acting in accordance with the procedure referred to in Article 189c, shall adopt the measures necessary to further the objectives referred to in Article 130u. Such measures may take the form of multiannual programmes.

2 The European Investment Bank shall contribute, under the terms laid down in its Statute, to the implementation of the measures referred to in paragraph 1.

3 The provisions of this Article shall not affect co-operation with the African, Caribbean and Pacific countries in the framework of the ACP-EEC Convention.

Article 130x

1 The Community and the Member States shall co-ordinate their policies on development co-operation and shall consult each other on their aid programmes, including in international organisations and during international conferences. They may undertake joint action. Member

States shall contribute if necessary to the implementation of Community aid programmes.

2 The Commission may take any useful initiative to promote the co-ordination referred to in paragraph 1.

Article 130y

Within their respective spheres of competence, the Community and the Member States shall co-operate with third countries and with the compe-tent international organisations. The arrangements for Community co-operation may be the subject of agreements between the Community and the third parties concerned, which shall be negotiated and con-cluded in accordance with Article 228.

The previous paragraph shall be without prejudice to Member States' competence to negotiate in interna-tional bodies and to conclude inter-national agreements.

Part Four
Association of the Overseas Countries and Territories

Article 131

The Member States agree to associ-ate with the Community the non-European countries and territories which have special relations with Belgium, Denmark, France, Italy, the Netherlands and the United Kingdom. These countries and ter-ritories (hereinafter called the "countries and territories") are listed in Annex IV to this Treaty.

The purpose of association shall be to promote the economic and social development of the countries and territories and to establish close economic relations between them and the Community as a whole.

In accordance with the principles set out in the Preamble to this Treaty, association shall serve pri-marily to further the interests and prosperity of the inhabitants of these countries and territories in order to lead them to the economic, social and cultural devel-opment to which they aspire.

Article 132

Association shall have the follow-ing objectives:

1 Member States shall apply to their trade with the countries and territories the same treatment as they accord each other pursuant to this Treaty.

2 Each country or territory shall apply to its trade with Member States and with the other countries and territories the same treatment as that which it applies to the European State with which it has special relations.

3 The Member States shall contri-bute to the investments required for the progressive development of these countries and territories.

4 For investments financed by the Community, participation in tenders and supplies shall be open on equal terms to all natural and legal persons who are nationals of a Member State or of one of the countries and territories.

5 In relations between Member

States and the countries and territories the right of establishment of nationals and companies or firms shall be regulated in accordance with the provisions and procedures laid down in the Chapter relating to the right of establishment and on a non-discriminatory basis, subject to any special provisions laid down pursuant to Article 136.

Article 133

1 Customs duties on imports into the Member States of goods originating in the countries and territories shall be completely abolished in conformity with the progressive abolition of customs duties between Member States in accordance with the provisions of this Treaty.
2 Customs duties on imports into each country or territory from Member States or from the other countries or territories shall be progressively abolished in accordance with the provisions of Articles 12, 13, 14, 15 and 17.
3 The countries and territories may, however, levy customs duties which meet the needs of their development and industrialisation or produce revenue for their budgets.

The duties referred to in the preceding subparagraph shall nevertheless be progressively reduced to the level of those imposed on imports of products from the Member State with which each country or territory has special relations. The percentages and the timetable of the reductions provided for under this Treaty shall apply to the difference between the duty imposed on a product coming from the Member State which has special relations with the country or territory concerned and the duty imposed on the same product

coming from within the Community on entry into the importing country or territory.
4 Paragraph 2 shall not apply to countries and territories which, by reason of the particular international obligations by which they are bound, already apply a non-discriminatory customs tariff when this Treaty enters into force.
5 The introduction of or any change in customs duties imposed on goods imported into the countries and territories shall not, either in law or in fact, give rise to any direct or indirect discrimination between imports from the various Member States.

Article 134

If the level of the duties applicable to goods from a third country on entry into a country or territory is liable, when the provisions of Article 133(1) have been applied, to cause deflections of trade to the detriment of any Member State, the latter may request the Commission to propose to the other Member States the measures needed to remedy the situation.

Article 135

Subject to the provisions relating to public health, public security or public policy, freedom of movement within Member States for workers from the countries and territories, and within the countries and territories for workers from Member States, shall be governed by agreements to be concluded subsequently with the unanimous approval of Member States.

Article 136

For an initial period of five years

after the entry into force of this Treaty, the details of and procedure for the association of the countries and territories with the Community shall be determined by an Implementing Convention annexed to this Treaty.

Before the Convention referred to in the preceding paragraph expires, the Council shall, acting unanimously, lay down provisions for a further period, on the basis of the experience acquired and of the principles set out in this Treaty.

Article 136a

The provisions of Articles 131 to 136 shall apply to Greenland, subject to the specific provisions for Greenland set out in the Protocol on special arrangements for Greenland, annexed to this Treaty.

Part Five
Institutions of the Community

Title I
Provisions Governing the Institutions

Chapter 1
The Institutions

SECTION 1
THE EUROPEAN PARLIAMENT

Article 137

The European Parliament, which shall consist of representatives of the peoples of the States brought together in the Community, shall exercise [] the powers [] conferred upon it by this Treaty.

Article 138

(Paras. 1 and 2 as replaced by Direct Elections Act, Arts 1 and 2)
1 The representatives in the European Parliament of the peoples of the States brought together in the Community shall be elected by direct universal suffrage.
2 The number of representatives elected in each Member State is as follows:

Belgium	25
Denmark	16
Germany	99
Greece	25
Spain	64
France	87
Ireland	15
Italy	87
Luxembourg	6
Netherlands	31
Austria	*21*
Portugal	25
Finland	*16*
Sweden	*22*
United Kingdom	87

3 The European Parliament shall draw up proposals for elections by direct universal suffrage in accordance with a uniform procedure in all Member States.

The Council shall, acting unanimously **after obtaining the assent of the European Parliament, which shall act by a majority of its component members**, lay down the appropriate provisions, which it shall recommend to Member States for adoption in accordance with their respective constitutional requirements.

Article 138a

Political parties at European level are important as a factor for integration within the Union. They contribute to forming a European awareness and to expressing the political will of the citizens of the Union.

Article 138b

In so far as provided in this Treaty, the European Parliament shall participate in the process leading up to the adoption of Community acts by exercising its powers under the procedures laid down in Articles 189b and 189c and by giving its assent or delivering advisory opinions.

The European Parliament may, acting by a majority of its members, request the Commission to submit any appropriate proposal on matters on which it considers that a Community act is required for the purpose of implementing this Treaty.

Article 138c

In the course of its duties, the European Parliament may, at the request of a quarter of its members, set up a temporary Committee of Inquiry to investigate, without prejudice to the powers conferred by this Treaty on other institutions or bodies, alleged contraventions or maladministration in the implementation of Community law, except where the alleged facts are being examined before a court and while the case is still subject to legal proceedings.

The temporary Committee of Inquiry shall cease to exist on the submission of its report.

The detailed provisions governing the exercise of the right of inquiry shall be determined by common accord of the European Parliament, the Council and the Commission.

Article 138d

Any citizen of the Union, and any natural or legal person residing or having its registered office in a Member State, shall have the right to address, individually or in association with other citizens or persons, a petition to the European Parliament on a matter which comes within the Community's fields of activity and which affects him, her or it directly.

Article 138e

1 The European Parliament shall appoint an Ombudsman empowered to receive complaints from any citizen of the Union or any natural or legal person residing or having its registered office in a Member State concerning instances of maladministration in the activities of the Community institutions or bodies, with the exception of the Court of Justice and the Court of First Instance acting in their judicial role.

In accordance with his duties, the Ombudsman shall conduct inquiries for which he finds grounds, either on his own initiative or on the basis of complaints submitted to him direct or through a member of the European Parliament, except where the alleged facts are or have been the subject of legal proceedings. Where the Ombudsman establishes an instance of maladministration, he shall refer the matter to the institution concerned, which shall have a period of three months in which to inform him of its views. The Ombudsman shall then forward a report to the European Parliament and the institution concerned. The person lodging the complaint shall be informed of the outcome of such inquiries.

The Ombudsman shall submit an annual report to the European Parliament on the outcome of his inquiries.

2 The Ombudsman shall be appointed after each election of the European Parliament for the duration of its term of office. The Ombudsman shall be eligible for reappointment.

The Ombudsman may be dismissed by the Court of Justice at the request of the European Parliament if he no longer fulfils the conditions required for the performance of his duties or if he is guilty of serious misconduct.

3 The Ombudsman shall be completely independent in the performance of his duties. In the performance of those duties he shall neither seek nor take instructions from any body. The Ombudsman may not, during his term of office, engage in any other occupation, whether gainful or not.

4 The European Parliament shall, after seeking an opinion from the Commission and with the approval of the Council acting by a qualified majority, lay down the regulations and general conditions governing the performance of the Ombudsman's duties.

Article 139

The European Parliament shall hold an annual session. It shall meet, without requiring to be convened, on the second Tuesday in March.

The European Parliament may meet in extraordinary session at the request of a majority of its members or at the request of the Council or of the Commission.

Article 140

The European Parliament shall elect its President and its officers from among its members.

Members of the Commission may attend all meetings and shall, at their request, be heard on behalf of the Commission.

The Commission shall reply orally or in writing to questions put to it by the European Parliament or by its members.

The Council shall be heard by the European Parliament in accordance with the conditions laid down by the Council in its rules of procedure.

Article 141

Save as otherwise provided in this Treaty, the European Parliament shall act by an absolute majority of the votes cast.

The rules of procedure shall determine the quorum.

Article 142

The European Parliament shall adopt its rules of procedure, acting by a majority of its members.

The proceedings of the European Parliament shall be published in the manner laid down in its rules of procedure.

Article 143

The European Parliament shall discuss in open session the annual general report submitted to it by the Commission.

Article 144

If a motion of censure on the activities of the Commission is tabled before it, the European Parliament shall not vote thereon until at least three days after the motion has been tabled and only by open vote. If the motion of censure is carried by a two-thirds majority of the votes cast, representing a majority of the members of the European Parliament, the members of the Commission shall resign as a body. They shall continue to deal with current business until they are replaced in accordance with Article 158. **In this case, the term of office of the members of the Commission appointed to replace them shall expire on the date on which the term of office of the members of the Commission obliged to resign as a body would have expired.**

SECTION 2
THE COUNCIL

Article 145

To ensure that the objectives set out in the Treaty are attained, the Council shall, in accordance with the provisions of this Treaty:
- ensure co-ordination of the general economic policies of the Member States;
- have power to take decisions;
- confer on the Commission, in the acts which the Council adopts, powers for the implementation of the rules which the Council lays down. The Council may impose certain requirements in respect of the exercise of these powers. The Council may also reserve the right, in specific cases, to exercise directly implementing powers itself. The procedures referred to above must be consonant with principles and rules to be laid down in advance by the Council, acting unanimously on a proposal from the Commission and after

obtaining the Opinion of the European Parliament.

Article 146

The Council shall consist of [] a **representative** of **each** Member State **at ministerial level, authorised to commit the government of that Member State.** []
The office of President shall be held in turn by each Member State in the Council for a term of six months in the order decided by the Council acting unanimously.

Article 147

The Council shall meet when convened by its President on his own initiative or at the request of one of its members or of the Commission.

Article 148

1 Save as otherwise provided in this Treaty, the Council shall act by a majority of its members.
2 Where the Council is required to act by a qualified majority, the votes of its members shall be weighted as follows:

Belgium	5
Denmark	3
Germany	10
Greece	5
Spain	8
France	10
Ireland	3
Italy	10
Luxembourg	2
Netherlands	5
Austria	*4*
Portugal	5
Finland	*3*
Sweden	*4*
United Kingdom	10

For their adoption, acts of the Council shall require at least:

- *62* votes in favour where this Treaty requires them to be adopted on a proposal from the Commission,
- *62* votes in favour, cast by at least *10* members, in other cases.

3 Abstentions by members present in person or represented shall not prevent the adoption by the Council of acts which require unanimity.

Article 149 (repealed by Maastricht Treaty)

Article 150

Where a vote is taken, any member of the Council may also act on behalf of not more than one other member.

Article 151

1 A committee consisting of the Permanent Representatives of the Member States shall be responsible for preparing the work of the Council and for carrying out the tasks assigned to it by the Council.

2 The Council shall be assisted by a General Secretariat, under the direction of a Secretary-General. The Secretary-General shall be appointed by the Council acting unanimously.

The Council shall decide on the organisation of the General Secretariat.

3 The Council shall adopt its rules of procedure.

Article 152

The Council may request the Commission to undertake any studies the Council considers desirable for the attainment of the common objectives, and to submit to it any appropriate proposals.

Article 153

The Council shall, after receiving an opinion from the Commission, determine the rules governing the committees provided for in this Treaty.

Article 154

The Council shall, acting by a qualified majority, determine the salaries, allowances and pensions of the President and members of the Commission, and of the President, Judges, Advocates-General and Registrar of the Court of Justice. It shall also, again by a qualified majority, determine any payment to be made instead of remuneration.

SECTION 3
THE COMMISSION

Article 155

In order to ensure the proper functioning and development of the common market, the Commission shall:

- ensure that the provisions of this Treaty and the measures taken by the institutions pursuant thereto are applied;
- formulate recommendations or deliver opinions on matters dealt with in this Treaty, if it expressly so provides or if the Commission considers it necessary;
- have its own power of decision and participate in the shaping of measures taken by the Council and by the European Parliament in the manner provided for in this Treaty;

- exercise the powers conferred on it by the Council for the implementation of the rules laid down by the latter.

Article 156

The Commission shall publish annually, not later than one month before the opening of the session of the European Parliament, a general report on the activities of the Community.

Article 157

1 The Commission shall consist of **20** members, who shall be chosen on the grounds of their general competence and whose independence is beyond doubt.

The number of members of the Commission may be altered by the Council, acting unanimously.

Only nationals of Member States may be members of the Commission.

The Commission must include at least one national of each of the Member States, but may not include more than two members having the nationality of the same State.

2 The members of the Commission shall, in the general interest of the Community, be completely independent in the performance of their duties. In the performance of these duties, they shall neither seek nor take instructions from any government or from any other body. They shall refrain from any action incompatible with their duties. Each Member State undertakes to respect this principle and not to seek to influence the members of the Commission in the performance of their tasks.

The members of the Commission may not, during their term of office, engage in any other occupation, whether gainful or not. When entering upon their duties they shall give a solemn undertaking that, both during and after their term of office, they will respect the obligations arising therefrom and in particular their duty to behave with integrity and discretion as regards the acceptance, after they have ceased to hold office, of certain appointments or benefits. In the event of any breach of these obligations, the Court of Justice may, on application by the Council or the Commission, rule that the member concerned be, according to the circumstances, either compulsorily retired in accordance with Article 160 or deprived of his right to a pension or other benefits in its stead.

Article 158

1 **The members of the Commission shall be appointed, in accordance with the procedure referred to in paragraph 2, for a period of five years, subject, if need be, to Article 144.**

Their term of office shall be renewable.

2 **The governments of the Member States shall nominate by common accord, after consulting the European Parliament, the person they intend to appoint as President of the Commission.**

The governments of the Member States shall, in consultation with the nominee for President, nominate the other persons whom they intend to appoint as members of the Commission.

The President and the other members of the Commission thus nominated shall be subject as a body to a vote of approval by the

European Parliament. After approval by the European Parliament, the President and the other members of the Commission shall be appointed by common accord of the governments of the Member States.

3 Paragraphs 1 and 2 shall be applied for the first time to the President and the other members of the Commission whose term of office begins on 7 January 1995.

The President and the other members of the Commission whose term of office begins on 7 January 1993 shall be appointed by common accord of the governments of the Member States. Their term of office shall expire on 6 January 1995.

Article 159

Apart from normal replacement, or death, the duties of a member of the Commission shall end when he resigns or is compulsorily retired.

The vacancy thus caused shall be filled for the remainder of the member's term of office by a new member appointed by common accord of the governments of the Member States. The Council may, acting unanimously, decide that such a vacancy need not be filled.

In the event of resignation, compulsory retirement or death, the President shall be replaced for the remainder of his term of office. The procedure laid down in Article 158(2) shall be applicable for the replacement of the President.

Save in the case of compulsory retirement under [] Article 160, members of the Commission shall remain in office until they have been replaced.

Article 160

If any member of the Commission no longer fulfils the conditions required for the performance of his duties or if he has been guilty of serious misconduct, the Court of Justice may, on application by the Council or the Commission, compulsorily retire him.

Article 161

[] The Commission may appoint a Vice-President or two Vice-Presidents from among its members.

Article 162

1 The Council and the Commission shall consult each other and shall settle by common accord their methods of co-operation.

2 The Commission shall adopt its rules of procedure so as to ensure that both it and its departments operate in accordance with the provisions of this Treaty. [] It shall ensure that these rules are published.

Article 163

The Commission shall act by a majority of the number of members provided for in [] Article 157.

A meeting of the Commission shall be valid only if the number of members laid down in its rules of procedure is present.

SECTION 4
THE COURT OF JUSTICE

Article 164

The Court of Justice shall ensure that in the interpretation and application of this Treaty the law is observed.

Article 165

The Court of Justice shall consist of *15* Judges.

The Court **of Justice** shall sit in plenary session. It may, however, form chambers, each consisting of three, *five or seven* Judges, either to undertake certain preparatory inquiries or to adjudicate on particular categories of cases in accordance with rules laid down for these purposes.

[] **The Court of Justice shall sit in plenary session when a Member State or a Community institution that is a party to the proceedings so requests.**

Should the Court of Justice so request, the Council may, acting unanimously, increase the number of Judges and make the necessary adjustments to the second and third paragraphs of this Article and to the second paragraph of Article 167.

Article 166

The Court of Justice shall be assisted by *eight* Advocates-General. *However, a ninth Advocate-General shall be appointed as from the date of accession until 6 October 2000.*

It shall be the duty of the Advocate-General, acting with complete impartiality and independence, to make, in open court, reasoned submissions on cases brought before the Court of Justice, in order to assist the Court in the performance of the task assigned to it in Article 164.

Should the Court of Justice so request, the Council may, acting unanimously, increase the number of Advocates-General and make the necessary adjustments to the third paragraph of Article 167.

Article 167

The Judges and Advocates-General shall be chosen from persons whose independence is beyond doubt and who possess the qualifications required for appointment to the highest judicial offices in their respective countries or who are jurisconsults of recognised competence; they shall be appointed by common accord of the governments of the Member States for a term of six years.

Every three years there shall be a partial replacement of the Judges. *Eight* and *seven* Judges shall be replaced alternately.

Every three years there shall be a partial replacement of the Advocates-General. *Four* Advocates-General shall be replaced on each occasion.

Retiring Judges and Advocates-General shall be eligible for re-appointment.

The Judges shall elect the President of the Court of Justice from among their number for a term of three years. He may be re-elected.

Article 168

The Court of Justice shall appoint its Registrar and lay down the rules governing his service.

Article 168a

1 [] **A Court of First Instance shall be attached to the Court of Justice** with jurisdiction to hear and determine at first instance, subject to a right of appeal to the Court of Justice on points of law only and in accordance with the conditions laid down by the Statute, certain classes of action or proceeding [] **defined in accordance with the conditions laid down in paragraph 2**. []

The Court of First Instance shall not be competent to hear and determine [] questions referred for a preliminary ruling under Article 177.

2 **At the request of the Court of Justice and after consulting the European Parliament and the Commission, the Council, [] acting unanimously, shall determine the classes of action or proceeding referred to in paragraph 1 and the composition of the Court of First Instance and shall** adopt the necessary adjustments and additional provisions to the Statute of the Court of Justice. Unless the Council decides otherwise, the provisions of this Treaty relating to the Court of Justice, in particular the provisions of the Protocol on the Statute of the Court of Justice, shall apply to [] **the Court of First Instance.**

3 The members of [] **the Court of First Instance** shall be chosen from persons whose independence is beyond doubt and who possess the ability required for appointment to judicial office; they shall be appointed by common accord of the governments of the Member States for a term of six years. The membership shall be partially renewed every three years. Retiring members shall be eligible for re-appointment.

4 [] **The Court of First Instance** shall establish its rules of procedure in agreement with the Court of Justice. Those rules shall require the unanimous approval of the Council.

Article 169

If the Commission considers that a Member State has failed to fulfil an obligation under this Treaty, it shall deliver a reasoned opinion on the matter after giving the State concerned the opportunity to submit its observations.

If the State concerned does not comply with the opinion within the period laid down by the Commission, the latter may bring the matter before the Court of Justice.

Article 170

A Member State which considers that another Member State has failed to fulfil an obligation under this Treaty may bring the matter before the Court of Justice.

Before a Member State brings an action against another Member State for an alleged infringement of an obligation under this Treaty, it shall bring the matter before the Commission.

The Commission shall deliver a reasoned opinion after each of the States concerned has been given the opportunity to submit its own case and its observations on the other party's case both orally and in writing.

If the Commission has not delivered an opinion within three months of the date on which the matter was brought before it, the absence of such opinion shall not prevent the matter from being brought before the Court of Justice.

Article 171

1 If the Court of Justice finds that a Member State has failed to fulfil an obligation under this Treaty, the State shall be required to take the necessary measures to comply with the judgment of the Court of Justice.

2 **If the Commission considers that the Member State concerned has not taken such measures it shall, after**

giving that State the opportunity to submit its observations, issue a reasoned opinion specifying the points on which the Member State concerned has not complied with the judgment of the Court of Justice.

If the Member State concerned fails to take the necessary measures to comply with the Court's judgment within the time-limit laid down by the Commission, the latter may bring the case before the Court of Justice. In so doing it shall specify the amount of the lump sum or penalty payment to be paid by the Member State concerned which it considers appropriate in the circumstances.

If the Court of Justice finds that the Member State concerned has not complied with its judgment it may impose a lump sum or penalty payment on it.

This procedure shall be without prejudice to Article 170.

Article 172

Regulations **adopted jointly by the European Parliament and the Council, and** by the Council, pursuant to the provisions of this Treaty, may give the Court of Justice unlimited jurisdiction [] **with** regard to the penalties provided for in such regulations.

Article 173

The Court of Justice shall review the legality **of acts adopted jointly by the European Parliament and the Council**, of acts of the Council, of the Commission **and of the ECB**, other than recommendations and opinions, [] **and of acts of the European Parliament intended to produce legal effects vis-à-vis third parties.**

It shall for this purpose have jurisdiction in actions brought by a Member State, the Council or the Commission on grounds of lack of competence, infringement of an essential procedural requirement, infringement of this Treaty or of any rule of law relating to its application, or misuse of powers.

The Court shall have jurisdiction under the same conditions in actions brought by the European Parliament and by the ECB for the purpose of protecting their prerogatives.

Any natural or legal person may, under the same conditions, institute proceedings against a decision addressed to that person or against a decision which, although in the form of a regulation or a decision addressed to another person, is of direct and individual concern to the former.

The proceedings provided for in this Article shall be instituted within two months of the publication of the measure, or of its notification to the plaintiff, or, in the absence thereof, of the day on which it came to the knowledge of the latter, as the case may be.

Article 174

If the action is well founded, the Court of Justice shall declare the act concerned to be void.

In the case of a regulation, however, the Court of Justice shall, if it considers this necessary, state which of the effects of the regulation which it has declared void shall be considered as definitive.

Article 175

Should **the European Parliament**, the Council or the Commission, in infringement of this Treaty, fail to act, the Member States and the other institutions of the Community may bring an action before the Court of Justice to have the infringement established.

The action shall be admissible only if the institution concerned has first been called upon to act. If, within two months of being so called upon, the institution concerned has not defined its position, the action may be brought within a further period of two months.

Any natural or legal person may, under the conditions laid down in the preceding paragraphs, complain to the Court of Justice that an institution of the Community has failed to address to that person any act other than a recommendation or an opinion.

The Court of Justice shall have jurisdiction, under the same conditions, in actions or proceedings brought by the ECB in the areas falling within the latter's field of competence and in actions or proceedings brought against the latter.

Article 176

The institution **or institutions** whose act has been declared void or whose failure to act has been declared contrary to this Treaty shall be required to take the necessary measures to comply with **the judgment of** the Court of Justice.

This obligation shall not affect any obligation which may result from the application of the second paragraph of Article 215.

This Article shall also apply to the ECB.

Article 177

The Court of Justice shall have jurisdiction to give preliminary rulings concerning:

(a) the interpretation of this Treaty;

(b) the validity and interpretation of acts of the institutions of the Community **and of the ECB;**

(c) the interpretation of the statutes of bodies established by an act of the Council, where those statutes so provide.

Where such a question is raised before any court or tribunal of a Member State, that court or tribunal may, if it considers that a decision on the question is necessary to enable it to give judgment, request the Court of Justice to give a ruling thereon.

Where any such question is raised in a case pending before a court or tribunal of a Member State against whose decisions there is no judicial remedy under national law, that court or tribunal shall bring the matter before the Court of Justice.

Article 178

The Court of Justice shall have jurisdiction in disputes relating to compensation for damage provided for in the second paragraph of Article 215.

Article 179

The Court of Justice shall have jurisdiction in any dispute between the Community and its servants within the limits and under the conditions laid down in the Staff Regulations or the Conditions of Employment.

Article 180

The Court of Justice shall, within the limits hereinafter laid down, have jurisdiction in disputes concerning:

(a) the fulfilment by Member States of obligations under the Statute of the European Investment Bank. In this connection, the Board of Directors of the Bank shall enjoy the powers conferred upon the Commission by Article 169;

(b) measures adopted by the Board of Governors of the **European Investment** Bank. In this connection, any Member State, the Commission or the Board of Directors of the Bank may institute proceedings under the conditions laid down in Article 173;

(c) measures adopted by the Board of Directors of the **European Investment** Bank. Proceedings against such measures may be instituted only by Member States or by the Commission, under the conditions laid down in Article 173, and solely on the grounds of non-compliance with the procedure provided for in Article 21(2), (5), (6) and (7) of the Statute of the Bank.

(d) **the fulfilment by national central banks of obligations under this Treaty and the Statute of the ESCB. In this connection the powers of the Council of the ECB in respect of national central banks shall be the same as those conferred upon the Commission in respect of Member States by Article 169. If the Court of Justice finds that a national central bank has failed to fulfil an obligation under this Treaty, that bank shall be required to take the necessary measures to**

comply with the judgment of the Court of Justice.

Article 181

The Court of Justice shall have jurisdiction to give judgment pursuant to any arbitration clause contained in a contract concluded by or on behalf of the Community, whether that contract be governed by public or private law.

Article 182

The Court of Justice shall have jurisdiction in any dispute between Member States which relates to the subject matter of this Treaty if the dispute is submitted to it under a special agreement between the parties.

Article 183

Save where jurisdiction is conferred on the Court of Justice by this Treaty, disputes to which the Community is a party shall not on that ground be excluded from the jurisdiction of the courts or tribunals of the Member States.

Article 184

Notwithstanding the expiry of the period laid down in the [] **fifth** paragraph of Article 173, any party may, in proceedings in which a regulation **adopted jointly by the European Parliament and the Council, or a regulation** of the Council, of the Commission **or of the ECB** is [] **at** issue, plead the grounds specified in the [] **second** paragraph of Article 173 in order to invoke before the Court of Justice the inapplicability of that regulation.

Article 185

Actions brought before the Court of Justice shall not have suspensory effect. The Court of Justice may, however, if it considers that circumstances so require, order that application of the contested act be suspended.

Article 186

The Court of Justice may in any cases before it prescribe any necessary interim measures.

Article 187

The judgments of the Court of Justice shall be enforceable under the conditions laid down in Article 192.

Article 188

The Statute of the Court of Justice is laid down in a separate Protocol.

The Council may, acting unanimously at the request of the Court of Justice and after consulting the Commission and the European Parliament, amend the provisions of Title III of the Statute.

The Court of Justice shall adopt its rules of procedure. These shall require the unanimous approval of the Council.

SECTION 5
THE COURT OF AUDITORS

Article 188a

The Court of Auditors shall carry out the audit.

Article 188b

1 The Court of Auditors shall consist of *15* members.
2 The members of the Court of Auditors shall be chosen from among persons who belong or have belonged in their respective countries to external audit bodies or who are especially qualified for this office. Their independence must be beyond doubt.
3 The members of the Court of Auditors shall be appointed for a term of six years by the Council, acting unanimously after consulting the European Parliament.

However, when the first appointments are made, four members of the Court of Auditors, chosen by lot, shall be appointed for a term of office of four years only.

The members of the Court of Auditors shall be eligible for reappointment.

They shall elect the President of the Court of Auditors from among their number for a term of three years. The President may be re-elected.
4 The members of the Court of Auditors shall, in the general interest of the Community, be completely independent in the performance of their duties.

In the performance of these duties, they shall neither seek nor take instructions from any government or from any other body. They shall refrain from any action incompatible with their duties.
5 The members of the Court of Auditors may not, during their term of office, engage in any other occupation, whether gainful or not. When entering upon their duties they shall give a solemn undertaking that, both during and after their term of office, they will respect the obligations arising therefrom and in particular their duty to behave with integrity and discretion as regards the acceptance, after they have ceased to hold office, of certain appointments or benefits.

6 Apart from normal replacement, or death, the duties of a member of the Court of Auditors shall end when he resigns, or is compulsorily retired by a ruling of the Court of Justice pursuant to paragraph 7.

The vacancy thus caused shall be filled for the remainder of the member's term of office.

Save in the case of compulsory retirement, members of the Court of Auditors shall remain in office until they have been replaced.

7 A member of the Court of Auditors may be deprived of his office or of his right to a pension or other benefits in its stead only if the Court of Justice, at the request of the Court of Auditors, finds that he no longer fulfils the requisite conditions or meets the obligations arising from his office.

8 The Council, acting by a qualified majority, shall determine the conditions of employment of the President and the members of the Court of Auditors and in particular their salaries, allowances and pensions. It shall also, by the same majority, determine any payment to be made instead of remuneration.

9 The provisions of the Protocol on the Privileges and Immunities of the European Communities applicable to the Judges of the Court of Justice shall also apply to the members of the Court of Auditors.

Article 188c

1 The Court of Auditors shall examine the accounts of all revenue and expenditure of the Community. It shall also examine the accounts of all revenue and expenditure of all bodies set up by the Community in so far as the relevant constituent instrument does not preclude such examination.

The Court of Auditors shall provide the European Parliament and the Council with a statement of assurance as to the reliability of the accounts and the legality and regularity of the underlying transactions.

2 The Court of Auditors shall examine whether all revenue has been received and all expenditure incurred in a lawful and regular manner and whether the financial management has been sound.

The audit of revenue shall be carried out on the basis both of the amounts established as due and the amounts actually paid to the Community.

The audit of expenditure shall be carried out on the basis both of commitments undertaken and payments made.

These audits may be carried out before the closure of accounts for the financial year in question.

3 The audit shall be based on records and, if necessary, performed on the spot in the other institutions of the Community and in the Member States. In the Member States the audit shall be carried out in liaison with the national audit bodies or, if these do not have the necessary powers, with the competent national departments. These bodies or departments shall inform the Court of Auditors whether they intend to take part in the audit.

The other institutions of the Community and the national audit bodies or, if these do not have the necessary powers, the competent national departments, shall forward to the Court of Auditors, at its request, any document or information necessary to carry out its task.

4 The Court of Auditors shall draw up an annual report after the close of each financial year. It shall be forwarded to the other institutions of

the Community and shall be published, together with the replies of these institutions to the observations of the Court of Auditors, in the Official Journal of the European Communities.

The Court of Auditors may also, at any time, submit observations, particularly in the form of special reports, on specific questions and deliver opinions at the request of one of the other institutions of the Community.

It shall adopt its annual reports, special reports or opinions by a majority of its members.

It shall assist the European Parliament and the Council in exercising their powers of control over the implementation of the budget.

Chapter 2
Provisions Common to Several Institutions

Article 189

In order to carry out their task and in accordance with the provisions of this Treaty, the European Parliament acting jointly with the Council, the Council and the Commission shall make regulations and issue directives, take decisions, make recommendations or deliver opinions.

A regulation shall have general application. It shall be binding in its entirety and directly applicable in all Member States.

A directive shall be binding, as to the result to be achieved, upon each Member State to which it is addressed, but shall leave to the national authorities the choice of form and methods.

A decision shall be binding in its entirety upon those to whom it is addressed.

Recommendations and opinions shall have no binding force.

Article 189a

1 Where, in pursuance of this Treaty, the Council acts on a proposal from the Commission, unanimity shall be required for an act constituting an amendment to that proposal, subject to Article 189b(4) and (5).

2 As long as the Council has not acted, the Commission may alter its proposal at any time during the procedures leading to the adoption of a Community act.

Article 189b

1 Where reference is made in this Treaty to this Article for the adoption of an act, the following procedure shall apply.

2 The Commission shall submit a proposal to the European Parliament and the Council.

The Council, acting by a qualified majority after obtaining the opinion of the European Parliament, shall adopt a common position. The common position shall be communicated to the European Parliament. The Council shall inform the European Parliament fully of the reasons which led it to adopt its common position. The Commission shall inform the European Parliament fully of its position.

If, within three months of such communication, the European Parliament:

(a) approves the common position, the Council shall definitively adopt the act in question in accordance with that common position;

(b) has not taken a decision, the Council shall adopt the act in question in accordance with its common position;

(c) indicates, by an absolute majority of its component members, that it intends to reject the common position, it shall immediately inform the Council. The Council may convene a meeting of the Conciliation Committee referred to in paragraph 4 to explain further its position. The European Parliament shall thereafter either confirm, by an absolute majority of its component members, its rejection of the common position, in which event the proposed act shall be deemed not to have been adopted, or propose amendments in accordance with sub-paragraph (d) of this paragraph;

(d) proposes amendments to the common position by an absolute majority of its component members, the amended text shall be forwarded to the Council and to the Commission, which shall deliver an opinion on those amendments.

3 If, within three months of the matter being referred to it, the Council, acting by a qualified majority, approves all the amendments of the European Parliament, it shall amend its common position accordingly and adopt the act in question; however, the Council shall act unanimously on the amendments on which the Commission has delivered a negative opinion. If the Council does not approve the act in question, the President of the Council, in agreement with the President of the European Parliament, shall forthwith convene a meeting of the Conciliation Committee.

4 The Conciliation Committee, which shall be composed of the members of the Council or their representatives and an equal number of representatives of the European Parliament, shall have the task of reaching agreement on a joint text, by a qualified majority of the members of the Council or their representatives and by a majority of the representatives of the European Parliament. The Commission shall take part in the Conciliation Committee's proceedings and shall take all the necessary initiatives with a view to reconciling the positions of the European Parliament and the Council.

5 If, within six weeks of its being convened, the Conciliation Committee approves a joint text, the European Parliament, acting by an absolute majority of the votes cast, and the Council, acting by a qualified majority, shall have a period of six weeks from that approval in which to adopt the act in question in accordance with the joint text. If one of the two institutions fails to approve the proposed act, it shall be deemed not to have been adopted.

6 Where the Conciliation Committee does not approve a joint text, the proposed act shall be deemed not to have been adopted unless the Council, acting by a qualified majority within six weeks of expiry of the period granted to the Conciliation Committee, confirms the common position to which it agreed before the conciliation procedure was initiated, possibly with amendments proposed by the European Parliament. In this case, the act in question shall be finally adopted unless the European Parliament, within six weeks of the date of confirmation by the Council, rejects the

text by an absolute majority of its component members, in which case the proposed act shall be deemed not to have been adopted.

7 The periods of three months and six weeks referred to in this Article may be extended by a maximum of one month and two weeks respectively by common accord of the European Parliament and the Council. The period of three months referred to in paragraph 2 shall be automatically extended by two months where paragraph 2(c) applies.

8 The scope of the procedure under this Article may be widened, in accordance with the procedure provided for in Article N(2) of the Treaty on European Union, on the basis of a report to be submitted to the Council by the Commission by 1996 at the latest.

Article 189c

Where reference is made in this Treaty to this Article for the adoption of an act, the following procedure shall apply:

(a) The Council, acting by a qualified majority on a proposal from the Commission and after obtaining the Opinion of the European Parliament, shall adopt a common position.

(b) The Council's common position shall be communicated to the European Parliament. The Council and the Commission shall inform the European Parliament fully of the reasons which led the Council to adopt its common position and also of the Commission's position.

If, within three months of such communication, the European Parliament approves this common position or has not taken a decision within that period, the Council shall definitively adopt the act in question in accordance with the common position.

(c) The European Parliament may, within the period of three months referred to in point (b), by an absolute majority of its component members, propose amendments to the Council's common position.

The European Parliament may also, by the same majority, reject the Council's common position. The result of the proceedings shall be transmitted to the Council and the Commission.

If the European Parliament has rejected the Council's common position, unanimity shall be required for the Council to act on a second reading.

(d) The Commission shall, within a period of one month, re-examine the proposal on the basis of which the Council adopted its common position, by taking into account the amendments proposed by the European Parliament.

The Commission shall forward to the Council, at the same time as its re-examined proposal, the amendments of the European Parliament which it has not accepted, and shall express its opinion on them. The Council may adopt these amendments unanimously.

(e) The Council, acting by a qualified majority, shall adopt the proposal as re-examined by the Commission.

Unanimity shall be required for the Council to amend the proposal as re-examined by the Commission.

(f) In the cases referred to in points (c), (d) and (e), the Council shall be required to act within a period of three months. If no decision is taken within this period, the Commission proposal shall be deemed not to have been adopted.

(g) The periods referred to in points (b) and (f) may be extended by a maximum of one month by common accord between the Council and the European Parliament.

Article 190

Regulations, directives and decisions **adopted jointly by the European Parliament and the Council, and such acts adopted by []** the Council or the Commission, shall state the reasons on which they are based and shall refer to any proposals or opinions which were required to be obtained pursuant to this Treaty.

Article 191

1 Regulations, **Directives and Decisions adopted in accordance with the procedure referred to in Article 189b shall be signed by the President of the European Parliament and by the President of the Council and** published in the Official Journal of the Community. They shall enter into force on the date specified in them or, in the absence thereof, on the twentieth day following **that of** their publication.

2 **Regulations of the Council and of the Commission, as well as directives of those institutions which are addressed to all Member States, shall be published in the Official Journal of the Community. They shall enter into force on the date** specified in them or, in the absence

thereof, on the twentieth day following that of their publication.

3 **Other** directives, and decisions, shall be notified to those to whom they are addressed and shall take effect upon such notification.

Article 192

Decisions of the Council or of the Commission which impose a pecuniary obligation on persons other than States, shall be enforceable.

Enforcement shall be governed by the rules of civil procedure in force in the State in the territory of which it is carried out. The order for its enforcement shall be appended to the decision, without other formality than verification of the authenticity of the decision, by the national authority which the Government of each Member State shall designate for this purpose and shall make known to the Commission and to the Court of Justice.

When these formalities have been completed on application by the party concerned, the latter may proceed to enforcement in accordance with the national law, by bringing the matter directly before the competent authority.

Enforcement may be suspended only by a decision of the Court of Justice. However, the courts of the country concerned shall have jurisdiction over complaints that enforcement is being carried out in an irregular manner.

Chapter 3
The Economic and Social Committee

Article 193

An Economic and Social Committee is hereby established. It shall have advisory status.

The Committee shall consist of representatives of the various categories of economic and social activity, in particular, representatives of producers, farmers, carriers, workers, dealers, craftsmen, professional occupations and representatives of the general public.

Article 194

The number of members of the Economic and Social Committee shall be as follows:

Belgium	12
Denmark	9
Germany	24
Greece	12
Spain	21
France	24
Ireland	9
Italy	24
Luxembourg	6
Netherlands	12
Austria	*12*
Portugal	12
Finland	*9*
Sweden	*12*
United Kingdom	24

The members of the Committee shall be appointed by the Council, acting unanimously, for four years. Their appointments shall be renewable.

The members of the Committee [] may not be bound by any mandatory instructions. **They shall be completely independent in the performance of their duties, in the general interest of the Community.**

The Council, acting by a qualified majority, shall determine the allowances of members of the Committee.

Article 195

1 For the appointment of the members of the Committee, each Member State shall provide the Council with a list containing twice as many candidates as there are seats allotted to its nationals.

The composition of the Committee shall take account of the need to ensure adequate representation of the various categories of economic and social activity.

2 The Council shall consult the Commission. It may obtain the opinion of European bodies which are representative of the various economic and social sectors to which the activities of the Community are of concern.

Article 196

The Committee shall elect its chairman and officers from among its members for a term of two years.

It shall adopt its rules of procedure. []

The Committee shall be convened by its chairman at the request of the Council or of the Commission. **It may also meet on its own initiative.**

Article 197

The Committee shall include specialised sections for the principal fields covered by this Treaty.

In particular, it shall contain an agricultural section and a transport section, which are the subject of special provisions in the Titles relating to agriculture and transport.

These specialised sections shall operate within the general terms of a reference of the Committee. They may not be consulted independently of the Committee.

Sub-committees may also be established within the Committee to prepare on specific questions or in specific fields, draft opinions to be submitted to the Committee for its consideration.

The rules of procedure shall lay down the methods of composition and the terms of reference of the specialised sections and of the sub-committees.

Article 198

The Committee must be consulted by the Council or by the Commission where this Treaty so provides. The Committee may be consulted by these institutions in all cases in which they consider it appropriate. **It may issue an opinion on its own initiative in cases in which it considers such action appropriate.**

The Council or the Commission shall, if it considers it necessary, set the Committee, for the submission of its opinion, a time limit which may not be less than [] **one month** from the date **on** which the chairman receives notification to this effect. Upon expiry of the time limit, the absence of an opinion shall not prevent further action.

The opinion of the Committee and that of the specialised section, together with a record of the proceedings, shall be forwarded to the Council and to the Commission.

Chapter 4
The Committee of the Regions

Article 198a

A Committee consisting of representatives of regional and local bodies, hereinafter referred to as "the Com-

mittee of the Regions", is hereby established with advisory status.

The number of members of the Committee of the Regions shall be as follows:

Belgium	12
Denmark	9
Germany	24
Greece	12
Spain	21
France	24
Ireland	9
Italy	24
Luxembourg	6
Netherlands	12
Austria	*12*
Portugal	12
Finland	*9*
Sweden	*12*
United Kingdom	24

The members of the Committee and an equal number of alternate members shall be appointed for four years by the Council acting unanimously on proposals from the respective Member States. Their term of office shall be renewable.

The members of the Committee may not be bound by any mandatory instructions. They shall be completely independent in the performance of their duties, in the general interest of the Community.

Article 198b

The Committee of the Regions shall elect its chairman and officers from among its members for a term of two years.

It shall adopt its rules of procedure and shall submit them for approval to the Council, acting unanimously.

The Committee shall be convened by its chairman at the request of the Council or of the Commission. It may also meet on its own initiative.

Article 198c

The Committee of the Regions shall be consulted by the Council or by the Commission where this Treaty so provides and in all other cases in which one of these two institutions considers it appropriate.

The Council or the Commission shall, if it considers it necessary, set the Committee, for the submission of its opinion, a time-limit which may not be less than one month from the date on which the chairman receives notification to this effect. Upon expiry of the time-limit, the absence of an opinion shall not prevent further action.

Where the Economic and Social Committee is consulted pursuant to Article 198, the Committee of the Regions shall be informed by the Council or the Commission of the request for an opinion. Where it considers that specific regional interests are involved, the Committee of the Regions may issue an opinion on the matter.

It may issue an opinion on its own initiative in cases in which it considers such action appropriate.

The opinion of the Committee, together with a record of the proceedings, shall be forwarded to the Council and to the Commission.

Chapter 5
European Investment Bank

Article 198d

The European Investment Bank shall have legal personality.

The members of the European Investment Bank shall be the Member States.

The Statute of the European Investment Bank is laid down in a Protocol annexed to this Treaty.

Article 198e

The task of the European Investment Bank shall be to contribute, by having recourse to the capital market and utilising its own resources, to the balanced and steady development of the common market in the interest of the Community. For this purpose the Bank shall, operating on a non-profit-making basis, grant loans and give guarantees which facilitate the financing of the following projects in all sectors of the economy:

(a) projects for developing less-developed regions;

(b) projects for modernising or converting undertakings or for developing fresh activities called for by the progressive establishment of the common market, where these projects are of such a size or nature that they cannot be entirely financed by the various means available in the individual Member States;

(c) projects of common interest to several Member States which are of such a size or nature that they cannot be entirely financed by the various means available in the individual Member States.

In carrying out its task, the Bank shall facilitate the financing of investment programmes in conjunction with assistance from the structural funds and other Community financial instruments.

Title II
Financial provisions

Article 199

All items of revenue and expenditure of the Community, including those relating to the European

Social Fund, shall be included in estimates to be drawn up for each financial year and shall be shown in the budget.

The administrative expenditure occasioned for the institutions by the provisions of the Treaty on European Union relating to common foreign and security policy and to co-operation in the fields of justice and home affairs shall be charged to the budget. The operational expenditure occasioned by the implementation of the said provisions may, under the conditions referred to therein, be charged to the budget.

The revenue and expenditure shown in the budget shall be in balance.

Article 200 (repealed at Maastricht)

Article 201

[] Without prejudice to other revenue, the budget shall be financed wholly from own resources.

The Council, acting unanimously on a proposal from the Commission and after consulting the European Parliament, shall lay down provisions relating to the system of own resources of the Community, which it shall recommend to the Member States for adoption in accordance with their respective constitutional requirements.

Article 201a

With a view to maintaining budgetary discipline, the Commission shall not make any proposal for a Community act, or alter its proposals, or adopt any implementing measure which is likely to have appreciable implications for the budget without providing the assurance that that proposal or that measure is capable of being financed within the limit of the Community's own resources arising under provisions laid down by the Council pursuant to Article 201.

Article 202

The expenditure shown in the budget shall be authorised for one financial year, unless the regulations made pursuant to Article 209 provide otherwise.

In accordance with conditions to be laid down pursuant to Article 209, any appropriations, other than those relating to staff expenditure, that are unexpended at the end of the financial year may be carried forward to the next financial year only.

Appropriations shall be classified under different chapters grouping items of expenditure according to their nature or purpose and subdivided, as far as may be necessary, in accordance with the regulations made pursuant to Article 209.

The expenditure of the European Parliament, the Council, the Commission and the Court of Justice shall be set out in separate parts of the budget, without prejudice to special arrangements for certain common items of expenditure.

Article 203

1   The financial year shall run from 1 January to 31 December.

2   Each institution of the Community shall, before 1 July, draw up estimates of its expenditure. The Commission shall consolidate these estimates in a preliminary draft budget. It shall attach thereto an opinion which may contain different estimates.

The   preliminary   draft   budget

shall contain an estimate of revenue and an estimate of expenditure.

3 The Commission shall place the preliminary draft budget before the Council not later than 1 September of the year preceding that in which the budget is to be implemented.

The Council shall consult the Commission and, where appropriate, the other institutions concerned whenever it intends to depart from the preliminary draft budget.

The Council, acting by a qualified majority, shall establish the draft budget and forward it to the European Parliament.

4 The draft budget shall be placed before the European Parliament not later than 5 October of the year preceding that in which the budget is to be implemented.

The European Parliament shall have the right to amend the draft budget, acting by a majority of its members, and to propose to the Council, acting by an absolute majority of the votes cast, modifications to the draft budget relating to expenditure necessarily resulting from this Treaty or from acts adopted in accordance therewith.

If, within 45 days of the draft budget being placed before it, the European Parliament has given its approval, the budget shall stand as finally adopted. If within this period the European Parliament has not amended the draft budget nor proposed any modifications thereto, the budget shall be deemed to be finally adopted.

If within this period the European Parliament has adopted amendments or proposed modifications, the draft budget together with the amendments or proposed modifications shall be forwarded to the Council.

5 After discussing the draft budget with the Commission and, where appropriate, with the other institutions concerned, the Council shall act under the following conditions:

(a) The Council may, acting by a qualified majority, modify any of the amendments adopted by the European Parliament;

(b) With regard to the proposed modifications:

• where a modification proposed by the European Parliament does not have the effect of increasing the total amount of the expenditure of an institution, owing in particular to the fact that the increase in expenditure which it would involve would be expressly compensated by one or more proposed modifications correspondingly reducing expenditure, the Council may, acting by a qualified majority, reject the proposed modification. In the absence of a decision to reject it, the proposed modification shall stand as accepted;

• where a modification proposed by the European Parliament has the effect of increasing the total amount of the expenditure of an institution, the Council may, acting by a qualified majority, accept this proposed modification. In the absence of a decision to accept it, the proposed modification shall stand as rejected;

• where, in pursuance of one of the two preceding subparagraphs, the Council has rejected a proposed modification, it may, acting by a qualified majority, either retain the amount shown in the draft budget or fix another amount.

The draft budget shall be

modified on the basis of the proposed modifications accepted by the Council.

If, within 15 days of the draft being placed before it, the Council has not modified any of the amendments adopted by the European Parliament and if the modifications proposed by the latter have been accepted, the budget shall be deemed to be finally adopted. The Council shall inform the European Parliament that it has not modified any of the amendments and that the proposed modifications have been accepted.

If within the period the Council has modified one or more of the amendments adopted by the European Parliament or if the modifications proposed by the latter have been rejected or modified, the modified draft budget shall again be forwarded to the European Parliament. The Council shall inform the European Parliament of the results of its deliberations.

6 Within 15 days of the draft budget being placed before it, the European Parliament, which shall have been notified of the action taken on its proposed modifications, may, acting by a majority of its members and three-fifths of the votes cast, amend or reject the modifications to its amendments made by the Council and shall adopt the budget accordingly. If within this period the European Parliament has not acted, the budget shall be deemed to be finally adopted.

7 When the procedure provided for in this Article has been completed, the President of the European Parliament shall declare that the budget has been finally adopted.

8 However, the European Parliament, acting by a majority of its members and two-thirds of the votes cast, may, if there are important reasons, reject the draft budget and ask for a new draft to be submitted to it.

9 A maximum rate of increase in relation to the expenditure of the same type to be incurred during the current year shall be fixed annually for the total expenditure other than that necessarily resulting from this Treaty or from acts adopted in accordance therewith.

The Commission shall, after consulting the Economic Policy Committee, declare what this maximum rate is as it results from:

- the trend, in terms of volume, of the gross national product within the Community;
- the average variation in the budgets of the Member States; and
- the trend of the cost of living during the preceding financial year.

The maximum rate shall be communicated, before 1 May, to all the institutions of the Community. The latter shall be required to conform to this during the budgetary procedure, subject to the provisions of the fourth and fifth subparagraphs of this paragraph.

If, in respect of expenditure other than that necessarily resulting from this Treaty or from acts adopted in accordance therewith, the actual rate of increase in the draft budget established by the Council is over half the maximum rate, the European Parliament may, exercising its right of amendment, further increase the total amount of that expenditure to a limit not exceeding half the maximum rate.

Where the European Parliament, the Council or the Commission consider that the activities of the Communities require that the rate determined according to the procedure laid down in this paragraph should be exceeded, another rate may be fixed by agreement between the Council, acting by a qualified majority, and the European Parliament, acting by a majority of its members and three-fifths of the votes cast.

10 Each institution shall exercise the powers conferred upon it by this Article, with due regard for the provisions of the Treaty and for acts adopted in accordance therewith, in particular those relating to the Communities' own resources and to the balance between revenue and expenditure.

Article 204

If at the beginning of a financial year, the budget has not yet been voted, a sum equivalent to not more than one-twelfth of the budget appropriations for the preceding financial year may be spent each month in respect of any chapter or other subdivision of the budget in accordance with the provisions of the Regulations made pursuant to Article 209; this arrangement shall not, however, have the effect of placing at the disposal of the Commission appropriations in excess of one-twelfth of those provided for in the draft budget in course of preparation.

The Council may, acting by a qualified majority, provided that the other conditions laid down in the first subparagraph are observed, authorise expenditure in excess of one-twelfth.

If the decision relates to expenditure which does not necessarily result from this Treaty or from acts adopted in accordance therewith, the Council shall forward it immediately to the European Parliament; within 30 days the European Parliament, acting by a majority of its members and three-fifths of the votes cast, may adopt a different decision on the expenditure in excess of the one-twelfth referred to in the first subparagraph. This part of the decision of the Council shall be suspended until the European Parliament has taken its decision. If within the said period the European Parliament has not taken a decision which differs from the decision of the Council, the latter shall be deemed to be finally adopted.

The decisions referred to in the second and third subparagraphs shall lay down the necessary measures relating to resources to ensure application of this Article.

Article 205

The Commission shall implement the budget, in accordance with the provisions of the regulations made pursuant to Article 209, on its own responsibility and within the limits of the appropriations, **having regard to the principles of sound financial management.**

The regulations shall lay down detailed rules for each institution concerning its part in effecting its own expenditure.

Within the budget, the Commission may, subject to the limits and conditions laid down in the regulations made pursuant to Article 209, transfer appropriations from one chapter to another or from one sub-division to another.

Article 205a

The Commission shall submit annually to the Council and to the European Parliament the accounts of the preceding financial year relating to the implementation of the budget. The Commission shall also forward to them a financial statement of the assets and liabilities of the Community.

Article 206

1 [] The European Parliament, acting on a recommendation from the Council which shall act by a qualified majority, shall give a discharge to the Commission in respect of the implementation of the budget. To this end, the Council and the European Parliament in turn shall examine the accounts and the financial statement referred to in Article 205a, the annual report by the Court of Auditors together with the replies of the institutions under audit to the observations of the Court of Auditors and any relevant special reports by the Court of Auditors.

2 Before giving a discharge to the Commission, or for any other purpose in connection with the exercise of its powers over the implementation of the budget, the European Parliament may ask to hear the Commission give evidence with regard to the execution of expenditure or the operation of financial control systems. The Commission shall submit any necessary information to the European Parliament at the latter's request.

3 The Commission shall take all appropriate steps to act on the observations in the decisions giving discharge and on other observations by the European Parliament relating to the execution of expenditure, as well as on comments accompanying the recommendations on discharge adopted by the Council.

At the request of the European Parliament or the Council, the Commission shall report on the measures taken in the light of these observations and comments and in particular on the instructions given to the departments which are responsible for the implementation of the budget. These reports shall also be forwarded to the Court of Auditors.

Article 206a (repealed by Maastricht Treaty)

Article 206b (repealed by Maastricht Treaty)

Article 207

The budget shall be drawn up in the unit of account determined in accordance with the provisions of the regulations made pursuant to Article 209.

The financial contributions provided for in Article 200(1) shall be placed at the disposal of the Community by the Member States in their national currencies.*

The available balances of these contributions shall be deposited with the Treasuries of Member States or with bodies designated by them. While on deposit, such funds shall retain the value corresponding to the parity, at the date of deposit, in relation to the unit of account referred to in the first paragraph.*

The balances may be invested on terms to be agreed between the Commission and the Member State concerned.*

[* No longer relevant in view of the fact that the budget shall be financed wholly from own resources. See Article 200 (repealed) and Article 201.]

The regulations made pursuant to Article 209 shall lay down the technical conditions under which financial operations relating to the European Social Fund shall be carried out.

Article 208

The Commission may, provided it notifies the competent authorities of the Member States concerned, transfer into the currency of one of the Member States its holdings in the currency of another Member State, to the extent necessary to enable them to be used for purposes which come within the scope of this Treaty. The Commission shall as far as possible avoid making such transfers if it possesses cash or liquid assets in the currencies which it needs.

The Commission shall deal with each Member State through the authority designated by the State concerned. In carrying out financial operations the Commission shall employ the services of the bank of issue of the Member State concerned or of any other financial institution approved by that State.

Article 209

The Council, acting unanimously on a proposal from the Commission and after consulting the European Parliament and obtaining the opinion of the Court of Auditors, shall:

(a) make Financial Regulations specifying in particular the procedure to be adopted for establishing and implementing the budget and for presenting and auditing accounts;

(b) determine the methods and procedure whereby the budget revenue provided under the arrangements relating to the Communities' own resources shall be made available to the Commission, and determine the measures to be applied, if need be, to meet cash requirements;

(c) lay down rules concerning the responsibility of **financial controllers**, authorising officers and accounting officers, and concerning appropriate arrangements for inspection.

Article 209a

Member States shall take the same measures to counter fraud affecting the financial interests of the Community as they take to counter fraud affecting their own financial interests.

Without prejudice to other provisions of this Treaty, Member States shall co-ordinate their action aimed at protecting the financial interests of the Community against fraud. To this end they shall organise, with the help of the Commission, close and regular co-operation between the competent departments of their administrations.

Part Six
General and Final Provisions

Article 210

The Community shall have legal personality.

Article 211

In each of the Member States, the Community shall enjoy the most extensive legal capacity accorded to legal persons under their laws; it may, in particular, acquire or dispose of moveable and immoveable property and may be a party to legal proceedings. To this end, the Community shall be represented by the Commission.

Article 212 (as replaced by Merger Treaty, Article 24(1))

The officials and other servants of the European Coal and Steel Community, the European Economic Community and the European Atomic Energy Community shall, at the date of entry into force of this Treaty, become officials and other servants of the European Communities and form part of the single administration of those Communities.

The Council shall, acting by a qualified majority on a proposal from the Commission and after consulting the other institutions concerned, lay down the Staff Regulations of officials of the European Communities and the Conditions of Employment of other servants of those Communities.

Article 213

The Commission may, within the limits and under conditions laid down by the Council in accordance with the provisions of this Treaty, collect any information and carry out any checks required for the performance of the tasks entrusted to it.

Article 214

The members of the institutions of the Community, the members of committees, and the officials and other servants of the Community shall be required, even after their duties have ceased, not to disclose information of the kind covered by the obligation of professional secrecy, in particular information about undertakings, their business relations or their cost components.

Article 215

The contractual liability of the Community shall be governed by the law applicable to the contract in question.

In the case of non-contractual liability, the Community shall, in accordance with the general principles common to the laws of the Member States, make good any damage caused by its institutions or by its servants in the performance of their duties.

The preceding paragraph shall apply under the same conditions to damage caused by the ECB or by its servants in the performance of their duties.

The personal liability of its servants towards the Community shall be governed by the provisions laid down in their Staff Regulations or in the Conditions of Employment applicable to them.

Article 216

The seat of the institutions of the Community shall be determined by common accord of the Governments of the Member States.

Article 217

The rules governing the languages of the institutions of the Community shall, without prejudice to the provisions contained in the rules of procedure of the Court of Justice, be determined by the Council, acting unanimously.

Article 218 (as replaced by Merger Treaty, Article 28(1))

The European Communities shall enjoy in the territories of the Member States such privileges and immunities as are necessary for the performance of their tasks, under the conditions laid down in the Protocol annexed to this Treaty. The same shall apply to the European Investment Bank.

Article 219

Member States undertake not to submit a dispute concerning the interpretation or application of this Treaty to any method of settlement other than those provided for therein.

Article 220

Member States shall, so far as is necessary, enter into negotiations with each other with a view to securing for the benefit of their nationals:

- the protection of persons and

the enjoyment and protection of rights under the same conditions as those accorded by each State to its own nationals;
- the abolition of double taxation within the Community;
- the mutual recognition of companies or firms within the meaning of the second paragraph of Article 58, the retention of legal personality in the event of transfer of their seat from one country to another, and the possibility of mergers between companies or firms governed by the laws of different countries;
- the simplification of formalities governing the reciprocal recognition and enforcement of judgments of courts or tribunals and of arbitration awards.

Article 221

Within three years of the entry into force of this Treaty, Member States shall accord nationals of the other Member States the same treatment as their own nationals as regards participation in the capital of companies or firms within the meaning of Article 58, without prejudice to the application of the other provisions of this Treaty.

Article 222

This Treaty shall in no way prejudice the rules in Member States governing the system of property ownership.

Article 223

1 The provisions of this Treaty shall not preclude the application of the following rules:

(a) No Member State shall be obliged to supply information

the disclosure of which it considers contrary to the essential interests of its security;

(b) Any Member State may take such measures as it considers necessary for the protection of the essential interests of its security which are connected with the production of or trade in arms, munitions and war material; such measures shall not adversely affect the conditions of competition in the common market regarding products which are not intended for specifically military purposes.

2   During the first year after the entry into force of this Treaty, the Council shall, acting unanimously, draw up a list of products to which the provisions of paragraph 1(b) shall apply.

3   The Council may, acting unanimously on a proposal from the Commission, make changes in this list.

Article 224

Member States shall consult each other with a view to taking together the steps needed to prevent the functioning of the common market being affected by measures which a Member State may be called upon to take in the event of serious internal disturbances affecting the maintenance of law and order, in the event of war, serious international tension constituting a threat of war, or in order to carry out obligations it has accepted for the purpose of maintaining peace and international security.

Article 225

If measures taken in the circum-stances referred to in Articles 223 and 224 have the effect of distorting the conditions of competition in the Common Market, the Commission shall, together with the State concerned, examine how these measures can be adjusted to the rules laid down in this Treaty.

By way of derogation from the procedure laid down in Articles 169 and 170, the Commission or any Member State may bring the matter directly before the Court of Justice if it considers that another Member State is making improper use of the powers provided for in Articles 223 and 224. The Court of Justice shall give its ruling "in camera".

Article 226

1   If, during the transitional period, difficulties arise which are serious and liable to persist in any sector of the economy or which could bring about serious deterioration in the economic situation of a given area, a Member State may apply for authorisation to take protective measures in order to rectify the situation and adjust the sector concerned to the economy of the common market.

2   On application by the State concerned, the Commission shall, by emergency procedure, determine without delay the protective measures which it considers necessary, specifying the circumstances and the manner in which they are to be put into effect.

3   The measures authorised under paragraph 2 may involve derogations from the rules of this Treaty, to such an extent and for such periods as are strictly necessary in order to attain the objectives referred to in paragraph 1. Priority

shall be given to such measures as will least disturb the functioning of the common market.

Article 227

1 This Treaty shall apply to the Kingdom of Belgium, the Kingdom of Denmark, the Federal Republic of Germany, the Hellenic Republic, the Kingdom of Spain, the French Republic, Ireland, the Italian Republic, the Grand Duchy of Luxembourg, the Kingdom of the Netherlands, *the Republic of Austria*, the Portuguese Republic, *the Republic of Finland, the Kingdom of Sweden* and the United Kingdom of Great Britain and Northern Ireland.

2 With regard to [] the French overseas departments, the general and particular provisions of this Treaty relating to:
- the free movement of goods;
- agriculture, save for Article 40(4);
- the liberalisation of services;
- the rules on competition;
- the protective measures provided for in Articles [] **109h, 109i** and 226;
- the institutions,

shall apply as soon as this Treaty enters into force.

The conditions under which the other provisions of this Treaty are to apply shall be determined, within two years of the entry into force of this Treaty, by decisions of the Council, acting unanimously on a proposal from the Commission.

The institutions of the Community will, within the framework of the procedures provided for in this Treaty, in particular Article 226, take care that the economic and social development of these areas is made possible.

3 The special arrangements for association set out in Part Four of this Treaty shall apply to the overseas countries and territories listed in Annex IV to this Treaty.

This Treaty shall not apply to those overseas countries and territories having special relations with the United Kingdom of Great Britain and Northern Ireland which are not included in the aforementioned list.

4 The provisions of this Treaty shall apply to the European territories for whose external relations a Member State is responsible.

5 Notwithstanding the preceding paragraphs:

(a) **This Treaty shall not apply to the Faroe Islands. []**

(b) This Treaty shall not apply to the Sovereign Base Areas of the United Kingdom of Great Britain and Northern Ireland in Cyprus.

(c) This Treaty shall apply to the Channel Islands and the Isle of Man only to the extent necessary to ensure the implementation of the arrangements for those islands set out in the Treaty concerning the accession of new Member States to the European Economic Community and to the European Atomic Energy Community signed on 22 January 1972.

(d) This Treaty shall not apply to the Åland islands. The Government of Finland may, however, give notice, by a declaration deposited when ratifying this Treaty with the Government of the Italian Republic, that the Treaty shall apply to the Åland islands in accordance with the provisions set out in Protocol No 2 to the Act concerning the conditions of accession of the

Republic of Austria, the Republic of Finland and the Kingdom of Sweden and the adjustments to the Treaties on which the European Union is founded. The Government of the Italian Republic shall transmit a certified copy of any such declaration to the Member States.

Article 228

1 Where this Treaty provides for the conclusion of agreements between the Community and one or more States or [] international organisations, the Commission shall make recommendations to the Council, which shall authorise the Commission to open the necessary negotiations. The Commission shall conduct these negotiations in consultation with special committees appointed by the Council to assist it in this task and within the framework of such directives as the Council may issue to it.

In exercising the powers conferred upon it by this paragraph, the Council shall act by a qualified majority, except in the cases provided for in the second sentence of paragraph 2, for which it shall act unanimously.

2 Subject to the powers vested in the Commission in this field, the agreements shall be concluded by the Council, acting by a qualified majority on a proposal from the Commission. The Council shall act unanimously when the agreement covers a field for which unanimity is required for the adoption of internal rules, and for the agreements referred to in Article 238.

3 The Council shall conclude agreements after consulting the European Parliament, except for the agreements referred to in Article 113(3), including cases where the agreement covers a field for which the procedure referred to in Article 189b or that referred to in Article 189c is required for the adoption of internal rules. The European Parliament shall deliver its opinion within a time limit which the Council may lay down according to the urgency of the matter. In the absence of an opinion within that time limit, the Council may act.

By way of derogation from the previous subparagraph, agreements referred to in Article 238, other agreements establishing a specific institutional framework by organising co-operation procedures, agreements having important budgetary implications for the Community and agreements entailing amendment of an act adopted under the procedure referred to in Article 189b shall be concluded after the assent of the European Parliament has been obtained.

The Council and the European Parliament may, in an urgent situation, agree upon a time limit for the assent.

4 When concluding an agreement, the Council may, by way of derogation from paragraph 2, authorise the Commission to approve modifications on behalf of the Community where the agreement provides for them to be adopted by a simplified procedure or by a body set up by the agreement; it may attach specific conditions to such authorisation.

5 When the Council envisages concluding an agreement which calls for amendments to this Treaty, the amendments must first be adopted in accordance with the procedure laid down in Article N of the Treaty on European Union.

6 The Council, the Commission or

a Member State may obtain the opinion of the Court of Justice as to whether an agreement envisaged is compatible with the provisions of this Treaty. Where the opinion of the Court of Justice is adverse, the agreement may enter into force only in accordance with Article N of the Treaty on European Union.

7 Agreements concluded under the conditions set out in this Article shall be binding on the institutions of the Community and on Member States.

Article 228a

Where it is provided, in a common position or in a joint action adopted according to the provisions of the Treaty on European Union relating to the common foreign and security policy, for an action by the Community to interrupt or to reduce, in part or completely, economic relations with one or more third countries, the Council shall take the necessary urgent measures. The Council shall act by a qualified majority on a proposal from the Commission.

Article 229

It shall be for the Commission to ensure the maintenance of all appropriate relations with the organs of the United Nations, of its specialised agencies and of the General Agreement on Tariffs and Trade.

The Commission shall also maintain such relations as are appropriate with all international organisations.

Article 230

The Community shall establish all appropriate forms of co-operation with the Council of Europe.

Article 231

The Community shall establish close co-operation with the Organisation for [] Economic Co-operation and Development, the details of which shall be determined by common accord.

Article 232

1 The provisions of this Treaty shall not affect the provisions of the Treaty establishing the European Coal and Steel Community, in particular as regards the rights and obligations of Member States, the powers of the institutions of that Community and the rules laid down by that Treaty for the functioning of the common market in coal and steel.

2 The provisions of this Treaty shall not derogate from those of the Treaty establishing the European Atomic Energy Community.

Article 233

The provisions of this Treaty shall not preclude the existence or completion of regional unions between Belgium and Luxembourg, or between Belgium, Luxembourg and the Netherlands, to the extent that the objectives of these regional unions are not attained by application of this Treaty.

Article 234

The rights and obligations arising from agreements concluded before the entry into force of this Treaty between one or more Member States on the one hand, and one or more third countries on the other, shall not be affected by the provisions of this Treaty.

To the extent that such agreements are not compatible with this Treaty, the Member State or States concerned shall take all appropriate steps to eliminate the incompatibilities established. Member States shall, where necessary, assist each other to this end and shall, where appropriate, adopt a common attitude.

In applying the agreements referred to in the first paragraph, Member States shall take into account the fact that the advantages accorded under this Treaty by each Member State form an integral part of the establishment of the Community and are thereby inseparably linked with the creation of common institutions, the conferring of powers upon them and the granting of the same advantages by all the other Member States.

Article 235

If action by the Community should prove necessary to attain, in the course of the operation of the common market, one of the objectives of the Community and this Treaty has not provided the necessary powers, the Council shall, acting unanimously on a proposal from the Commission and after consulting the European Parliament, take the appropriate measures.

Article 236 (repealed by Maastricht Treaty)

Article 237 (repealed by Maastricht Treaty)

Article 238

The Community may conclude with [] **one or more States or interna-**

tional organisations agreements establishing an association involving reciprocal rights and obligations, common action and special procedures. []

Article 239

The Protocols annexed to this Treaty by common accord of the Member States shall form an integral part thereof.

Article 240

This Treaty is concluded for an unlimited period.

Setting up of the institutions

Article 241

The Council shall meet within one month of the entry into force of this Treaty.

Article 242

The Council shall, within three months of its first meeting, take all appropriate measures to constitute the Economic and Social Committee.

Article 243

The Assembly shall meet within two months of the first meeting of the Council, having been convened by the President of the Council, in order to elect its officers and draw up its rules of procedure. Pending the election of its officers, the oldest member shall take the chair.

Article 244

The Court of Justice shall take up its duties as soon as its members have been appointed. Its first President shall be appointed for three years in the same manner as its members.

The Court of Justice shall adopt its rules of procedure within three months of taking up its duties.

No matter may be brought before the Court of Justice until its rules of procedure have been published. The time within which an action must be brought shall run only from the date of this publication.

Upon his appointment, the President of the Court of Justice shall exercise the powers conferred upon him by this Treaty.

Article 245

The Commission shall take up its duties and assume the responsibilities conferred upon it by this Treaty as soon as its members have been appointed.

Upon taking up its duties, the Commission shall undertake the studies and arrange the contacts needed for making an overall survey of the economic situation of the Community.

Article 246

1 The first financial year shall run from the date on which this Treaty enters into force until 31 December following. Should this Treaty, however, enter into force during the second half of the year, the first financial year shall run until 31 December of the following year.

2 Until the budget for the first financial year has been established, Member States shall make the Community interest-free advances which shall be deducted from their financial contributions to the implementation of the budget.

3 Until the Staff Regulations of officials and the Conditions of

Employment of other servants of the Community provided for in Article 212 have been laid down, each institution shall recruit the Staff it needs and to this end conclude contracts of limited duration.

Each institution shall examine together with the Council any question concerning the number, remuneration and distribution of posts.

Final provisions

Article 247

This Treaty shall be ratified by the High Contracting Parties in accordance with their respective constitutional requirements. The instruments of ratification shall be deposited with the Government of the Italian Republic.

This Treaty shall enter into force on the first day of the month following the deposit of the instrument of ratification by the last signatory State to take this step. If, however, such deposit is made less than 15 days before the beginning of the following month, this Treaty shall not enter into force until the first day of the second month after the date of such deposit.

Article 248

This Treaty, drawn up in a single original in the Dutch, French, German and Italian languages, all four texts being equally authentic, shall be deposited in the archives of the Government of the Italian Republic, which shall transmit a certified copy to each of the Governments of the other signatory States.

Protocol
on the excessive deficit procedure

THE HIGH CONTRACTING PARTIES,

DESIRING to lay down the details of the excessive deficit procedure referred to in Article 104c of the Treaty establishing the European Community,

HAVE AGREED upon the following provisions, which shall be annexed to the Treaty establishing the European Community:

Article 1

The reference values referred to in Article 104c(2) of this Treaty are:
- 3% for the ratio of the planned or actual government deficit to gross domestic product at market prices;
- 60% for the ratio of government debt to gross domestic product at market prices.

Article 2

In Article 104c of this Treaty and in this Protocol:
- government means general government, that is central government, regional or local government and social security funds, to the exclusion of commercial operations, as defined in the European System of Integrated Economic Accounts;
- deficit means net borrowing as defined in the European System of Integrated Economic Accounts;
- investment means gross fixed capital formation as defined in the European System of Integrated Economic Accounts;
- debt means total gross debt at nominal value outstanding at the end of the year and consolidated between and within the sectors of general government as defined in the first indent.

Article 3

In order to ensure the effectiveness of the excessive deficit procedure, the governments of the Member States shall be responsible under this procedure for the deficits of general government as defined in the first indent of Article 2. The Member States shall ensure that national procedures in the budgetary area enable them to meet their obligations in this area deriving from this Treaty. The Member States shall report their planned and actual deficits and the levels of their debt promptly and regularly to the Commission.

Article 4

The statistical data to be used for the application of this Protocol shall be provided by the Commission.

Protocol
on the convergence criteria referred to in Article 109j of the Treaty establishing the European Community

THE HIGH CONTRACTING PARTIES,

DESIRING to lay down the details of the convergence criteria which shall guide the Community in taking decisions on the passage to the third stage of economic and monetary union, referred to in Article 109j(1) of this Treaty,

HAVE AGREED upon the following provisions, which shall be annexed to the Treaty establishing the European Community:

Article 1

The criterion on price stability referred to in the first indent of Article 109j(1) of this Treaty shall mean that a Member State has a price performance that is sustainable and an average rate of inflation, observed over a period of one year before the examination, that does not exceed by more than 1½ percentage points that of, at most, the three best performing Member States in terms of price stability. Inflation shall be measured by means of the consumer price index on a comparable basis, taking into account differences in national definitions.

Article 2

The criterion on the government budgetary position referred to in the second indent of Article 109j(1) of this Treaty shall mean that at the time of the examination the Member State is not the subject of a Council decision under Article 104c(6) of this Treaty that an excessive deficit exists.

Article 3

The criterion on participation in the Exchange Rate Mechanism of the European Monetary System referred to in the third indent of Article 109j(1) of this Treaty shall mean that a Member State has respected the normal fluctuation margins provided for by the Exchange Rate Mechanism of the European Monetary System without severe tensions for at least the last two years before the examination. In particular, the Member State shall not have devalued its currency's bilateral central rate against any other Member State's currency on its own initiative for the same period.

Article 4

The criterion on the convergence of interest rates referred to in the fourth indent of Article 109j(1) of this Treaty shall mean that, observed over a period of one year before the examination, a Member State has had an average nominal long-term interest rate that does not exceed by more than 2 percentage points that of, at most, the three best performing Member States in terms of price stability. Interest rates shall be measured on the basis of long-term government bonds or comparable securities, taking into account differences in national definitions.

Article 5

The statistical data to be used for the application of this Protocol shall be provided by the Commission.

Article 6

The Council shall, acting unanimously on a proposal from the Commission and after consulting the European Parliament, the EMI or the ECB as the case may be, and the Committee referred to in Article 109c, adopt appropriate provisions to lay down the details of the convergence criteria referred to in Article 109j of this Treaty, which shall then replace this Protocol.

Protocol
on the transition to the third stage of Economic and Monetary Union

THE HIGH CONTRACTING PARTIES,

Declare the irreversible character of the Community's movement to the third stage of Economic and Monetary Union by signing the new Treaty provisions on Economic and Monetary Union.

Therefore all Member States shall, whether they fulfil the necessary conditions for the adoption of a single currency or not, respect the will for the Community to enter swiftly into the third stage, and therefore no Member State shall prevent the entering into the third stage.

If by the end of 1997 the date of the beginning of the third stage has not been set, the Member States concerned, the Community institutions and other bodies involved shall expedite all preparatory work during 1998, in order to enable the Community to enter the third stage irrevocably on 1 January 1999 and to enable the ECB and the ESCB to start their full functioning from this date.

This Protocol shall be annexed to the Treaty establishing the European Community.

Protocol
on certain provisions relating to the United
Kingdom of Great Britain and Northern Ireland

THE HIGH CONTRACTING PARTIES,

RECOGNISING that the United Kingdom shall not be obliged or committed to move to the third stage of Economic and Monetary Union without a separate decision to do so by its government and Parliament,

NOTING the practice of the government of the United Kingdom to fund its borrowing requirement by the sale of debt to the private sector,

HAVE AGREED the following provisions, which shall be annexed to the Treaty establishing the European Community;

1 The United Kingdom shall notify the Council whether it intends to move to the third stage before the Council makes its assessment under Article 109j(2) of this Treaty.
   Unless the United Kingdom notifies the Council that it intends to move to the third stage, it shall be under no obligation to do so.
   If no date is set for the beginning of the third stage under Article 109j(3) of this Treaty, the United Kingdom may notify its intention to move to the third stage before 1 January 1998.
2 Paragraphs 3 to 9 shall have effect if the United Kingdom notifies the Council that it does not intend to move to the third stage.
3 The United Kingdom shall not be included among the majority of Member States which fulfil the necessary conditions referred to in the second indent of Article 109j(2) and the first indent of Article 109j(3) of this Treaty.
4 The United Kingdom shall retain its powers in the field of monetary policy according to national law.
5 Articles 3a(2), 104c(1), (9) and (11), 105(1) to (5), 105a, 107, 108, 108a, 109, 109a(1) and (2)(b) and 109l(4) and (5) of this Treaty shall not apply to the United Kingdom. In these provisions references to the Community or the Member States shall not include the United Kingdom and references to national central banks shall not include the Bank of England.
6 Articles 109e(4) and 109h and i of this Treaty shall continue to apply to the United Kingdom. Articles 109c(4) and 109m shall apply to the United Kingdom as if it had a derogation.
7 The voting rights of the United Kingdom shall be suspended in respect of acts of the Council referred to in the Articles listed in paragraph 5. For this purpose the weighted votes of the United Kingdom shall be excluded from any calculation of a qualified majority under Article 109k(5) of this Treaty.
   The United Kingdom shall also have no right to participate in the appointment of the President, the Vice-President and the other members of the Executive Board of the ECB under Articles 109a(2)(b) and 109l(1) of this Treaty.

8   Articles 3, 4, 6, 7, 9.2, 10.1, 10.3, 11.2, 12.1, 14, 16, 18 to 20, 22, 23, 26, 27, 30 to 34, 50 and 52 of the Protocol on the Statute of the European System of Central Banks and of the European Central Bank ("the Statute") shall not apply to the United Kingdom.

In those Articles, references to the Community or the Member States shall not include the United Kingdom and references to national central banks or shareholders shall not include the Bank of England.

References in Articles 10.3 and 30.2 of the Statute to "subscribed capital of the ECB" shall not include capital subscribed by the Bank of England.

9   Article 109l(3) of this Treaty and Articles 44 to 48 of the Statute shall have effect, whether or not there is any Member State with a derogation, subject to the following amendments:

(a)   References in Article 44 to the tasks of the ECB and the EMI shall include those tasks that still need to be performed in the third stage owing to any decision of the United Kingdom not to move to that stage.

(b)   In addition to the tasks referred to in Article 47 the ECB shall also give advice in relation to and contribute to the preparation of any decision of the Council with regard to the United Kingdom taken in accordance with paragraphs 10(a) and 10(c).

(c)   The Bank of England shall pay up its subscription to the capital of the ECB as a contribution to its operational costs on the same basis as national central banks of Member States with a derogation.

10   If the United Kingdom does not move to the third stage, it may change its notification at any time after the beginning of that stage. In that event:

(a)   The United Kingdom shall have the right to move to the third stage provided only that it satisfies the necessary conditions. The Council, acting at the request of the United Kingdom and under the conditions and in accordance with the procedure laid down in Article 109k(2) of this Treaty, shall decide whether it fulfils the necessary conditions.

(b)   The Bank of England shall pay up its subscribed capital, transfer to the ECB foreign reserve assets and contribute to its reserves on the same basis as the national central bank of a Member State whose derogation has been abrogated.

(c)   The Council, acting under the conditions and in accordance with the procedure laid down in Article 109l(5) of this Treaty, shall take all other necessary decisions to enable the United Kingdom to move to the third stage.

If the United Kingdom moves to the third stage pursuant to the provisions of this protocol, paragraphs 3 to 9 shall cease to have effect.

11   Notwithstanding Articles 104 and 109e(3) of this Treaty and Article 21.1 of the Statute, the government of the United Kingdom may maintain its Ways and Means facility with the Bank of England if and so long as the United Kingdom does not move to the third stage.

Protocol
on social policy

THE HIGH CONTRACTING PARTIES,

NOTING that eleven Member States, that is to say the Kingdom of Belgium, the Kingdom of Denmark, the Federal Republic of Germany, the Hellenic Republic, the Kingdom of Spain, the French Republic, Ireland, the Italian Republic, the Grand Duchy of Luxembourg, the Kingdom of the Netherlands and the Portuguese Republic, wish to continue along the path laid down in the 1989 Social Charter; that they have adopted among themselves an Agreement to this end; that this Agreement is annexed to this Protocol; that this Protocol and the said Agreement are without prejudice to the provisions of this Treaty, particularly those relating to social policy which constitute an integral part of the "acquis communautaire":

1 Agree to authorise those eleven Member States to have recourse to the institutions, procedures and mechanisms of the Treaty for the purposes of taking among themselves and applying as far as they are concerned the acts and decisions required for giving effect to the abovementioned Agreement.

2 The United Kingdom of Great Britain and Northern Ireland shall not take part in the deliberations and the adoption by the Council of Commission proposals made on the basis of this Protocol and the abovementioned Agreement.

By way of derogation from Article 148(2) of the Treaty, acts of the Council which are made pursuant to this Protocol and which must be adopted by qualified majority shall be deemed adopted if they have received at least 52 votes in favour. The unanimity of the members of the Council, with the exception of the United Kingdom of Great Britain and Northern Ireland, shall be necessary for acts of the Council which must be adopted unanimously and for those amending the Commission proposal.

Acts adopted by the Council and any financial consequences other than administrative costs entailed for the institutions shall not be applicable to the United Kingdom of Great Britain and Northern Ireland.

3 This Protocol shall be annexed to the Treaty establishing the European Community.

Agreement
on social policy concluded between the Member States of the European Community with the exception of the United Kingdom of Great Britain and Northern Ireland

The undersigned eleven HIGH CONTRACTING PARTIES, that is to say the Kingdom of Belgium, the Kingdom of Denmark, the Federal Republic of Germany, the Hellenic Republic, the Kingdom of Spain, the French Republic, Ireland, the Italian Republic, the Grand Duchy of Luxembourg, the Kingdom of the Netherlands and the Portuguese Republic (hereinafter referred to as "the Member States"),

WISHING to implement the 1989 Social Charter on the basis of the "acquis communautaire",

CONSIDERING the Protocol of social policy,

HAVE AGREED as follows:

Article 1

The Community and the Member States shall have as their objectives the promotion of employment, improved living and working conditions, proper social protection, dialogue between management and labour, the development of human resources with a view to lasting high employment and the combatting of exclusion. To this end the Community and the Member States shall implement measures which take account of the diverse forms of national practices, in particular in the field of contractual relations, and the need to maintain the competitiveness of the Community economy.

Article 2

1 With a view to achieving the objectives of Article 1, the Community shall support and complement the activities of the Member States in the following fields:

- improvement in particular of the working environment to protect workers' health and safety;
- working conditions;
- the information and consultation of workers;
- equality between men and women with regard to labour market opportunities and treatment at work;
- the integration of persons excluded from the labour market, without prejudice to Article 127 of the Treaty establishing the European Community (hereinafter referred to as "the Treaty").

2 To this end, the Council may adopt, by means of directives, minimum requirements for gradual implementation, having regard to the conditions and technical rules obtaining in each of the Member States. Such directives shall avoid imposing administrative, financial and legal constraints in a way

which would hold back the creation and development of small and medium-sized undertakings.

The Council shall act in accordance with the procedure referred to in Article 189c of the Treaty after consulting the Economic and Social Committee.

3   However, the Council shall act unanimously on a proposal from the Commission, after consulting the European Parliament and the Economic and Social Committee, in the following areas:

- social security and social protection of workers;
- protection of workers where their employment contract is terminated;
- representation and collective defence of the interests of workers and employers, including co-determination, subject to paragraph 6;
- conditions of employment for third-country nationals legally residing in Community territory;
- financial contribution for promotion of employment and job-creation, without prejudice to the provisions relating to the Social Fund.

4   A Member State may entrust management and labour, at their joint request, with the implementation of directives adopted pursuant to paragraphs 2 and 3.

In this case, it shall ensure that, no later than the date on which a directive must be transposed in accordance with Article 189, management and labour have introduced the necessary measures by agreement, the Member State concerned being required to take any necessary measure enabling it at any time to be in a position to guarantee the results imposed by that directive.

5   The provisions adopted pursuant to this Article shall not prevent any Member State from maintaining or introducing more stringent protective measures compatible with the Treaty.

6   The provisions of this Article shall not apply to pay, the right of association, the right to strike or the right to impose lock-outs.

Article 3

1   The Commission shall have the task of promoting the consultation of management and labour at Community level and shall take any relevant measure to facilitate their dialogue by ensuring balanced support for the parties.

2   To this end, before submitting proposals in the social policy field, the Commission shall consult management and labour on the possible direction of Community action.

3   If, after such consultation, the Commission considers Community action advisable, it shall consult management and labour on the content of the envisaged proposal. Management and labour shall forward to the Commission an opinion or, where appropriate, a recommendation.

4   On the occasion of such consultation, management and labour may inform the Commission of their wish to initiate the process provided for in Article 4. The duration of the procedure shall not exceed nine months, unless the management and labour concerned and the Commission decide jointly to extend it.

Article 4

1   Should management and labour so desire, the dialogue between

them at Community level may lead to contractual relations, including agreements.

2 Agreements concluded at Community level shall be implemented either in accordance with the procedures and practices specific to management and labour and the Member States or, in matters covered by Article 2, at the joint request of the signatory parties, by a Council decision on a proposal from the Commission.

The Council shall act by qualified majority, except where the agreement in question contains one or more provisions relating to one of the areas referred to in Article 2(3), in which case it shall act unanimously.

Article 5

With a view to achieving the objectives of Article 1 and without prejudice to the other provisions of the Treaty, the Commission shall encourage cooperation between the Member States and facilitate the coordination of their action in all social policy fields under this Agreement.

Article 6

1 Each Member State shall ensure that the principle of equal pay for male and female workers for equal work is applied.

2 For the purpose of this Article, "pay" means the ordinary basic or minimum wage or salary and any other consideration, whether in cash or in kind, which the worker receives directly or indirectly, in respect of his employment, from his employer.

Equal pay without discrimination based on sex means:

(a) that pay for the same work at piece rates shall be calculated on the basis of the same unit of measurement;

(b) that pay for work at time rates shall be the same for the same job.

3 This Article shall not prevent any Member State from maintaining or adopting measures providing for specific advantages in order to make it easier for women to pursue a vocational activity or to prevent or compensate for disadvantages in their professional careers.

Article 7

The Commission shall draw up a report each year on progress in achieving the objectives of Article 1, including the demographic situation in the Community. It shall forward the report to the European Parliament, the Council and the Economic and Social Committee.

The European Parliament may invite the Commission to draw up reports on particular problems concerning the social situation.

Declarations

1. Declaration on Article 2(2)

The eleven High Contracting Parties note that in the discussions on Article 2(2) of the Agreement it was agreed that the Community does not intend, in laying down minimum requirements for the protection of the safety and health of employees, to discriminate in a manner unjustified by the circumstances against employees in small and medium-sized undertakings.

2. Declaration on Article 4(2)

The eleven High Contracting Parties declare that the first of the arrangements for application of the agreements between management and labour at Community level – referred to in Article 4(2) – will consist in developing, by collective bargaining according to the rules of each Member State, the content of the agreements, and that consequently this arrangement implies no obligation on the Member States to apply the agreements directly or to work out rules for their transposition, nor any obligation to amend national legislation in force to facilitate their implementation.

Protocol
on economic and social cohesion

THE HIGH CONTRACTING PARTIES,

RECALLING that the Union has set itself the objective of promoting economic and social progress, *inter alia*, through the strengthening of economic and social cohesion;

RECALLING that Article 2 of the Treaty establishing the European Community includes the task of promoting economic and social cohesion and solidarity between Member States and that the strengthening of economic and social cohesion figures among the activities of the Community listed in Article 3;

RECALLING that the provisions of Part Three, Title XIV, on economic and social cohesion as a whole provide the legal basis for consolidating and further developing the Community's action in the field of economic and social cohesion, including the creation of a new fund;

RECALLING that the provisions of Part Three, Title XII on trans-European networks and Title XVI on environment envisage a Cohesion Fund to be set up before 31 December 1993;

STATING their belief that progress towards Economic and Monetary Union will contribute to the economic growth of all Member States;

NOTING that the Community's Structural Funds are being doubled in real terms between 1987 and 1993, implying large transfers, especially as a proportion of GDP of the less prosperous Member States;

NOTING that the European Investment Bank is lending large and increasing amounts for the benefit of the poorer regions;

NOTING the desire for greater flexibility in the arrangements for allocations from the Structural Funds;

NOTING the desire for modulation of the levels of Community participation in programmes and projects in certain countries;

NOTING the proposal to take greater account of the relative prosperity of Member States in the system of own resources;

REAFFIRM that the promotion of economic and social cohesion is vital to the full development and enduring success of the Community, and underline the importance of the inclusion of economic and social cohesion in Articles 2 and 3 of this Treaty;

REAFFIRM their conviction that the Structural Funds should continue to play a considerable part in the achievement of Community objectives in the field of cohesion;

REAFFIRM their conviction that the European Investment Bank should continue to devote the majority of its resources to the promotion of economic and social cohesion, and declare their willingness to review the capital needs of the European Investment Bank as soon as this is necessary for that purpose;

REAFFIRM the need for a thorough evaluation of the operation and effectiveness of the Structural Funds in 1992, and the need to review, on that occasion, the appropriate size of these Funds in the light of the tasks of the Community in the area of economic and social cohesion;

AGREE that the Cohesion Fund to be set up before 31 December 1993 will provide Community financial contributions to projects in the fields of environment and trans-European networks in Member States with a per capita GNP of less than 90% of the Community average which have a programme leading to the fulfilment of the conditions of economic convergence as set out in Article 104c;

DECLARE their intention of allowing a greater margin of flexibility in allocating financing from the Structural Funds to specific needs not covered under the present Structural Funds regulations;

DECLARE their willingness to modulate the levels of Community participation in the context of programmes and projects of the Structural Funds, with a view to avoiding excessive increases in budgetary expenditure in the less prosperous Member States;

RECOGNISE the need to monitor regularly the progress made towards achieving economic and social cohesion and state their willingness to study all necessary measures in this respect;

DECLARE their intention of taking greater account of the contributive capacity of individual Member States in the system of own resources, and of examining means of correcting, for the less prosperous Member States, regressive elements existing in the present own resources system;

AGREE to annex this Protocol to the Treaty establishing the European Community.

Protocol
on the Economic and Social Committee and the Committee of the Regions

THE HIGH CONTRACTING PARTIES,

HAVE AGREED upon the following provision, which shall be annexed to this Treaty establishing the European Community:

The Economic and Social Committee and the Committee of the Regions shall have a common organisational structure.

Protocol
annexed to the Treaty on European Union and to the Treaties establishing the European Communities

THE HIGH CONTRACTING PARTIES,

HAVE AGREED upon the following provision, which shall be annexed to the Treaty on European Union and to the Treaties establishing the European Communities:

Nothing in the Treaty on European Union, or in the Treaties establishing the European Communities, or in the Treaties or Acts modifying or supplementing those Treaties, shall affect the application in Ireland of Article 40.3.3. of the Constitution of Ireland.

INDEX

References in *italic* figures are to Article numbers of the EC Treaty set out in Appendix D

235

developing countries, 50
Eastern Europe, 50
economic and social cohesion, 49, *130a-130e*
energy, 49, *129c*
environment, 46, 49
European Investment Bank, 46-47
information technology, 49
infrastructure projects, 46, 49, *129c*
research and development, 49
role of Court of Auditors, 43-44
small businesses, 46, 49-50
technology transfer, 49-50
telecommunications, 46, 49, *129c*
training, 49-50
trans-European networks, 46, *129c*
transport, 46, 49, *129c*

G
GATT
members, 14
relations with European Community, *229*
Government Deficits. *See* **Budget Deficits**
Grievances. *See* **Complaints**

H
Harmonisation of Laws, *99-102*
Health and Safety of Workers, 13, *117, 118a*
Agency for Health and Safety at Work, 47
Health Policy, *129*
Home Affairs Policy, 22-23, 35
ECJ jurisdiction, 42
Human Rights, 66, 68-69, 76

I
IGC, 8-9, 10
Immigration Controls, 12-13, 23, *100c*
complaints, 38
jurisdiction of ECJ, 42
See also **Free Movement of Persons; Right of Establishment**
Import Charges, *98*
Imports
abolition of customs duties, *9, 12-15*

elimination of restrictions, *30-33, 35-37*
See also **Quantitative Restrictions**
India, 79
Individual Action. *See* **Enforcement**
Industrial and Commercial Policy, *110-115, 130*
Directorate-General, 89
Industrial Relations, *117, 118a*
Inflation Rate, 7
Information Technology
Directorate-General, 89
funding programmes, 49
Infrastructure Projects, *129b-129d*
funding programmes, 46, 49, *129c*
Infringement. *See* **Enforcement**
Insurance Services, *61*
Inter-Governmental Conference, 8-9, 10
Interim Relief, 42, 62, 64, *186*
Internal Market, 2-3
Directorate-General, 92
establishment, *7-7c*
extent, 70
regulatory agencies, 47-48
role of ECJ, 42
role of ECOSOC, 44-45
See also **Customs; Free Movement of Capital; Free Movement of Goods; Free Movement of Persons; Free Movement of Services**
Internal Market Council, 15
Internal Security. *See* **Judicial and Home Affairs Policy**
Investment Programmes. *See* **Funding Programmes**

J
Judicial and Home Affairs Policy, 22-23, 35
ECJ jurisdiction, 42
Judicial Review, 63-64, *173-177*

L
Labour Law. *See* **Employment Law**
Languages, 10, *217*